Finding the 'Ring of Truth'

The story of a Scottish Spitfire pilot from RAF 234 Squadron,
Missing in Action in late July 1944, and the odyssey of
2003–2015 to identify his war grave in southern Brittany

ERNEST RUSSELL LYON
(19 December 1922–27 July 1944)

Finding the 'Ring of Truth'

The story of a Scottish Spitfire pilot from RAF 234 Squadron, Missing in Action in late July 1944, and the odyssey of 2003–2015 to identify his war grave in southern Brittany

ERNEST RUSSELL LYON
(19 December 1922–27 July 1944)

Richard Lyon and Jean-Yves Le Lan

JANUS PUBLISHING COMPANY LTD
Cambridge, England

First published in Great Britain 2019
by Janus Publishing Company Ltd
The Studio
High Green
Great Shelford
Cambridge CB22 5EG

www.januspublishing.co.uk

ISBN 978-1-85756-892-9

Cover Design: Janus Publishing Company Ltd

Cover images: Lyon family collection, David Ferguson collection,
Darren Harbar Photography and Jahoo Clouseau from Pexels

Printed and bound in Great Britain

Reviews for *Finding the 'Ring of Truth'*

'There is something profoundly moving about the way Richard Lyon fought to identify his beloved kinsman, Flying Officer Ernest Russell Lyon, and to ensure that he forever rests in peace under his own name. Following "The Few", who fought to defend freedom in the British Empire & Commonwealth's "Finest Hour", Russell Lyon deserved nothing but the best memorial, and through his family's tireless efforts he has finally received it. This is a story of heroic persistence, to the extent that Richard Lyon even managed to get the regulations changed so that other servicemen can be recognized in the way that Russell now has been. Readers will be full of admiration for the refusal of a loving, proud family to take no for an answer.'

Professor Andrew Roberts
author: *Churchill: Walking with Destiny*

'A superb and beautifully compiled book written with intense determination, perseverance, admiration and family pride against constant officialdom, by the nephew of Russell Lyon, Richard Lyon.

Russell, with me, was a fighter pilot on 234 (F) Squadron RAF flying Spitfires during World War II, with whom I flew numerous sorties against our common enemy.

Russell, always known as Ben by us all in the Squadron, was my dearest friend and when on leave together at my home my parents treated him like a second son with care and love.

Ben had been in an unmarked grave for very many years but with the incredible efforts of Richard, who has strived for so long, his headstone now bears his name, and may he rest in peace.

I am honoured indeed, and proud to have not only been mentioned but pictured too in this memorable book, and also was to have been on the same sortie as my dear friend Ben when he was shot down on the 27th July 1944.'

Squadron Leader Alan Frost
WWII Spitfire Pilot, RAF 234 Squadron

'"Heroic persistence" indeed – but an inspirational book in other ways too. It highlights the power of family loyalties across generations, resulting in a mission for recognition. It reminds the post-war generation of the sacrifices made on our behalf by young men like Russell Lyon, cut off in their prime, which we were never called upon to repeat.

It sheds interesting light on the chaotic situation in Northern France as the German troops retreated after D-Day – resulting in major challenges for those who sought to bury, and only later to identify, the bodies of allied forces. Over the succeeding decades this led to the complex procedural decisions about narrative, forensic and other evidence facing the war graves' authorities: an issue which the book describes with admirable objectivity.

As the authors acknowledge, on-the-ground historical research owes much to the Internet, and as in all feats of historical detective work there were elements of good fortune. However, these were greatly outweighed by the forging of friendships which led to a generous collaborative spirit across national borders. As a result, this book is a powerful example of the individual contributions made by dedicated local historians to the bigger-picture events and trends recorded by those whose careers are spent writing about the past.'

Dr Nigel Richardson
author: *Thring of Uppingham: Victorian Educator*

'A 234 Squadron commander in 1964, and now a military historian, I took an early interest in this story, drove to Brittany to meet the eyewitnesses and those who dug up the wreckage, confirmed that this could be from a Spitfire Mk 5b and left France convinced that Russell Lyon lay below the unnamed gravestone at Guidel. I then followed the many abortive attempts to name Russell's gravestone until I concluded that the establishment would remain intransigent; but Richard Lyon would have none of it, and he reaped his just reward. In this very well presented and readable book he has treated us to a lesson on how exhaustive research and honest persistence can pay off, and he should be applauded for his diligence.'

Group Captain Nigel J.R. Walpole OBE BA FRAeS
author: *Dragon Rampant: The Story of 234 Fighter Squadron*

'The official body that needed to be convinced "beyond all reasonable doubt" that F/O Lyon lay in Grave 33, Row 6 in Guidel was the MoD's Joint Casualty and Compassionate Centre (JCCC). Years of battling with "the authorities" achieved the desired result, and, as well as the story of the grave, this book is something of a manual in how to tackle officialdom.

The author is meticulous in detailing his researches and equally diligent in including in the book maps, tables, copies of documents, glossaries, a bibliography and almost 100 pages of appendices.

Every "Known unto God" casualty should have a nephew like the author, with his persistence in dealing with authority.'

Stella Pedersen
The Aberdeen and North East Scotland Family History Society

'Both Richard Lyon and Jean-Yves Le Lan (along with many others) should be commended for "Finding the 'Ring of Truth'" and their endeavours to remember the contribution and sacrifice of Flying

Officer Ernest Russell Lyon. The story features many subjects that authors rarely feature and members of the public take for granted.

It reminds us of the Commonwealth War Graves Commission's continuing work to maintain the physical state of cemeteries across the world and the memory of all those who made the ultimate sacrifice. This book records the friendship and collaboration between people of different nations to achieve recognition for a young Scottish pilot who died upholding freedom that we all benefit from to the current day.'

Daniel Scott-Davies
The Spitfire Society

'On July 27 1944, just a few weeks after D-Day, a Spitfire pilot of 234 Squadron failed to return from a sortie over Brittany. Posted missing, F/O Russell Lyon was later recorded as 'having no known grave'. This truly moving book records the life and brief service of the 21-year-old Scot, but the bulk of it describes the forensic research by a family member and dedicated French civilians to finding his grave. This compelling book painstakingly takes the reader through the detail of establishing the burden of proof that meant that finally an 'unknown' grave was indeed that of the missing pilot. This is a valiant story of endeavour to ensure that the final resting place of F/O E.R. Lyon RAF is marked and duly honoured. A brilliant, inspiring story.'

Andrew Thomas
Wing Commander

Andrew Thomas is one of Britain's most pre-eminent RAF researchers, having published numerous squadron histories

Dedication

This story is firstly dedicated to the memory of Flying Officer Russell Lyon, 1922–1944. Secondly, it is dedicated to some 20,400 Allied Airmen of World War II who have no known grave. Thirdly, the story is dedicated to Russell Lyon's father and mother, Ernest and Elizabeth, and brothers, Stanley and Jimmy, who sadly did not live to hear the 21st-century story that unfolds in the following pages.

Acknowledgements

Many people have been involved with the research behind this story, or in roles connected with it, and in particular, I would like to thank the following for the part they have played to bring it to a successful conclusion.

In and around Plœmeur, Kercavès and Guidel in southern Brittany I am most grateful to my co-author Jean-Yves Le Lan, to Jean Robic, and to their families; to Claude Hélias, Gérard Penobert and to Général d'Armée aérienne (*2e section*) Jean Fleury GC; to the late Joseph Le Corroller; to the Mayor of Larmor-Plage, Victor Tonnerre; of Plœmeur, Loïc Le Meur and Ronan Loas; and of Guidel, François Aubertin; and to the local populace who were so generous with their hospitality.

To all the members of the RAF 234 Squadron Association, but especially to the President, Air Marshal Sir Richard Garwood KBE CB DFC MA RAF, without whom this story would have barely left the ground; to the Lifetime Honorary Secretary, Derek Colborne; to the current Association Secretary, Rob Sargent; to Group Captain Nigel Walpole OBE BA RAF, the author of *Dragon Rampant: the Story of No. 234 Fighter Squadron*; and to 234 Squadron WWII Spitfire pilots Squadron Leader Alan Frost, the late F/O Dave Ferguson and the families of the late F/O George Sparrow and the late F/O Jackson Dymond.

To the Director of the RAF Legal Branch, Air Vice Marshal Lindsay Irvine CB, and to the (then) Defence Services Secretary, Rear Admiral Simon Williams CVO, who chaired the final review panel.

To the staff of the Commonwealth War Graves Commission at Maidenhead, the Joint Casualty and Compassionate Centre at

RAF Innsworth, and the RAF Air Historical Branch at RAF Northolt, who have had to endure my enquiries and stubbornness in not taking no for an answer, and who undertook their work with a professional but sympathetic approach.

To George Watson's College, Edinburgh, for their interest and involvement.

I thank Ken Sewell, Barbara Legg, Tina Brand and all at Janus Publishing for their roles in the production of this book.

I thank my daughter Amelia who patiently went through the draft making numerous valuable comments, bringing coherence and clarity to the text. I thank my daughter-in-law Becky and my friend and neighbour, Professor Don Broom, for kindly reading early drafts of some parts of the story, and for the helpful comments they gave. I also thank Colin Walsh for the advice he gave to me with regard to potential publishing. I thank Trish and Mick Le Moignan for their interest, reading and comments on the proof copy of this book.

I thank Andy Saunders for his interest and support.

I thank my two brothers, Alastair and Bob, and our extended family for their interest in the story as it developed over the years.

I also thank my four children, Alex, Amelia, Vicky and Charlie for their forbearance and patience with me over the years as the story, and then this book, developed.

Most of all I thank my dear wife Anne deeply for her support and patience as the story took over the first few years of my retirement.

Contents

Glossary

Air Gnr	Air Gunner
AM	Air Marshal
AVM	Air Vice Marshal
CWGC	Commonwealth War Graves Commission, Maidenhead
DORIS	Department of Research and Information Services at the Royal Air Force Museum, Hendon, London
Fl/Lt	Flight Lieutenant
Fl/Sgt	Flight Sergeant
Flt Engr	Flight Engineer
F/O	Flying Officer
Gp Capt	Group Captain
JCCC	(MoD) Joint Casualty and Compassionate Centre, RAF Innsworth
JOMOC	Joint Operational Meteorology and Oceanography Centre, Northwood Headquarters, Eastbury, Hertfordshire.
MoD	Ministry of Defence, Whitehall, London
Nav	Navigator
NCAP	National Collection of Aerial Photography, Edinburgh
Obs	Observer
PLT	*Plutowny*, Platoon Leader (Polish)

RAF   Royal Air Force

RAF MREU   Royal Air Force Missing Research and Enquiry Unit

RCAF   Royal Canadian Air Force

Rhubarb 323   RAF low-level offensive fighter actions, seeking targets of opportunity, at times of low cloud and poor visibility

RNZAF   Royal New Zealand Air Force

Sgt   Sergeant

Sqn   Squadron

Sqn Ldr   Squadron Leader

W/Op   Wireless Operator

WWI   World War I 1914–1918

WWII   World War II 1939–1945

Glossary: English–French

Able Seaman	*Quartier maître*
Air Gunner	*Artilleur aérien*
Flight Engineer	*Ingénieur volant*
Flight Lieutenant (Pilot)	*Capitaine (pilote)*
Flight Sergeant	*Sergent aviateur*
Flying Officer (Pilot)	*Lieutenant (pilote)*
Navigator/Bomber	*Navigateur/bombardier*
Observer	*Observateur*
Pilot Officer (Pilot)	*Sous-lieutenant (pilote)*
Private	*Soldat*
Sergeant	*Sergent*
Squadron	*Escadron*
Squadron Leader (Pilot)	*Major (pilote)*
Warrant Officer Class II (Pilot)	*Adjudant (pilote)*
Wireless Operator	*Radiotélégraphiste*

Foreword

I have been delighted to be part of Richard Lyon's campaign to have the final resting place of his uncle, Flying Officer Russell Lyon, finally recognised. This is not only a story of a brave young airman tragically killed on operations at the age of 21 years but a story about a family's endeavour to make sure that their relative did not rest in France, unrecognised for his sacrifice, in an unnamed grave. Being involved for many years with 234 Squadron, with which Russell was serving when he died, I first heard about the 'Spitfire pilot in the unnamed grave' back in 2004. Like many others, the more you understand about this story then the more compelling it becomes. There is absolutely no doubt in my mind and that of many of my senior colleagues that this young man, Russell Lyon, who fought for his country and gave his life on the evening of 27 July 1944, lies below the white Commonwealth War Grave headstone now inscribed with his name in the Guidel Communal Cemetery.

This has been a true David and Goliath epic, with Richard having to challenge the MOD over an extended period of time with true grit and persistence to achieve what is without doubt the right answer. Organisations do not always like to be challenged but I knew from the very first meeting I had with Richard Lyon that if the MOD thought a comforting letter about his uncle with the wrong answer was going to impress him then they had unfortunately miscalculated. Following setback after setback, Richard's persistence won through when an MOD high-level review panel agreed that the grave at Guidel should now be marked with Russell's name.

I was fortunate enough to attend the re-dedication ceremony in October 2015, having visited the crash site, the roundabout propeller-memorial and the site of the German Flak battery that shot the Flying Officer down; I was delighted to meet and be shown these sites by the French researchers, Jean Robic and Jean-Yves Le Lan, who have devoted so much time and energy to this project. I congratulate Richard Lyon and his family for persisting against the odds to get this well-deserved recognition for Richard's uncle's grave. I believe, in turn, Russell would be pleased to think that all these years later, people care about the sacrifice that he and so many other young men ultimately made for this country.

Air Marshal Sir Richard Garwood KBE CB DFC MA RAF

Preface

I was moved to write down this story in its entirety for a number of reasons. Firstly, as an account of a family history story about a single individual, my uncle, who, like many of his generation, died at the young age of 21 in the latter stages of World War II.

Secondly, I was moved to do so because of the extraordinary sequence of events that led to the name of my uncle at long last being put on to the CWGC gravestone that had previously just said 'RAF Officer 29th July 1944 "Known unto God"'.

Thirdly, to share the story into a wider sphere which, perhaps, may encourage others to pursue their aims relentlessly despite the obstacles, bureaucratic and otherwise, that are put in their path.

The story could hardly have started or finished without the Internet. This vehicle cut through logjams of connectivity and enabled connections to be made and relationships to be formed, occasionally by acts of pure serendipity. More than once I had to pinch myself to check that I was not dreaming as the story pitched one way or another.

There are many books written about famous fighter pilots who have greater prominence as aces in the pack than the pilot whose experiences are covered by this story. There are a handful of pilots from RAF 234 Squadron who so feature, amongst whom Bob Doe and Pat Hughes are examples. The Squadron itself is believed to have shot down more enemy aircraft in the Battle of Britain than any other Squadron. As this is being written, in early 2017, the now disbanded Squadron, whose motto is '*Ignem Mortemque Despuimus*' ('We Spit Fire and Death') and which was founded in 1917, is planning its Centenary Celebrations.

So this account is about someone who, like many other young pilots, undertook his job with bravery, with skill, with fear, with a belief in the right cause, and with little thought for himself and out of the glare of publicity afforded to the fighter ace pilots.

Had Russell not volunteered in 1943 to be posted back, from the relative safety of his role as flying instructor in Canada, to an operational Squadron in England, then he might well still be with us today and attending the Squadron reunions with his old pals.

I am writing about someone that I have never met. Now I feel that I know him well from the years that I have worked on this story and from all that has been unearthed or heard from others.

That was not the case at the start of this journey. He was then only a memory, from a framed photograph of this young man in RAF uniform standing on my father's desk.

I hope that readers of this story will come to know Russell as I have.

Richard Lyon

List of Illustrations

Chapter 1

Chapter 2

Chapter 3

Chapter 4

6.19   The official party at the Stele unveiling. Photo by the official photographer (name not known) for the Commune of Larmor-Plage, reproduced by kind permission of the City of Larmor-Plage.

6.20   Jean-Yves Le Lan reading Russell's biography in French. Photo Alain Terras.

6.21, 6.22 Charles Lyon reading Russell's biography in English. Photo 6.21 by Alain Terras. Photo 6.22 by David Webster.

6.23, 6.24 Richard Lyon thanking all for the occasion of the Stele creation and unveiling. Photos Jean-Yves Le Lan.

6.25, 6.26 The unveiling of the Stele by the Mayor of Larmor-Plage, Victor Tonnerre, and Richard Lyon. Photos David Webster.

6.27   The Lyon family wreath. Photo by Anne Lyon.

6.28   Children wreath laying. Photo by the official photographer (name not known) for the Commune of Larmor-Plage, reproduced by kind permission of the City of Larmor-Plage.

6.29, 6.30 Local children completing the planting of Scottish heathers around the Stele. Photo 6.29 by a photographer known only as Michel. Photo 6.30 by the official photographer (name not known) for the Commune of Larmor-Plage, reproduced by kind permission of the City of Larmor-Plage.

6.31   L to R, Sébastien Le Coupanec, Jean Robic, Victor Tonnerre and Jean-Yves Le Lan and Richard Lyon. Photo by the official photographer (name not known) for the Commune of Larmor-Plage, reproduced by kind permission of the City of Larmor-Plage.

6.32   L to R, David Webster, Russell Lyon, Richard Lyon, Anne Lyon, Charles Lyon, Victoria Windmill (née Lyon), Pamela Lyon and Alastair Lyon. Photo Mark Windmill, son-in-law of author.

Chapter 10

Appendices

A 8.1   *The Little Prince* welcomes Russell to his home on Asteroid B-612. Created by Gérard Pénobert. Richard Lyon Collection.

A9.1, A9.2 Jean Robic with parts recovered, and Jean Robic, centre, with Nigel Walpole, right, and Jean-Michael Lepretre, left. Photos N. Walpole.

A9.3   The gearing part of the Merlin engine on display over the 234 Squadron colours.

A9.4   The view in the main entrance of the RAF College at Cranwell, between the portraits of HM Queen Elizabeth II and HRH The Duke of Edinburgh. Derek Colborne, Secretary of the 234 Squadron Association with back to the camera, Alan Frost extreme right. Photos Lyon family collection.

A9.5   An exhaust from the Merlin engine mounted for display by Jean Robic. Photo Richard Lyon.

A9.6, A9.7 The 2008 Stele at the new roundabout at Kercavès, mounted on a piece of granite taken from the roof of the U-boat pens at Keroman. Photo J.-Y. Le Lan.

Chapter 1

Early Life and Family History

1.1 Russell, age 6 months. Lyon family collection.

Ernest Russell Lyon was born in Edinburgh on 19 December 1922 to Ernest Hutcheon Lyon (1891–1985) and his second wife, Elizabeth Wright Lyon (née Pealling) (1886–1935). Christened Ernest Russell Lyon, he was known as Russell.

He had an older brother, my father, Stanley Douglas Lyon (1917–1991), and a younger brother, James Gordon Lyon (1927–1956). Stanley's mother, Helen Wilson Kelly (1890–1919), died (of Bright's Disease) when he was still an infant. Helen Kelly's family came from Foveran, Aberdeenshire.

Ernest then married Elizabeth Pealling in 1920, whose family originated from Kirkcudbrightshire and south-west Scotland, and who gave him his second and third sons, Russell and Jimmy. The Christian name Russell came from the surname of his maternal line great-grandfather, Samuel Russell, from Sanquhar, Dumfriesshire. The

three boys grew up in Edinburgh and attended local schools including
George Heriot's School and George Watson's College.

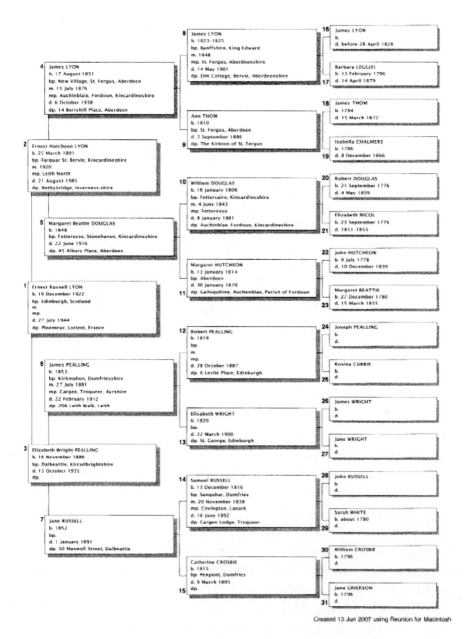

1.2 Russell Lyon's family tree. Lyon family collection.

Their father Ernest was born in 1891 in Inverbervie, Kincardineshire, and was the youngest of six children. He had two sisters, Jane Christie Lyon (1878–1966) and Margaret Ann Lyon (1883–1971), and three brothers, James Lyon (1881–1918), George David Lyon (1884–1972) and Arthur William Douglas Lyon (1886–1958).

Their grandfather, James Lyon (1851–1938), a landscape gardener, was born in St. Fergus and their grandmother, Margaret Beattie Douglas (1848–1916), was born in Fetteresso.

1.3 Russell with elder and younger brothers, Stanley and Jimmy. Lyon family collection.

1.4 Russell with father, brothers and grandparents.
Lyon family collection.

Their great-grandfather, also James Lyon (*c*.1823–1901), was born in King Edward Parish. At the time of the 1851 census, this James Lyon is at St. Fergus, address Londerton, which is a 343-acre farm in the southern portion of St. Fergus Parish, just north of Mains of Inverugie, owned by the Thomson family in 1881.

By the 1881 census this James is aged 57, a shepherd living at a dwelling in Seatown, Crimond, Aberdeen with Ann Lyon (nee Thom) age 70.

Studies to find earlier antecedents on the Lyon line have just one more James Lyon, whose origins and dates are unknown. His spouse, Barbara Legg(e) (1796–1879), is shown to have married for a second time to George Finnie in Pitsligo in 1828. Her death certificate indicates that she was the widow of James Lyon. There is no record yet found of this James Lyon other than his marriage to Barbara Legg(e) in 1822 in Pitsligo, and an assumed death before 1828.

The birth parishes for Russell's great-grandparents on his father's side, James Lyon, Ann Thom, William Douglas and Margaret Hutcheon, are, respectively, the Parish of King Edward, the Kirkton of St. Fergus, Fordoun and Fordoun.

Moving back a generation earlier to the great-great-grandparents of Russell shows there are birth parishes including Gamrie, St. Fergus, Fordoun, Fettercairn and Stonehaven.

Many of Russell's antecedents on his father's side are from the farming communities of north-east Scotland. They will have endured hardships that are long forgotten. From the same area of north-east Scotland, the contents of *A Scots Quair* by Lewis Grassic Gibbon have provided me, comfortable now in 21st-century East Anglia, with much flavour of how hard existence was a hundred years or so ago.

Russell can be seen as a 'grandson' if not son of north-east Scotland.

Research on other members of this Lyon line shows that some, like many during the 19th century, emigrated from north-east Scotland to distant lands, including to Regina, Saskatchewan, Canada; to Vancouver, Canada; and to Millicent, Adelaide, Australia.

1.5 Russell with father and mother, brothers and cousins, at Braemar *c.*1932. Lyon family collection.

Russell's great-uncle, George Chalmers Lyon (1849–1929), moved south to live in Hastings, Kent, where he was the Head Park Gardener. In 1906, Russell's uncle, George David, emigrated to Pennsylvania, USA, where he was also a landscape gardener.

Holidays from Edinburgh for Stanley, Russell and James in the 1920s and 1930s often took them to Braemar, Deeside, where they holidayed together with various cousins and where their uncle, the well known Aberdeen and Deeside artist George Melvin Rennie (1875–1953), had a summer studio adjacent to the Invercauld Arms Hotel.

1.6 Russell with family at the Falls of Garbh Allt, Royal Deeside *c.*1934. Lyon family collection.

George married Margaret Ann Lyon (1883–1971), aunt to Russell, in Aberdeen in 1919, with whom he had two sons and a daughter. George's first wife, Isabella Allan, with whom he had four sons and two daughters, had died in 1916.

Around Braemar and Deeside is the area where Clan Farquharson originates from, dating back many centuries. Clan Farquharson is comprised of a number of small septs including one sept of people with the Lyon surname.

Russell's early school years were spent firstly at Gillespie's and then at George Heriot's School in Edinburgh. He entered Heriot's on 23 September 1930. In July 1932, he left George Heriot's School and started his next phase of education on 22 September 1932 at George Watson's College, also in Edinburgh.

George Heriot's School, Edinburgh

1.7 George Heriot's School, Edinburgh, seen from the Grassmarket just below Edinburgh Castle.
Copyright Wikipedia, Dave Morris from Oxford, England, FlickrLickr.

Founded in 1628 as a hospital school for impoverished orphan children, with an endowment from George Heriot, the school is located in central Edinburgh. The original charitable aim to provide free education to fatherless children continues today although the school has also taken fee-paying pupils from the 1880s onwards. The school is now co-educational with 1,600 pupils.

Motto: '*Impendo*' ('I Distribute Chearfullie')

The George Watson's College record shows:

> He got the bronze medal for swimming in fourth year and by the time he was in sixth year he was in the rugby First XV where he gained his colours. He studied English, French, Physics and Chemistry in sixth year, was a patrol leader in the Scouts and was in the Army Training Corps and played tennis and cricket. He was also a prefect.

George Watson's College, Edinburgh

1.8 George Watson's College. Copyright Website Watsonians Online –
https://www.watsonians.org/page.aspx?pid=329.

Founded in 1741 as a hospital school, with an endowment from George Watson, the school is located in Colinton in south-west Edinburgh. As the hospital school system fell into disrepute, the school was re-formed in 1870 as a fee-paying day school for 800 boys. Amalgamated with George Watson's Ladies College in the 1970s, the school now has some 2,400 pupils.

Motto: '*Ex Corde Caritas*' ('Love from the Heart')

On 15 October 1935, when Russell was approaching his 13th birthday, his mother, Elizabeth, died following a sudden and severe stroke.

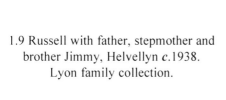

1.9 Russell with father, stepmother and brother Jimmy, Helvellyn *c*.1938. Lyon family collection.

Amongst family history possessions is a Scout logbook from Russell's teenage years in Colinton in Edinburgh.

Written in 1939/1940, this shows, amongst other comment, Russell's wry observations on the disruption to everyday life caused by WWII. For instance, he blames the low turnout for an evening patrol meeting on 'that chap on the opposite page' (he is referring to his cartoon of Hitler). He also sets out for each meeting of his troop, those who are present, those who have not been able to attend, and what the group has accomplished.

The page shows four lifelike cartoon figures of Churchill, Roosevelt, Hitler and Mussolini.

The logbook is well illustrated with stick-figure diagrams, several of which have cartoon characters displaying his artistic talents, and includes photographs of the troop's camping excursions.

Another entry in the Scout logbook records that 'my pals think I look like Clark Gable', so Russell clearly, handsome as he was, had a sense of humour.,

1.10 Page from Russell's Scout logbook. Lyon family collection.
The page shows four lifelike cartoon figures of Churchill,
Roosevelt Hitler and Mussolini.

1.11 Russell Lyon *c.* 1940.
Lyon family collection.

Chapter 2
RAF Career 1941–1944

2.1 Russell Lyon, RAF Wings
awarded, 1942.
Lyon family collection.

Soon after his 18th birthday, Russell Lyon volunteered to join the RAF, and he enlisted in the RAF Volunteer Reserve on 1 March 1941.

His full Service Record, obtained from the RAF Personnel Management Agency at RAF Innsworth, upon payment of a nominal fee, is:

- 1 March 1941, enlistment Royal Air Force Volunteer Reserve
- Held in reserve 7 July 1941 L.A.C.R.C. July to September 1941
- Basic Training October 1941 to May 1942
- Canada and the USA training 20 May 1942
- Awarded pilot's wings, promoted to Sergeant

- May 1942–March 1943, Pilot Instructor USA and Canada
- 4 March 1943, promoted to Flying Officer
- June to October 1943, Pilot Operational training
- 26 September 1943, RAF Hutton Cranswick, 12 Group
- 20 October 1943, posted to 234 Squadron December 1943, RAF Church Fenton 2
- 9 January 1944, RAF Coltishall
- 19 March 1944, RAF Bolt Head, 10 Group
- 30 April 1944, RAF Deanland, 85 Group
- 19 June 1944, RAF Predannack,10 Group
- 27 July 1944, Missing in Action

Around March 1943, Russell volunteered to return to the UK and to be posted to an operational squadron. When he joined 234 Squadron, he acquired the nickname 'Ben' Lyon (after the Hollywood actor and agent Ben Lyon).

Brief History of RAF 234 Squadron

2.2 RAF 234 Squadron Badge.
Copyright Site RAF.

The squadron was formed in August 1918, from Flights 350, 351, 352 and 353. Based in the Scilly Isles at RNAS Tresco, the squadron flew Felixtowe F3 and Curtiss H12 flying boats to patrol the Western Approaches to the English Channel. Missions continued until the Armistice on 11 November 1918, after which the squadron was disbanded.

On 30 October 1939, 234 Squadron was re-formed at RAF Leconfield, again flying coastal patrols. For this work of giving protection to shipping, the squadron was equipped with Magisters, a Battle, Gauntlets and Blenheim Mk1fs until March 1940. Then, it began to be re-equipped with Spitfires that became operational on 11 May 1940. During the Battle of Britain, the squadron was based in the south of Great Britain. The squadron suffered heavy losses but also high success rates with ace pilots such as Pat Hughes, Bob Doe and Keith Lawrence. In April 1941, the squadron carried out missions in the north of France. It continued providing defensive patrols until January 1943. The squadron was active over northern France during and after the Normandy Invasion. On 1 May 1945, 234 Squadron was equipped with jets, new American Mustang F4s, and undertook long-range bomber escort missions.

A few days before the end of the war, the squadron moved to the north of Scotland, operating with RAF Coastal Command along the Norwegian coast. It then returned to East Anglia in July and was re-equipped with Spitfire MkIXs. In February 1946 these were replaced by Meteor F3s and on 1 September 1946, the squadron was renumbered as 266 Squadron.

On 1 August 1952, the squadron was re-formed in RAF Oldenbourg, in Germany, providing for a ground attack role, and was equipped with Vampire FB5s and FB9s. In November 1953, the squadron received Sabre F4s, with these being replaced in May 1956 by Hunter F4s. On 15 July 1957, the squadron was dissolved.

The squadron Motto is '*Ignem mortemque despuimus*' ('We spit fire and death'). Nicknamed 'The Dragons', the squadron's insignia shows a Dragon Rampant, with flames issuing from the mouth.

From this period the family has a series of postcards written by Russell and addressed to his younger brother James (Jimmy). These are all sent from the deep south of the United States. They have also passed through the Censor's Office. Some of these show airplanes and aerodromes in Alabama and Georgia. One group, which would be considered not to be at all politically correct today, show images of people of colour at work in the cotton fields.

2.3 Front of postcard from Russell Lyon (Advance Trainer preparing for Night Flight, Maxwell Field, Montgomery, Ala.). Lyon family collection.

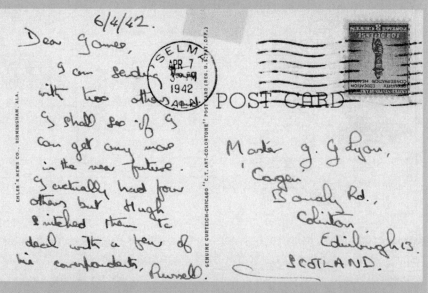

2.4 Reverse of postcard from Russell Lyon starting with text '6/4/42 – Dear James, I am sending this with…'. Lyon family collection.

2.5 Front of postcard from Russell Lyon (Advance Trainers Taking Off for Flight, Maxwell Field, Montgomery, Ala.). Lyon family collection.

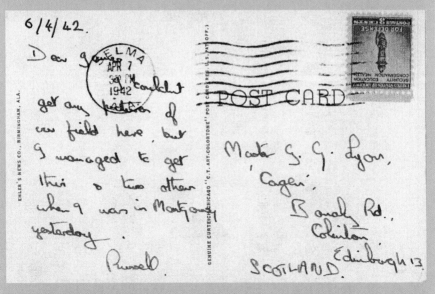

2.6 Reverse of postcard from Russell Lyon with the text '6/4/42 – Dear James, …'. Lyon family collection.

2.7 Front of postcard from Russell Lyon (Post Operation's Building,
Maxwell Field, Montgomery Ala.). Lyon family collection.

2.8 Reverse of postcard from Russell Lyon with the text '15/4/42 –
Dear James, …'. Lyon family collection.

Russell records in a cheery fashion what he is able to say without, apparently, raising the Censor's umbrage.

RAF 234 Squadron performed strongly in the Battle of Britain but by June 1943 it nearly disappeared. However, in August 1943, an overseas posting was cancelled and the squadron was re-formed and equipped with some rather old Spitfire MkVbs, often converted from Mk Is and Mk IIs. Russell joined the squadron in September when they were posted to RAF Hutton Cranswick in East Yorkshire, and then to RAF Church Fenton in North Yorkshire.

By this time Flight Lieutenant 'Wally' Walton (a veteran of the Defence of Malta) was Flight Commander and Squadron Leader Phil Arnott had taken command of the squadron.

2.9 'A' Flight, RAF 234 Squadron, Russell Lyon fifth from right.
Collection: the late David Ferguson.

In 1944, when stationed at Bolt Head in the South Hams area of Devon, as part of 10 Group, the officers of 234 Squadron were billeted at The Cottage Hotel in Hope Cove.

On D-Day, 6 June 1944, the Operations Record Book shows that Russell flew with the squadron before dawn, escorting the tug aircraft and gliders that were landing troops behind the invasion beaches in France, and then later in the day, giving air cover over Gold and

Omaha beaches. The biggest risk to their lives then was friendly fire, despite the Black and White D-Day wing markings. The story goes that when these were first painted on the 234 Squadron MkVbs, it poured with rain and all the paint, being water based, was washed off. A second paint application was then made.

RAF Bolt Head

A satellite of RAF Exeter, RAF Bolt Head was a grass airfield located one mile south-west of Salcombe, Devon. Nearby was The Ground Control Interceptor Station (CGI), RAF Hope Cove, where, from 1941, Fighter Operations in the English Channel were directed. The installation and development of this radar station in 1941 was carried out by a young radar technician, Jack Nissenthal.

The airfield at Bolt Head was notoriously difficult for planes to land as the approach was often from the seaward side, where wind currents on the high and steep cliff face of Bolt Head were unpredictable. Landings in poor weather often resulted in fatal crashes into the cliffs.

It is recounted that:

> One night the airfield was totally non-operational because of thick sea mist. A squadron of Polish fighters returned from France; two were damaged and all were short of fuel. They asked us to help them to land at Bolt Head. They insisted they could get no further. The runways ran straight from the cliff edges, and in no time 10 had crashed into the cliffs. Two crashed on the runway and one pilot survived. The carnage on the sides of the cliff, found next morning, was appalling, and the words and cries of the pilots over the radio transmitter as they crashed were unforgettable, said Pam McNicol.

After D-Day, 234 Squadron was posted to RAF Predannack, on the Lizard Peninsula, so that the pilots would have areas of Brittany within combat range. The MkVb Spitfire has fuel tank capacity of 282 gallons, providing for a total flight length of 1,135 miles in fair weather. A 20 per cent reserve would be normal for pilots to hold. This would not give pilots much time over a target such as one near Lorient, in southern Brittany. At best, pilots might have some ten

2.10 1944, RAF 234 Squadron members, Russell Lyon back row left.
The late George Sparrow family collection.

minutes over a target in the Lorient area before they would have to return to base.

There are two fuel tanks in the Spitfire MkVb. One is located immediately behind the Merlin engine, thus placing it immediately in front of the pilot's cockpit. The second is located just behind the pilot's seat.

Characteristics of the Spitfire MkVb

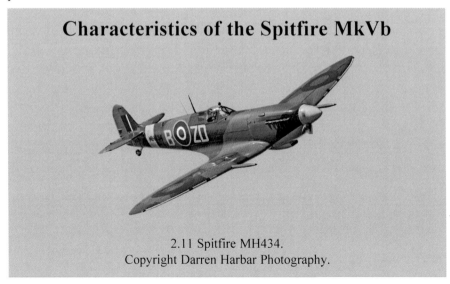

2.11 Spitfire MH434.
Copyright Darren Harbar Photography.

Type: Hunter Fighter Monoplane.
Dimensions: wingspan: 36 ft 10 in (11.23 m); length 29 ft 11 in (9.12 m); height 11 ft 5 in (3.48 m); wing area 242.1 sq.ft. (22.48 m²).
Powerplant: 1 x Rolls-Royce Merlin 45 supercharged V12 engine, 1,470 hp (1,096 kW) at 9,250 ft (2,819 m).
Performance: Maximum speed: 370 mph (595 km/h) at 20,000 ft (6095 m) altitude; service ceiling: 36,500 ft (11,200 m); combat range: 470 miles (760 km).
Armament: 2 x 20 mm Hispano Mk I/II and 4 x .303mm Browning machine guns placed in the wings.
Anon. Press Cutting:

The word 'spitfire' originally meant a fiery tempered person, one easily aroused to anger. In the late 1930s Sir Robert McLean, chairman of Vickers, the company co-ordinating supplies to the government, wanted a name for their new fighter plane which suggested something 'venomous' and started with an 's', the first letter of the manufacturer, Supermarine. Other suggestions were Shrike and Shrew. The plane's designer, R.J. Mitchell, who died young in 1937, wasn't impressed: 'It's just the sort of bloody silly name they would choose.'

In the period from May to July 1945, RAF 234 Squadron were posted to RAF Peterhead, also known as Longside Airfield. A fuller list of the squadron's role and postings is shown below, including two in north-east Scotland:
RAF 234 Squadron duty:

- Role: 1939–1945: Home based Fighter Squadron
- 8 August 1940: No.10 Group; Fighter Command
- 6 June 1944: No.11 Group; Air Defence of Great Britain; Allied Expeditionary Air Force
- May–July 1945: Peterhead
- July 1945: Dyce

On 1 April 1994, 234 Squadron was disbanded.

RAF Predannack

RAF Predannack is on the Lizard Peninsula in Cornwall. It opened in 1941 as a satellite for RAF Portreath. Squadrons posted there initially undertook a defence role for the South-West. There were occasional raids by the Luftwaffe, but later the squadrons stationed at RAF Predannack took on more offensive roles including anti-shipping strikes over the Bay of Biscay. The base was used as a build-up location for the European bomber offensive, and it was used as an emergency landing location and as a jumping-off point for operations in North Africa. As World War II receded, fighter squadrons were posted there, including RAF 234 Squadron, as the location of the base allowed Spitfires the range to attack Axis Forces as far south as Lorient. Use of the base in the 21st century continues with use by RAF 626 Volunteer Gliding Squadron Unit and by the Royal Navy School of Flight Deck Operations for fire drill and crash rescue training on a number of older dummy, or now redundant, aircraft.

2.12 Memorial at the RAF Predannack site.

The inscription reads:

RAF Predannack

This memorial honours all ranks and nationalities that served here during World War II.

While casting your eyes on this memorial spare a thought for those who flew from here and failed to return, many have no known grave.

'Like a breath of wind, gone in a fleeting second only the memories remain'

Simply dedicated June 2002.

Another 'Ben' Lyon

Meanwhile Russell's brother Stanley, born 1917, was serving in another theatre of WWII.

Stanley had studied engineering at Edinburgh University and he then worked for a year with an engineering consultancy in Edinburgh. In November 1939, two months after the Declaration of War, he joined the Royal Engineers and soon was posted to 128 Company (Tyne Electrical Engineers) E. and M. Company, Royal Engineers (Territorial), formed in 1940. This company had a battledress flash showing a fist holding an arrow against a background of thistles that led to the company's nickname – the 'Nig-Nogs'.

The Story of the Tyne Electrical Engineers recounts 'And why were we called the "Nig-Nogs"? Because on the shoulders of our battledress was the Crest of the Tyne Electrical Engineers.' 'What is that?' asked the blonde bombshell from Scarborough. 'A Nig-Nog,' said our Tynesider. And this nickname then stuck.

2.13 'Nig-Nog'
Crest of 128 Company.

In the 128 Company Stanley Lyon acquired the nickname 'Ben', as had his younger brother Russell in the RAF.

Initially working on infrastructure installations around Cairnryan and Gareloch in 1942, the 128 Company joined the PAI force (British Army Persian and Iraq Command) and was posted to Basrah and Shaibah airbase in Iraq. The Company worked on provision of water supplies, refrigeration and ice plants as well as lighting and fan installations in both Iraq and Iran. The Company soon found itself spread between Mosul in the north, Andiminsk and Teheran in the east, to Basrah and Abadan in the south, before its HQ was moved to Baghdad.

Stanley was now appointed a Captain in the 128 Company and in 1943 this unit found itself in Palestine and then Egypt. Among their responsibilities was the maintenance of the Western Desert Pipeline. The *History of the Tyne Electrical Engineers* records:

> This line had, since the days of Montgomery at Alamein, supplied water to the garrisons up to Mersah Matruh and beyond; also to the entire Arab population of the Western Desert, who treated it as a gift from Allah, after finding that when struck sharply with a pick in Mosaic fashion it gushed forth water for the gardens, camels and ablutionary activities of the Chosen.

After six years of service with this Company of the Royal Engineers, Stanley ('Ben') Lyon was demobilised in December 1945 with the rank of Major.

In a reference letter written for Stanley Lyon at the end of World War II by a former Chaplain to HM Forces, attached to the Royal Engineers, W.G. Humphreys writes:

> Throughout the six years of service with the same company of Royal Engineers, at home and overseas, he has continuously attracted to himself the admiration of his fellow officers and the esteem of those under his command by reason of a nature that can happily infect men with a spirit of dogged persistence even in the face of untoward circumstances.

Upon demobilisation, Stanley joined the Dyestuffs Division of ICI in Huddersfield, Yorkshire, as a construction engineer. After two years he went to a similar post at ICI Billingham on Teesside. After another spell with ICI Dyestuffs he became Director of Engineering at ICI Wilton, south of the River Tees. He then moved back to ICI Billingham as Director of Production and then Chairman of the Agricultural Division. His obituary in *The Times* of 27 December 1991 records that 'the timing of this was propitious, for that division was wrestling with the problems of building a 300,000 tonne ammonia plant, nearly ten times the size of what had been attempted hitherto'. Lyon played a major role in the success of that project, which was to wreak one of the biggest engineering transformations at ICI in the post-war era. This led to the lowering of the price of ammonia and made the company one of the world's leaders in the production of fertilisers. It was a pillar of the group's profits for years to come. The group later used the Billingham plant as a blueprint for similar projects in India, Australia and other countries around the world. In 1968 he was part of a panel of businessmen and industrialists appointed by the government to investigate manpower savings in the non-industrial civil service. Stanley was appointed to the Main Board of ICI in 1968, responsible for organisation and services, and then for personnel. He rose to be a Deputy Chairman from 1972 to 1977.

The *Times* obituary records:

> Stanley Lyon was one of that phalanx of able managers on whom ICI depended in the 1960s and 1970s; they laid the foundations for the company's subsequent success in the 1980s. And many millions of people in poorer countries will have been unaware of his unobtrusive contribution to the improvement in their diets because of better and cheaper agricultural products.

2.14 Russell's elder brother, Stanley 'Ben' Lyon, 1917–1991.

Chapter 3
Mission of 27 July 1944 – Missing in Action

In the days leading up to 27 July, 234 Squadron pilots were involved in a number of missions.

On the afternoon of 22 July 1944, four aircraft went on a reconnaissance mission of the Nostang area east of Lorient, and also attacked locomotives at Hennebont. After the attack, one Spitfire, piloted by Flying Officer (F/O) John Coward, was reported as missing.

F/O Coward's Spitfire, AD470, crashed near Auray. His body was recovered by the Germans, identified and buried at Guidel, in Row 6, Grave 32. The Guidel Communal Cemetery Old Register Record lists the burial of this identified casualty on 24 July 1944.

Flying Officer John Liversedge Coward, RAF 234 Squadron Royal Air Force Volunteer Reserve

Son of Tom and Annie Coward of Barnsley, Yorkshire, and husband of Claire Coward of Barnsley.

Shot down piloting Spitfire AD470 and crashed near Auray, and killed in action at 16.45hrs on 22 July 1944, aged 29.

F/O John Coward was buried two days later, on 24 July 1944, by the Germans at Guidel in Row 6, Grave No. 32 at Guidel Communal Cemetery.

3.1 CWGC Graves 32 and 33, Row 6, Guidel Communal Cemetery. Photo Richard Lyon.

Auray is some 31 miles south east of Guidel.

On a later mission on the same day, eight RAF 234 Squadron Spitfires escorted three Mosquitoes of RAF 151 Squadron on a bombing mission of a German Naval HQ at Nostang, east of Lorient, the Spitfires attacking afterwards with cannon and machine gun. On that mission Fl/Lt Walton (BM200) and F/O Lyon (BL563) flew as Red 1 and Red 2.

On 23 July F/O Lyon flew with three others on a shipping reconnaissance mission between Morlaix and the Ile de Sein. On 24 July he flew with seven others on a bombing mission on rail infrastructure. Unusually, the Spitfires had been modified to carry 500lb bombs for these missions. Later the same day he flew on a shipping patrol mission west of Ushant. F/O Lyon, with seven Spitfires, flew a similar mission on the afternoon of 25 July, attacking locomotives and vehicle movements in Landivisiau and in the area north of Quimper, Finistère. The Squadron Record Book also notes that the weather over the Channel during this week was not good. This now declassified Squadron Record Book shows eight Spitfires flying from RAF Predannack Airfield at 19.00 hours on 27 July 1944.

The eight Spitfires from 234 Squadron were:

- Spitfire BM200, Fl/Lt. W.C. Walton, DFC, Mission Leader
- Spitfire [unknown] Fl/Sgt P.J. Mall
- Spitfire AR343 F/O E.R. Lyon
- Spitfire BL646 Fl/Sgt L.M. Stockwall
- Spitfire BL810 Fl/Lt F.E. Dymond
- Spitfire AR364 Fl/Sgt A. Morgan
- Spitfire BM238 F/O G.F. Sparrow
- Spitfire W3320 Fl/Sgt A.C. Buttler

This was a 'Rhubarb 323' mission to attack the Luftwaffe base at Kerlin-Bastard and to disrupt the Axis Forces that were retreating away from the Allied Forces who had now moved out of the Normandy beaches. On this mission each Spitfire was also adapted to carry a 500lb bomb.

3.2 The Spitfire MkVb.
Crown Copyright and from the Spitfire site.

The Spitfire MkVb was considerably less suited for dive-bombing missions than its more modern contemporaries equipped with C-type wing and had to be handled with care by the pilot during these missions. It could only carry one bomb under the fuselage and its wings were not sufficiently stressed for high-g loads.

After crossing the French coast at Plouescat, at 6,000ft altitude under clouds, the Spitfires set direction for an attack on the installations at the Luftwaffe base at Kerlin-Bastard. This air base is now known as Lann-Bihoué, a national base of the Marine and Air Forces of the French Ministry of Defence.

Place	Date	Time	Summary of Events	References to Appendices
R.A.F. Form 540 *See instructions for use of this form in K.R. and A.C.I. para. 2349 and War Manual, Pt. II., chapter XX. and also in R.A.F. Pocket Book.*			OPERATIONS RECORD BOOK of (Unit or Formation) No. 234 (Madras Presidency) Squadron. SECRET.	Page No. S E V E N No. of pages used for day
Predannack.	25.7.44		The other four aircraft attacked 20 trucks ten miles N.W. of Quimper. On returning, these aircraft again strafed Landivisiau. Weather was excellent.	
	26.7.44		No Ops. today, the weather clamped right down but duty flight maintained the necessary state.	
			Pilots went to the photographic section and saw our latest combat films. The ground crews also saw them. F/Lt. C.H. Lattimer and Lt. M. Bernard posted to HQ A D.G.B.	
	27.7.44		Another Shipping Recco this morning. Abervrach Goulet De Brest. Aircraft had to return when mid-channel due to bad weather. Rain from 0 - 6,000 feet.	
			At 19.00 hours, eight aircraft were airborne on Rhubarb 323. Squadron crossed in over Plouescat at 6,000 feet above cloud, this broke up in the S. Kerlin Bastard A/F was strafed and airikes were seen on hangers, dispersal area huts and watch office. No e/a were seen.	
			F/O. Lyon was hit over Lorient by heavy flak at 6,000 feet and his aircraft was seen to dive away out of control and crash in flames S.S.E. of A/D. No parachute was seen. F/Lt. Walton, DFC was hit also by L.A.A. defenses of A/D when at 0 feet. He climbed to 6,000 feet and successfully bailed out in Quimperle area. Remaining aircraft returned safely.	
			F/Lt. T.W. Berry posted from 611 Squadron. W/O. R.A. Fairweather posted non-effective to Predannack.	
	28.7.44		Just a Shipping Recco today at 21.05 hours. Morlaix - Ushant - Goulet De Brest. No shipping was sighted. Visibility good. Today we have heard that F/Sgt. Fargher had just got back to England from France. Good Show. Also F/Lt. Lattimer has received the D.F.C.	
			also a darn good show. F/Lt. Johnston has taken over as Flight Commander of "A" Flight. F/Sgt. W.A. Livesley posted from No. 64 Squadron.	
	29.7.44		At 07.04 hours twelve aircraft were airborne on Ramrod 158. We crossed the French Coast at Plouescat, located target, village of Scrigniac, which was supposed to be occupied by German troops. All bombs were dropped on the target at 07.46 hours, but results were not seen due to masses of smoke and dust. 2 aircraft then strafed the target with cannon and machine gun. Power cables, a factory and gun posts were hit in area. No enemy reaction apart from a little flak. All aircraft returned to base by 08.30 hours.	1

3.3 RAF 234 Squadron Operations Record Book, 27 July 1944,
National Archives, Kew.

One part of this mission was also to observe what aircraft the Luftwaffe might have at this airbase. Blue Section carried out a strafing attack, during which damage was caused to the watchtower, barracks and hangars. Following this, Red Section proceeded a little further down the coast towards Lorient. It was here that they were bracketed by accurate and heavy flak. At 19.54 hrs Spitfire AR343 (Red 3) was hit at 6,000ft by flak from the Quatre Chemins flak battery located south of Plœmeur.

A little later, Spitfire BM200 (Red 1) was also hit, by the flak battery at Kerlec, when flying at low level.

Red 3, piloted by F/O E.R. Lyon, was severely damaged and was seen to dive away out of control and crash in flames with no parachute seen.

Red 1 managed to retain control long enough to climb to a height where Walton was able to parachute out. He landed safely at Kerdanet, near Quimperlé, and Spitfire BM200 crashed to the ground in a fireball at Rédéné. At liberty for a short while, and being helped by the local resistance, Walton was captured by the Germans at around 21.00 hrs. He was a prisoner of war for the remainder of World War II.

3.4 RAF 234 Squadron Operations Record Book, 27 July 1944,
National Archives, Kew.

J

Dulag-Luft, Wetzler
Eingang 1 0.AUG 1944
Zentralkart. u. Meldest.

Formblatt 1

Angaben über Gefangennahme von feindlichen Luft-

waffenangehörigen.

Dienststelle: __Fliegerhorstkommandantur E (v)226/XII__
Ort: _____Lorient (Fliegerhorst)_____
Zeit: _____27.Juli 1944._____

Betr.: ~~Abschuß~~ ~~Notlandung~~ eines britischen Flugzeuges (Spitfires)

bei Ros -Spernez Strasse Lorient-Quimperle

am __27.7.44__ um __21,00__ Uhr.

Name: _____W o l t o n_____
Vorname: _____W i l l i a m_____
Dienstrang: _____Fl.Lt._____
Nr. der Erkennungsmarke: __119499(nach seinen Angaben die Marke
Verbleib: __gefangen__ verloren,wurde in Zivil gefangen
Ort und Zeit der Gefangennahme: __am 27.7.44 21,00 Uhr__
Bezeichnung des Lazaretts: _____ Strasse Lorient-Quimperle
Ort und Zeit der Beisetzung: _____
(Grablage evtl.nachzuldn!)

Hauptmann und Offz.z.b.V.

Verteiler:
Auswertestelle West.
FLGK.Wfr.Io
Astab Nord.
Kdo.Fl.H.B.8/XII (laval.
Entwurf.
Gefang.Vern.St.Chartres.

CAPTURE OF F. LT. W. WALTON
(SPITFIRE BM 200) AT 21.00 HRS
ON 27TH July 1944

3.5 German record of the capture of Fl/Lt W. Walton on 27 July 1944 at 21.00hrs.

30

The crash site location of Spitfire BM200 was found and excavated in 2004 by local French enthusiasts. The recovered and broken Spitfire BM200 Rolls-Royce Merlin engine was donated to the Salle des traditions (Musée) at the Base Aéronavale de Lann-Bihoué, where it has been cleaned by members of the French air and naval veterans' association and has been put on display in the Salle des Expositions.

Six Spitfires returned to base at RAF Predannack at 20.50 hours.

Anne Shelton and Glenn Miller

3.6 Anne Shelton CD Cover, *Thank You Captain Miller*.
Reproduced by kind permission of Kelly Richards, niece of Anne Shelton.

As the remaining six 234 Squadron pilots landed safely back at RAF Predannack at 20.50 hrs on 27 July 1944, they will have retired exhausted to their billets, no doubt contemplating the fate of their two fellow pilots who had not returned. Live on the radio, moments after their return, they would have heard Anne Shelton singing in a thirty-minute broadcast (in which Anne was the guest artist) of The American Band of the Supreme Allied Command under the direction of Captain Glenn Miller. A little later, in December 1944, Glenn Miller was the one for whom the luck ran out as his plane, a C-64 Norseman, went missing over the English Channel on a flight to Versailles. Anne Shelton was invited to accompany Glenn Miller on this flight but due to other commitments she declined the invitation.

A CD has been made from a recording of the thirty-minute broadcast of 27 July 1944, with the following tracks:

Tracks 1–7 The American Band of the Supreme Allied Command with Capt Miller

Tracks 8–18 all by Anne Shelton

Track 8 'Don't Misunderstand'

Track 9 'I Fall in Love with You Every Day'

Track 10 'Time May Change'

Track 11 'Take off the Coat'

Track 12 'Siberia'

Track 13 'I Ain't Got Nobody'

Track 14 'Easter Parade' (from 1944 broadcast with Bing Crosby)

Track 15 'If There are Stars in My Eyes' (Jo Shelton)

Track 16 'The Village of St. Bernadette'

Track 17 'Cross over the Bridge'

Track 18 'I'll be Seeing You'

Within the family papers are press cuttings from Scottish newspapers announcing Russell's fate. The cuttings indicated that Russell's Spitfire was seen to have been shot down, crashing in flames near Plœmeur, Lorient, Brittany, in western France. One cutting of 25 November 1944 in *The Scotsman* reports him as missing in action and then the next, of 30 June 1945, reports that he was now officially presumed killed.

In the immediate post-war era, Russell's name was recorded on the Runnymede Memorial amongst the 20,400 Royal Air Force personnel who fell in combat in Europe and the Atlantic and who have no known grave. His name is also on the WWII War Memorial in Colinton Parish Church Cemetery in Edinburgh, and on the gravestone nearby over his mother Elizabeth's grave, his mother having predeceased him in 1935.

Scotsman.

25 Nov^r, 1944.

Missing On Active Service

LYON.—Missing on operations near LORIENT, on 27th July 1944, Flying Officer RUSSELL LYON, R.A.F.V.R., Fighter Command, son of Ernest H. Lyon and the late Elizabeth W. Lyon, Cargen, Bonaly Road, Colinton.

TEDCASTLE.—Missing on operations off HOLLAND in November 1944, Lieutenant MAURICE W. TEDCASTLE, R.N.V.R., 6t Oaklands, Weston Favell, Northampton, and younger son of Mrs Tedcastle, Craigroyston, Glenfarg, Perth.

3.7 Scottish Press Cuttings 1944.
Lyon family collection.

WAR CASUALTIES

Wing Commander G. ("Peter") Panitz, D.F.C., "train-busting ace of the Royal Australian Air Force," is officially reported missing from air operations. He is 28. His home is at Dufftown, Banffshire. He enlisted from Southport, Queensland.

Flying Officer Russell Lyon, R.A.F.V.R. (Fighter Command), who is reported missing from air operations, is the son of Mr Ernest H. Lyon and the late Mrs Lyon, Cargen, Bonaly Road, Colinton, Edinburgh. Educated at George Watson's College, where he was a member of the 1st XV in 1940-41, Flying Officer Lyon joined the R.A.F. in July 1941. He trained as a pilot in the United States, and after getting his wings and being commissioned, he acted as a flying instructor at various air fields in the United States and in Canada, returning to this country in April 1943 for operational training. He was reported missing from operations near Lorient on July 27, his Spitfire having been seen to be hit by *flak* and to crash in flames.

3.8 Lyon family grave,
Colinton, Edinburgh,
before 1985.
Lyon family collection.

The War Memorial in Colinton Parish Church Cemetery in Edinburgh

Ernest Russell Lyon is remembered on this memorial, located near to his family home.

3.9 WWII War Memorial in Colinton Parish Church Cemetery in Edinburgh. Photo Andrew Paterson.

Runnymede Memorial

Also known as the Air Forces Memorial, it is located near Egham, Surrey, on high ground overlooking the Runnymede meadows on the south side of the River Thames, where the Magna Carta was sealed by King John on 15 June 1215.

The Memorial was opened on 17 October 1953 by HM Queen Elizabeth II, four months after her Coronation.

It commemorates some 20,400 Air Force men and women from the British Empire who lost their lives in WWII and who have no known grave.

3.10 Runnymede Memorial. Photo Richard Lyon.

3.11 Runnymede Memorial commemorating Missing Air Forces personnel
with no known grave. E.R. Lyon is remembered on this memorial.
Photo Richard Lyon.

On Saturday 29 July 1944 the remains of an *Inconnu* English Airman were buried by the German Military Forces in Grave No. 33 in Row 6 at Guidel Cemetery, just a few kilometres north-west of the crash site of Spitfire AR343. A witness statement made by the farmer on whose land the Spitfire had crashed records (1) that one of the French-speaking Germans clearing the crash site told him that the body of the pilot had been taken to Guidel to be buried and (2) that on a visit to Guidel two days after the crash on his land the farmer spoke with the gravedigger of Guidel Cemetery who said that a grave was ready and he was going to bury a pilot.

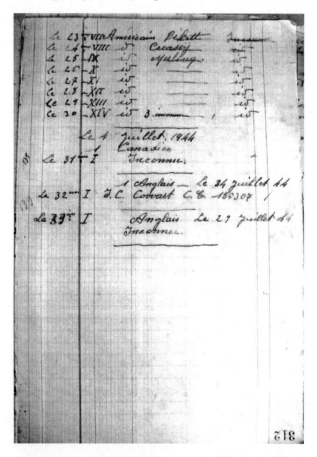

3.12 Guidel Communal Cemetery record book page shows
burial of F/O John Coward on 24 July 1944 and
'*Anglais Inconnu*' on 29 July 1944. Photo J.-Y. Le Lan.

It is poignant to note that on 20 July 1944, a few days before the mission, there was an attempt to assassinate the Fuhrer, Adolf Hitler, at the Wolf's Lair Field Headquarters in East Prussia. The code name of the conspirators' assassination attempt was Operation Valkyrie. The attempt was led by Claus von Stauffenberg. Had it succeeded, one wonders today how soon a negotiated peace would have followed with the consequent further saving of many innocent lives.

Posthumously, the following medals were awarded to Ernest Russell Lyon and were sent by the Air Ministry to his father:

- 1939–1945 Star
- Air Crew Europe Star (Atlantic or France and Germany)
- Defence Medal (Silver laurel leaves (King's Commendation for brave conduct. Civil))
- War Medal 1939–45 (Oak leaf)

3.13 Medals awarded posthumously to Russell Lyon, photo Richard Lyon.
Left to Right: 1939–45 Star; Air Crew Europe Star; Defence Medal;
War Medal 1939–45.

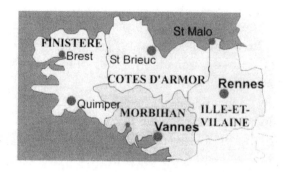

BRITTANY

THE MORBIHAN DEPARTMENT

1 ⭐ Guidel Cemetery

2 ⭐ Crash site at Kercaves, 27.7.1944, F/O Lyon, Spitfire AR343
Possible Burial " Anglais Inconnu in Row 6 Grave 33 at Guidel on 29th
July 1944

3 ⭐ Crash site at Auray, 22.7.1944, F/O Coward, Spitfire, Burial Row 6
Grave 32 at Guidel on 24th July 1944

3.14 Map of Brittany with Guidel, Kercavès and Auray marked.

Chapter 4

The Lorient Pocket, 7 August 1944–10 May 1945

A few days later, following the fatal shooting down of Spitfire AR343 at around 19.55 hrs on 27 July 1944, the area around the crash site, and the area of possible burial of the casualty at Guidel, were contained in what became known as the Lorient Pocket, Festung Lorient, or the Poche de Lorient.

After D-Day and the break-out from the invasion beaches into Normandy, the major thrust of the advancing Allied Forces was towards Paris. Many retreating German forces, estimated at 100,000 German soldiers, headed for the well-defended Atlantic Wall fortresses of Brest, Lorient and Saint-Nazaire on the western, Atlantic, coast of France where the U-boat bases had been heavily fortified. At Lorient there was the vast Keroman U-boat base.

The Keroman base was the largest on the French Atlantic coast and housed the German U-boat Headquarters, and accommodated the 2nd and 10th U-boat flotillas for much of the Battle of the Atlantic.

4.1 Keroman U-boat pens. Photo by Jean-Yves Le Lan.

In the winter of 1943/44 heavy bombing of the U-boat Base, ordered by Churchill, failed to make much impact on the vast concrete structures, so Churchill then ordered bombing attacks to remove much of the infrastructure around Keroman, resulting in almost total destruction of the city of Lorient. Before this phase of bombing took place, thousands of leaflets were dropped over the area, instructing and allowing time for residents to evacuate the area.

4.2 The East Dombunker, the first German U-boat enclosure at Lorient. Photo Jean-Yves Le Lan.

Admiral Karl Donitz was Commander in Chief of the German Navy until 1 May 1945 when he succeeded Hitler as Head of State of the German Reich. He had been based in a large house at Kernével, Larmor-Plage, across the estuary waters from the Keroman U-boat base. However, after the commando raid on Saint-Nazaire of March 1942, Hitler ordered Admiral Dönitz to move his headquarters to Paris.

Allied responsibility for clearing the Axis Forces from Brittany was given to General Patton and the US 3rd Army, who became operational on 1 August 1944 and brought the VIII Corps and the 6th Armoured Division together to clear the Brittany peninsula and especially the German forces in Brest.

The 4th Armoured Division initially followed, but they then headed for Rennes and Lorient. Once Brest had fallen, the senior German Commander, General Der Artillerie Wilhelm Fahrmbacher, took command of all the forces that were centred on Lorient.

In total there were some 25,000 German forces who, under their Commanders, including Konter Admiral Kaehler, were determined to hold out, backed by upwards of 500 artillery pieces. By 7 August 1944, these German forces were surrounded on three sides, and on their fourth side was the sea. With many diehards among them, they set about denying the Allies the use of the port of Lorient, and other fortifications making up the Atlantic Wall. Some 300 artillery pieces defended attack from the direction of the sea.

The Lorient Pocket was thus formed, with the Allied Forces, together with Free French Forces and the French Resistance Forces, holding the siege for the remainder of World War II. The area was some 850 sq. miles of territory. In this besieged area there were some 26,000 German soldiers and some 20,000 civilian population.

Brest was liberated on 19 September 1944, but at a cost of 10,000 American soldiers. Capturing the ports of Lorient and Saint-Nazaire intact had ceased to be of strategic importance to the Allies and the American Forces abandoned any further plans for attacking the two fortresses on 7 September 1944, and so the sieges continued until the end of World War II.

The German forces were cut off from the Reich but occasionally ships or U-boats reached the port to replenish supplies. Food was the major problem to those German forces within the Lorient Pocket.

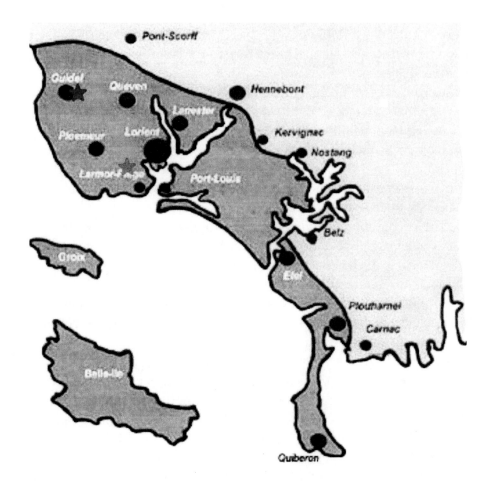

The Lorient Pocket

7th August 1944 to 10th May 1945

⭐ Guidel Cemetery burial of 'Anglais Inconnu' on 29.7.1944

CWGC Headstone of 1953 records RAF Officer, Known unto God.

⭐ Crash site at Kercavès, 27.7.1944, F/O Lyon, Spitfire AR343

4.3 The Lorient Pocket with Spitfire AR 343 Crash Site and Guidel Communal Cemetery marked by Richard Lyon.

The Black Panther Division, part of the US 12th Army Group, took over from the 94th Infantry Division on 1 January 1945. With a score to settle, months of skirmishing then followed.

Within the Lorient Pocket, French postage stamps had remained in use, and post continued between Lorient and liberated France, but re-supply caused problems as no new stamps were getting into the Pocket. In liberated France, the image of Marshall Petain on stamps was banned, but these were still in use in Lorient. To get around the problem, in 1945, the Lorient Pocket issued its own set of postage stamps, French stamps with Festung Lorient overprint, which are much sought after by collectors today.

4.4 Lorient Pocket, Vichy France postage stamp overprinted 'Festung Lorient'. Rights Reserved

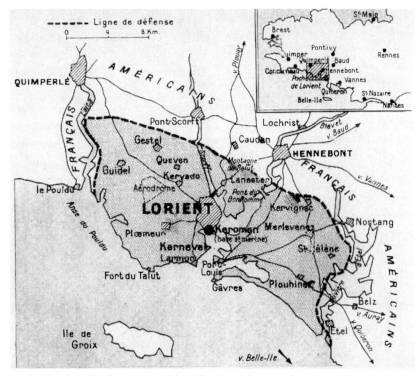

4.5 Lorient Pocket Map, with Allied positions, and regional thumbnail insert map, from 'La Poche de Lorient', by Jean Aubertin.

The US 66th Infantry Division was tasked with seeing that the German forces around Lorient and Saint-Nazaire, impregnably fortified, were not able to break out or menace other Allied Forces. There were 25,000 Americans and 10,000 Frenchmen in this little-known, or even orphan, division. The Commander was Major General Herna (Dutch) Kramer, who was chosen for the job as he had graduated from a German war college. Stalemate ensued. The Germans had plotted every bit of ground within the range of their guns and could obliterate any spot. The German Commander had a communication system in place enabling him to talk instantly to anyone, or to all his troops.

4.6 Lorient Pocket Defence Lines.

Day after day artillery skirmishes took place. With one shot the Allies sank a 5,000-ton ship in Lorient harbour. It looked as though the Germans could not be taken until two American officers, Col. James Hamilton and Lt. Col. Ralph Ganns, came up with an idea. They had carried out interrogations of captured Germans until they had the name and position of every German officer in the Lorient Pocket. Using a PA system that was loud enough for American announcements to be heard by all on the German side, with the aim of wearing down the German morale the Americans would give the name of the German unit or commanding officer that they were to target next.

The suicide of Adolf Hitler took place on 30 April 1945. With seven lines of defences, Fortress Lorient was a challenge for the Allied Forces to take on, but the plan to break the morale of the besieged forces started in early May.

On 1 May 1945, the announcement came: 'Watch Col. Schmidt's headquarters. In 10 minutes we will blow it to pieces.' The warning was repeated every minute until after ten minutes every American gun was turned on the colonel's headquarters, which was destroyed. 'We are now going to wipe out Capt Reuther's company – just look that way and watch it' the loudspeakers said next, and the threat was carried out. Thus, German units were destroyed one by one, and more and more surrenders took place until finally General Fahrmbacher of the Luftwaffe surrendered all his forces.

The surrender of the Lorient Pocket came on 8 May 1945. General Farhmbacher, who had defied the Allied order to surrender, as well as Admiral Donitz's order to lay down arms, surrendered to General Kramer. Kramer was in command of the 12th Army Coastal Sector and the 66th Infantry Division. There was then a two-day delay until 10 May, when the formal surrender actually took place.

It is recorded that food supplies in the last few months of the Lorient Pocket were desperately low. In order to supplement the meagre supplies General Fahrmbacher and his quartermaster are reported to have secretly organised sawdust obtained from railway sleepers to be used for bread making. A week after Germany surrendered the general asked his quartermaster how many sleepers were left, with the answer being given: 'one'. With no food left, surrender of those still holding out in the Lorient Pocket was inevitable.

The French resistance fighters and the American division were made responsible for making the blockade during nine long months, up to the signing of the act of surrender on 7 May 1945 in Étel.

Preparatory meetings for the surrender of the Lorient Pocket took place on the Right Bank of the river of Étel, in Magouer, in Plouhinec. On 4 May, a meeting between Germans and an Allied deputation had resulted in no agreement. General Fahrmbacher refused to capitulate. On Monday 7 May, he agreed to restart discussions, with officers of both camps meeting in the Café le Carour in Magouer (now the Café de la Barre) at 3 p.m. Colonel Keating led for the Americans, Colonel Joppé represented the French Army and Colonel Borst represented the German Army. The negotiations nearly failed once again. The Germans thought that they had not been conquered in battles.

Colonel Keating threatened the Germans then with massive bombing. The German colonel gave a report of his mission to General Fahrmbacher and came back to declare to the Allies that their requirements would be satisfied. To cross the river Étel a Red Cross boat was used.

It was the young captain André Villard who arranged the Surrender Ceremony. He told later his memory of this unforgettable day in these terms:

> I invited the three Germans to advance towards the Allied officers who waited not far from the 'Café Breton', for the public declaration to take place.
>
> Approaching our representatives, the Germans stood to attention, made Nazi salutes and bowed twice.
>
> The leader of the deputation turned to the Americans. It was very pale and solemn. He declared: Commander of the American Forces, in accordance with the orders of my leaders, I come to sign the capitulation. Then turning to the French officers, he began speaking the same statement, but was quickly interrupted by the Colonel Joppé who said to him: I understand, let us not waste time! And he made a gesture to advance towards the Café where the large room had been prepared for the signing of the capitulation.
>
> Nothing was changed on the pre-arranged surrender conditions. The Germans, who became more and more

emotional and resigned to the outcome, made signs that they had accepted the conditions.

Colonel Borst, in the name of General Fahrmbacher, took his pen and prepared to sign the document, his movement triggered off the flashes of light from the photographer's magnesium flares, but he hesitated and did not sign immediately. Then, believing the moment was advantageous to himself, he affixed his signature. But a photographer was ready and recorded the moment.

Without a word, Colonel Borst withdrew his gun from the holster and presented it to the American Colonel. This gesture finalised the complete submission of the German forces.

All matters were strictly regulated. It was 9 p.m. when the German Officers returned to the pier after saluting the Allied officers.

The Allied officers returned the salutes.

Ceasefire was envisaged the following day at 12:01 a.m. During the next two days, the Germans cleared mines from the main routes and removed roadblocks, but they also destroyed their archives. The Surrender Ceremony took place in a field in Caudan on 10 May at 4 p.m. General Fahrmbacher solemnly presented his revolver to General Kramer, Commander of the American Forces in the region. In the field at Caudan, General Borgnis-Desbordes, Colonel Morice and their officers represented the French Interior Forces.

At Étel, a memorial plaque is fixed to the facade above the Bar Breton signage recording that the signing of the German surrender took place in this building. The inscription on the plaque reads: 'HERE WAS SIGNED THE CAPITULATION GERMAN OF THE POCKET OF LORIENT 7 MAY 1945'.

The table at which the surrender was signed remained in place in the Bar Breton until 2006. Since then it has been moved to a Committee Room in Étel Town Hall and registers in the heritage of Étel. Much time was available to the German forces to destroy their records, so few German military records from the area survive today.

Throughout this period, from 7 August 1944 until 10 May 1945, the crash site of Spitfire AR343 near Plœmeur, and the cemetery at Guidel, were not accessible to the Allied Forces. Nor were any further Allied casualties buried in the cemetery at Guidel. The casualty buried there, in Row 6, Grave 33, on Saturday 29 July 1944 was the last World War II Allied RAF casualty to be buried at Guidel.

During WWII the International Red Cross acted to enable casualty reporting for both sides of the conflict using the 'Totenlist' exchange of information. This scheme of casualty reporting had originated at the time of the First World War. However, no Red Cross Totenlist records exist today reporting on the casualty from the shooting down of Spitfire AR343 on 27 July 1944.

Many of the local population were evacuated from the Lorient Pocket area before 7 August 1944. A few of the local population who remained in the Lorient Pocket for the nine months until the surrender took place suffered dreadfully under the German forces and it is therefore understandable that at this time some of the routine Red Cross humanitarian activities were severely curtailed.

4.7 The sign of the Bar Breton, with the plaque above recording the place of signature of the surrender of the Lorient Pocket. Photo Jean-Yves Le Lan.

4.8, 4.9 Signing of the surrender at the Bar Breton by Colonel Borst.
Collection Musée des thoniers/Association Autrefois Étel & sa région.
And www.alamy.com, ref. CW6FP4.

4.10 Lorient Pocket Surrender, near Caudan, General Fahrmbacher and staff with Allied Commanders. Copyright Droits Réservés.

4.11 General Fahrmbacher hands his pistol to General Kramer. Copyright Droits Réservés.

Chapter 5

The Immediate Post-War Period 1945–1950s

Following the German surrender in May 1945, both the US and the Allied Forces were soon in the Brittany area and, as time progressed, searches occurred for missing personnel. In December 1944 the RAF expanded the Missing Research Section (MRS) of the Air Ministry. The unit was then known as the Missing Research and Enquiry Service (MRES).

Searches for missing personnel were undertaken by the Missing Research and Enquiry Unit No. 1 (MREU 1), who were responsible for searches in the whole of France, and became operational from August 1945 onwards.

First into the area were the US search authorities who found their way into the Lorient area. In September 1945, the US 605th Quartermaster Corps Registration Company carried out an examination of the Guidel Cemetery, exhuming and transferring US casualties, some to the Brittany American Cemetery and Memorial at St. James, near Mont-Saint-Michel; some to the Normandy American Cemetery and Memorial at Colleville-sur-Mer near the Omaha Beach; and one to the Ardennes American Cemetery and Memorial at Neupré in Belgium.

In the late summer of 1945, the unit responsible for searches in France was rapidly expanded from around 14 to approximately 350 personnel, and this was split into six units with different geographical areas of responsibility. MREU 1 was responsible for work in France and Luxembourg, and this commenced in December 1945 (AIR 55/65), with the first task to sweep the Channel coast from Dunkerque to Brest. All sections were in the field by 15 December but delays occurred due to the mines still present in many areas along the coastline. Some areas were therefore not searched until later in 1946.

MREU 1 searched France *département* by *département* in accordance with instructions issued by the Air Ministry, a total of ninety *départements*.

The references below to AIR documents refer to the Catalogue Descriptions of a large series of Air Ministry documents dating from 1918 to 1964 which are held in the National Archives at Kew. These are generally available to the public in the reading rooms at Kew.

MREU 1 was divided into six sections, each responsible for different regions. (AIR 29/1598.)

MREU 1 Section 2 was initially located at Bayeux and later moved to Vannes covering the *départements* of Calvados and Morbihan. (Handwritten alteration over text in AIR 55/78.)

In July 1946, the RAF MREU 7 carried out examinations at Guidel. They examined Grave 33, Row 6, where the burial of the *inconnu* English airman had taken place on 29 July 1944, but they were unable to positively identify this casualty. The exhumation report indicated few bones present and a scrap of an RAF issue shirt. It also indicated that the skull was missing.

By 14 January 1947, work in Morbihan and Finistère, together with sixteen other *départements*, was reported as finished. (AIR 55/78.)

It was recorded that the long-term policy for MREUs working in NW Europe would be that they would continue at their present strength until 30 June 1947 and thereafter scale down until disbandment at the end of November 1947. (AIR 20/9050.)

MREU 1 was disbanded on 31 July 1947, leaving a detachment based in Paris that survived another year. (AIR 55/65.)

In the early 1950s the Commonwealth War Graves Commission (CWGC) installed headstones (replacing the original simple wooden crosses installed over each war grave) in the Commonwealth Section of the Guidel Cemetery.

Over grave No 33 in Row 6, where the burial took place on 29 July 1944, the inscription on the Commonwealth War Grave reads:

'An Airman of the 1939–1945 War, Royal Air Force, 29 July 1944, Known unto God'.

5.1 Guidel Communal Cemetery
during WWII, and with CWGC
headstones after WWII.
Collection Richard Lyon.

5.2, 5.3 CWGC headstone at Row 6,
Grave 33, Guidel Communal Cemetery.
Photos Richard Lyon.

Amongst other inscriptions put forward for war memorials in war cemeteries that were being created after World War I, Rudyard Kipling suggested that the phrase 'Known unto God' should be put on the headstones of all unknown soldiers. In the period after World War I, Kipling, who had lost his own son, Jack, with no known grave, worked with Sir Fabian Ware in the early days of the Imperial War Graves Commission, now the Commonwealth War Graves Commission. Kipling commented then that the work they had taken on was the single biggest piece of work since the time of the Pharaohs, and the Pharaohs only worked in their own country.

5.4, 5.5 CWGC sections at Kerentrech and Lanester.
Photos Jean-Yves Le Lan.

5.6 CWGC section at Gâvres. Photo Jean-Yves Le Lan.

At the Guidel Cemetery, in the CWGC section, there are five rows of graves with empty areas between certain graves corresponding to the places that were the graves of the American servicemen transferred to St. James in late 1945.

In Row 6 there are thirty-three graves; in Row 5, twenty-six graves; in Row 4, twenty-eight graves; in Row 3, twenty-two graves; and in Row 2 there are eight graves. There is no Row 1. This makes a total of one hundred and seventeen Commonwealth war graves.

At Guidel at the time of the study (See Appendix 3) there are one hundred and eight casualties whose identity is known and nine are unknown. Casualties come from the Commonwealth countries (United Kingdom, Canada, Australia, New Zealand) and one casualty is Polish. Almost all the casualties are airmen, with many resulting from the bombing raids over Lorient in the winter of 1942/43.

Winston Churchill was concerned that conventional bombing could not destroy the U-boat pens in Lorient, as their concrete structures were so massive. Instead he ordered that bombing was to be concentrated on all the surrounding areas to take out the infrastructure around the U-boat pens.

The graveyard of Guidel contains some tombs of 1941 and 1942 but the great majority of casualties correspond to the year 1943 and a few for the year 1944.

For casualties in the area around Lorient there were several cemeteries in use by the Germans. These included Lorient-Kerentrech, Lanester, Gâvres and Guidel. It was of concern to the German authorities that many of the local French population would turn up in silent protest when casualties were being buried. Accordingly, during the latter three years of World War II they chose to organise the burial of all casualties at Guidel alone, where the surrounding high wall prevented the local populace from making their silent protest known.

Henri Hado, who was then a teenager living locally to Guidel, often watched the burials of foreign servicemen at Guidel during the war years. His memory was that the Germans went about things with respect. Casualties were brought to the cemetery by the Germans in coffins and a ceremony was organised in the presence of a German military unit who fired a volley salute over the burial of each casualty. There were no local French people present except for the gravedigger.

In England, the RAF built the Runnymede Memorial, (see illustrations 3.10 and 3.11) designed by Edward Maufe and opened in 1953, listing some 20,400 names of airmen who lost their lives in WWII and who have no known grave. F/O Russell Lyon's name is included on this memorial.

During this era many other memorials were built across the United Kingdom in cities, towns, schools, universities and other institutions, commemorating Army, Navy, Air Force, Merchant Navy and civilian casualties of World War II.

Chapter 6
Events of 2001–2008

Fifty years later, in November 2006, a Scottish genealogical website (www.talkingscot.com) encouraged members to post memorials to relatives who had lost their lives fighting for their country in the two world wars, if not also earlier and later wars.

One such memorial had already been placed by the author's cousin, David Webster, for his uncle (who is also the author's maternal uncle), Flight Sergeant William McLennan Jack (1917–1944), who served in the RAF Volunteer Reserve. His unarmed transport plane had been shot down over the English Channel near Dieppe in March 1944, and his remains were recovered and buried at Whitley Bay (Hartley South) Cemetery, Northumberland.

Many such memorials were being posted on this Scottish website and the author decided to add one for his uncle, F/O Ernest Russell Lyon (1922–1944). The author's knowledge of his uncle was limited to little more than the bare facts taken from the newspaper cuttings (Missing in Action and later Assumed Dead classified notices; see Illustration 3.7) in his possession. The bare facts included his name, the date of 27 July 1944 and the name of the town of Plœmeur where, just a few weeks after D-Day, Russell's Spitfire had been seen to hit the ground.

Little was then known about Russell, with information coming only via the newspaper cuttings and photos in the family archive. In old family photograph albums there are several photos of Russell with his elder half-brother, Stanley, and his younger brother, James, as they grew up in Colinton, on the south-western edge of Edinburgh, in the late 1920s and 1930s.

A photo of Russell in RAF uniform had also stood prominently on Stanley's desk in the family room in his home in Danby, North Yorkshire. This photo is well remembered by Stanley's three sons, Alastair, Richard and Bob, as they grew up, and also by their wives and children during visits made to Danby in the last three decades of the 20th century.

At the beginning of April 2007, five months after posting the memorial on the TalkingScot website, the author received an email from a Frenchman, Jean-Yves Le Lan. Jean-Yves, and other local history and aviation enthusiasts including Claude Hélias and Jean Robic, worked to preserve aeronautical heritage and to conduct research into the history of aviation in Brittany. Their research into the WWII air war over Brittany included bombing raids, crashes of Allied and enemy aircraft, escape networks for airmen and similar subjects. The email received was in French, and was well illustrated with several photographs and pictures. With rudimentary 'O' level French skills and a handy French–English dictionary, this was soon translated.

One photograph was of 'A' Flight of 234 Squadron in the winter of 1943–44, showing a group of fifteen RAF pilots in front of a Spitfire, in which Russell Lyon is present. (See Chapter 2, photo 2.9.) The information received added greatly to the author's knowledge of Russell, including photographs not seen before.

The email revealed that a Spitfire crash site at Kercavès, near Plœmeur, Lorient, had been excavated by members of the group in 2001–3.

In 2001, a lady who was walking her dog in some woodland near Kercavès saw a 'pipe' sticking out of the ground, with other metal debris nearby. She reported this to local history and aviation

6.1 Metal wreckage at the Kercavès crash site. Photos by Jean Robic.

enthusiasts Jean Robic and his friends, who then excavated and found the remains of a Spitfire.

Archival research was then undertaken by Jean-Yves Le Lan, Jean Robic and another aviation historian, Claude Hélias.

6.2
L to R, Jean-Yves Le Lan, Alastair Lyon, Joseph Le Corroller, Jean Robic and Pamela Lyon. Photo by Catherine Le Lan.

The site was 4 km SSE of the aerodrome of Lorient-Lann-Bihoué which, in WWII and under German occupation, had been called Kerlin-Bastard. Lorient then was the heavily defended port and U-boat base.

The Spitfire at this crash site had been identified as a MkVb, registration number AR343. This was shown to be one of eight Spitfires from 234 Squadron that had embarked on a 'Rhubarb 323' code name mission on the evening of 27 July 1944. The pilot of AR343 was Flying Officer E.R. Lyon.

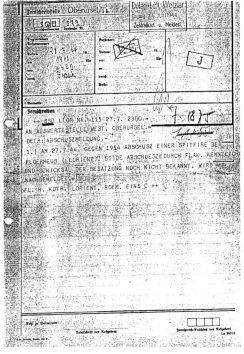

6.3 German record of a Spitfire shot down at 19.54 hrs on 27 July 1944 by Plœmeur, Lorient.

In the history of 234 Squadron, some of which is recorded in the book *Spitfire Mark V in Action: RAF Operations in Northern Europe* by Peter Caygill, the details of this Rhubarb 323 mission and the loss of F/O E.R. (Ben) Lyon, Red 3, are mentioned.

The French researchers had also discovered the German record (captured in 1945 by the Americans and now in the National Archives in Washington) which recorded a Spitfire being shot down, and also a contemporary French eyewitness account, all indicating that the crash site was to the SSE of the Kerlin-Bastard Luftwaffe base.

Larmor Plage le 29. 11. 2003

Je soussigné Joseph Le Corroller
Agriculteur retraité 80 ans
demeurant à Kercavés (Larmor Plage)

déclare avoir été témoin de la chute d'un avion Spitfire près de ma ferme en juillet 1944 en fin de journée c'était l'époque des moissons les allemands arrivés sur les lieux m'ont déclaré que cet avion était un spitfire –

le corps du pilote gisait à côté de la carcasse en feu et son parachute brûlait les militaires m'ont donné l'ordre de partir vite. À ma connaissance le corps du pilote repose à guidel

téléphone
7 33-60-67

Joseph Le CORROLLER
KERCAVES
56960 LARMOR-PLAGE

6.4 Witness Statement by Joseph Le Corroller.
Collection Richard Lyon.

From a handwritten statement:

LARMOR-PLAGE, 29 May 2003

I, the undersigned, Joseph Le Corroller, a retired farmer aged 80, residing at Kercaves (Larmor-Plage) declare that I was witness to a Spitfire coming down close to my farm in July 1944, at the end of the day.
This took place during harvest time. The Germans arrived on the scene and told me that the aircraft was a Spitfire.
The body of the pilot was lying by the side of the burning fuselage with his parachute on fire. The soldiers told me to leave immediately.
To my knowledge, the body of the pilot lies in Guidel.

(signature)

Joseph Le Corroller,
KERCAVES,
56960 LARMOR-PLAGE

Tel: 0 [illegible] 97 33 60 67

6.5 Translation of witness statement into English.

The eyewitness account, from Joseph Le Corroller, indicated that the RAF pilot had not survived – he had seen the pilot's body at a distance of some six metres from the cockpit wreckage – and that the Germans arrived quickly in the place where the Spitfire had crashed. He was ordered to leave. Later, as the Germans were clearing the above-ground wreckage, a soldier said to him that the pilot had been taken to Guidel.

Photographs of the remains of the Spitfire that were excavated in 2001–2003 were in the email, with several of the parts identified. A George V half-crown dated 1936 had also been found in the wreckage.

It was becoming abundantly clear that this particular Spitfire crash site was that in which Russell had lost his life, and it was due to the diligence and enthusiasm of a small group of Frenchmen that the flame in his memory could be rekindled some sixty-three years after the event. The French researchers were very pleased to have found a living relation of Russell, for whom they had been searching for some time.

Since the first email, much more correspondence flowed between the author and the French researchers (one of whom is now his co-author), between the author and the RAF Personnel Records, the RAF Air Historical Branch, and former members of 234 Squadron, to ensure that as complete a record as possible can now be made of the story of Russell Lyon, this young Scotsman, to hand down to future generations.

But it was another piece of research by the French group that aroused even more interest. They had researched all other crashes in the period before and after the AR343 Spitfire crash of 27 July 1944, and had recorded the fate of the respective pilots. One burial in a local cemetery, at Guidel 3km to the NW of the Luftwaffe airfield of Kerlin-Bastard, has been found where the original cemetery register records: '*Anglais Le 29 Juillet 1944, Inconnu*'. Unfortunately, there is no mention of the origin of the body in the register. The Germans probably did not say anything to the gravedigger when they brought the body on 29 July and he did not dare to ask.

A photograph of the grave showed the Commonwealth War Grave headstone from the 1950s marked: 'An Airman of the 1939–1945 War, Royal Air Force, 29th July 1944. Known unto God'.

6.6
Guidel Communal Cemetery
Row 6, Grave 33.
Photo Richard Lyon.

The French research showed that in the days close to 27 July 1944 there had been only three other Allied Forces crashes. One pilot, Flight Lieutenant E.C. Walton, the leader of the mission, had been captured after successfully baling out. A second pilot on a different mission had crashed near Morbihan; the pilot had been identified and was buried locally. That left just one other crash – that on the evening of 27 July of Spitfire AR343 – and the Guidel unidentified grave of 29 July.

The French researchers reported that they had been in contact with the French office of the CWGC at Beaurains with the results of their research but the CWGC had indicated to them that they would not change a headstone unless they were 100 per cent certain of its identification. The author then set out on a mission to get Russell Lyon's name on to the gravestone at Guidel, little then knowing what he had embarked upon.

An enquiry, including the new information now known to the family regarding the crash site, the unmarked grave at Guidel and the eyewitness account of Joseph Le Corroller, was made to the CWGC in June 2007. They replied confirming that the Ministry of Defence had agreed to reopen the investigation into the possible identification of the grave at Guidel.

An early administrative hurdle had to be overcome with formal consent required from Claude Hélias in order that the contents of all his letters to the CWGC (France Area) could be released to the author. This consent was readily granted on 26 November 2007.

Contact was also made with the RAF 234 Squadron Association, whose Secretary, Derek Colborne, immediately invited the author to the next Annual Reunion at RAF Cranwell.

Derek mentioned that the history of 234 Squadron, entitled *Dragon Rampant: the Story of No. 234 Fighter Squadron*, was about to be published. This included a short piece on the events of 27 July 1944. The author, Group Captain Nigel Walpole OBE BA RAF, had already visited Plœmeur and Guidel and had met with those involved in the story. At the time of publication, no contact had been made with any of the living kin of the pilot, Russell Lyon, despite attempts having been made to do so.

Russell's living kin (the author, the author's two brothers and one elderly cousin) and members of 234 Squadron then eagerly awaited the outcome of the reopened MoD inquiry. The author's elder brother, Alastair, visited the area in July 2007 and was shown around the crash site and the cemetery at Guidel. He also met Joseph Le Corroller, the retired elderly farmer on whose land the crash had occurred and who was the eyewitness to and first on the scene of the Spitfire crash in July 1944. His memories have been recorded (Illustrations 6.4 and 6.5) and formed part of the submission that had been made to the reopened inquiry for the possible grave identification.

In and around Plœmeur and this part of southern Brittany voluntary work on the subject was being done principally by three people, Claude Hélias, Jean-Yves Le Lan and Jean Robic.

Claude Hélias has undertaken wide-ranging research into the Allied air losses over the whole of Brittany from 1940 to 1944, and in 2003 had presented a dossier to the Beaurains Office of the CWGC seeking recognition of the grave at Guidel in the name of F/O E.R. Lyon. In 2004, some of his questions of 2003 had remained unanswered:

Question 1: On what basis was the death date of the casualty in the grave at Guidel of the '*inconnu*' given as 29 July 1944?

Question 2: Why has the testimony of M. Joseph Le Corroller that 'to my knowledge the body of the pilot lies at Guidel' been disregarded and the application for grave identification advanced no further?

Those questions continued to remain unanswered.

Jean-Yves Le Lan is President of the Comité d'Histoire du Pays de Plœmeur, the local history society for Plœmeur and the surrounding area.

Jean Robic is a local farmer whose farm is adjacent to the Lann-Bihoué (WWII Kerlin-Bastard) airbase. During WWII, his parents' farm was requisitioned by the Germans and occupied by them. On land around the Robic farmhouse, Ferme du Cosquéric, many underground bunkers and gun emplacements were built.

With the help of local colleagues Sébastien Le Coupanec and Alain Gargam, the crash site at Kercavès was excavated in 2003/4. The eyewitness, Joseph Le Corroller, still lived in his farmhouse near to the crash site.

6.7 L to R, Sébastien Le Coupanec, Jean Robic and
Jean-Yves Le Lan. Photo Richard Lyon.

The letter dated 7 June 2007 from the CWGC informing the
author that the inquiry had been reopened by the Ministry of Defence
included contact details of the Joint Casualty and Compassionate
Centre (JCCC) at RAF Innsworth, to whom the author was instructed
to send the material for review. The letter also included the comment
that evidence had to prove 'beyond all reasonable doubt' that the grave
casualty at Grave 33, Row 6 in Guidel was F/O Russell Lyon. To the
non-expert eye, the material seemed to form a very strong submission,
even to the extent that it might have been called a 'no brainer'. At this
stage another dossier was produced, and in September 2007 this was
sent off to the JCCC at RAF Innsworth.

In January 2008 a reply was received from the JCCC stating:

> In conclusion due to the lack of conclusive information which
> is required to identify beyond all reasonable doubt and despite
> the obvious efforts which have been made in respect of research
> by both yourself and Mr Hélias, the case will now be closed.
> However another review will be conducted if any additional
> information is received.

This was disappointing, but we were not going to give up. Our task was then to find new and fresh evidence. In Plœmeur it was decided to place notices in the local newspapers concerning the case, asking if there were other witnesses to the events of 27 July 1944.

Three elderly ladies responded, Mme Anne Le Corre, Mme Jeanne Ezvan and Mme Anne Guillou, whose witness statements were then taken.

Mme Anne Le Corre recollected that her fifteenth birthday occurred on 26 July, just the day before the Spitfire was shot down. She recounted that she was with her whole family in a field close to Quatre-Chemins when she saw the plane crash near Kercavès. The battery at Quatre-Chemins was some 30 metres away from where she was, and she heard the Germans shout out with joy that they had hit the plane. As the plane plunged from the sky, she flung herself onto the ground and also prayed. A dog called 'Policier' ran around barking but a horse nearby remained calm. Later gossip in the village mentioned that the pilot who had been killed was English.

Mme Jeanne Ezvan, also a teenager at the time, recollected that the crash occurred a few days before the closure of the Poche de Lorient. She was out with her mother in the early evening collecting turnips from a field near her family farm in Kercavès. She heard a large noise as the plane fell onto M. Le Corroller's land. The Germans secured the area and told everyone to leave. She recounted that a few days later her brother found, some 150–200 metres from the crash site, a flying boot with a piece of a human leg (tibia) and pieces of clothing scattered around. He did not touch or move these remains. No French police or ambulance came to the crash site.

Mme Anne Guillou (whose maiden name is Ezvan and who is a sister of Jeanne Ezvan) was then 22 years old. She recalled the events of the crash on one evening in July 1944. She was some 200 metres distant from the crash and recalled that the battery at Quatre-Chemins, located near the Maison Blayo, shot down the plane. She watched the smoking plane as it pirouetted to the ground after being hit. She said that in her opinion the pilot died on the spot. Anne recounts that her brother did not tell her about the flying boot that he had found. The Germans forbade anyone from approaching the crash site. After the crash she heard them cry out 'Canadian'.

6.8, 6.9 Jean Robic with Anne Guillou, and with
Jeanne Ezvan. Photos Jean-Yves Le Lan.

These statements added detail to the event of the evening of 27 July 1944, but they did not contain any more conclusive statements that would unlock the case. The reference to 'Canadian' is, perhaps, possible if Russell was wearing a badge or similar on his uniform relating to his time in 1942/1943 when he was a pilot instructor in Canada.

In January 2008, Joseph Le Corroller spoke further with Jean-Yves Le Lan and added comment that following the crash of the Spitfire at Kercavès he spoke with the Germans, who had brought a lorry and

6.10 WWII aerial photo of 10 March 1945 with position of crash site,
the Quatre-Chemins flak battery and the houses of two witnesses shown.
Source: The National Collection of Aerial Photography, Edinburgh.
The coast is just visible top left.

were clearing the wreckage from the site. One of the Germans spoke a little French and 'he told me that the body of the pilot had been taken to Guidel to be buried'. Joseph continued by saying that on Saturday 29 July, two days after the crash of the 27th, he went to see a cousin, Jean Quillien, who lived in the hamlet of Bilérit, by Guidel. On his way to meet his cousin he cycled through Guidel and spoke with the gravedigger who 'said to me that he was going to bury a pilot and that a grave was open for this'.

Through early 2008 further information was collated including:

(1) From the Department of Research and Information Services (DORIS) at the RAF Museum, Hendon who confirmed:

> The part numbers given are certainly in the format used by Supermarine. 30037, 30038 and 30050 denote parts for engine mounting, engine cowling and undercarriage respectively for a Spitfire 1. Many of the Spitfire 1 components were used, unchanged, in the Mark V, so it is entirely possible that this wreckage is from AR343 but it is not possible to link them to this specific aircraft.

(2) A statement from Claude Hélias:

> I have compiled a list of all Spitfire losses during operations in Brittany from 1941–1944. I figured it would be of interest for your reply because it shows that only one Spitfire, that is your uncle's AR343, crashed at Larmor-Plage from 1941–1944.

(3) A further German report was found in the Bundesarchiv (the German Federal Archive) in Freiburg by a German researcher who was engaged to see if other contemporary material from 1944 was on the record. This record was a German Army report of 6.00 a.m. on 28 July 1944 and recording from the AOK 7 HQ 7th Army, reported by Gefr. (Corp) Burzer to Receiver Uffz. (Sgt) Schaaf, at para d:

> Fighter bomber attack by 6 Spitfires on Lorient Airfield. Losses: None. 1 shot down near La Roche-Bernard, 1 shot down near Larmor-Plage (on the Plœmeur–Kernevel road).

German Army Report 6.00am 28th July 1944
One spitfire – Larmor-Plage- Street Ploemeur/Kernevel
from Bundesarchiv at Freiburg (Feb.2008)

Abt. Io

            Ic – Morgenmeldung vom 28.7.44.   *148*

An   Durchgegeben: Gefr. Burzer
                                    Uhrzeit   : 6.00 Uhr
A O K 7   Aufgenommen : Uffz. Schaaf

zu a) Von Alderney starker fdl. Schiffsverkehr von Kriegsschiffen,
      Transportern u. Tankern nach und von Cherbourg beobachtet.

zu d) 2 Aufklärer Raum Vannes, Nantes. Aufklärung von 10 Maschinen
      (Liberator) über Seegebiet Roscoff – Ile d'Ouessant. Jagdvor-
      stoss von 18 Spitfire im Raum Nantes, Lorient, Redon. Jaboan-
      griff von 6 Spitfire auf Fliegerhorst Lorient.
      Verluste: keine. 1 Abschuss bei La Roche Bernard, 1 Abschuss
      bei Larmor – Plage (anStrasse Plumeur-Kernevel).
      20 Sabotagemaschinen im Raum Redon.
      Einflug von 10 Versorgungsmaschinen über Ferros.

zu i) Bei Plumaudan (12 km SSW·Dinan) Festnahme von 2 Terroristen,
      darunter 1 Führer. Bei Brusvily (9 km SW Dinan) Festnahme eines
      spionageverdächtigen Franzosen. 1 km S Cleguerec Beschießung
      eines Wehrmacht-LKW durch Terroristen. 2 Soldaten verwundet.
      Streifen erfolglos. Entgleisung einer Lok mit Pakwagen bei
      Plaintel (12 km SSW St.Brieuc) infolge Laschenlösung. Sprengung
      eines Gleises zwischen Guingamp und Pedernec. Schaden am 28.7.
      vormittags beseitigt.

Verteiler:
K.G.   Ia
Chef   Ic

6.11 German Army report from the Bundesarchiv at Freiburg.
Lyon family collection.

This report confirms the shooting down of the two Spitfires, firstly BM 200 piloted by Walton, and secondly AR343 piloted by Russell Lyon. In April 2008 this additional material was sent to the JCCC for their further consideration.

In the same month came confirmation from the Mayor of Larmor-Plage, the Commune nearest to the crash site, that a roundabout would be named in memory of Russell Lyon, and a Stele would be erected beside the roundabout. The roundabout was being created to provide access for a new housing estate being built on the land near to the crash site. The news that this local Commune wished to honour Russell's sacrifice in this way was very thrilling for the family and for the 234 Squadron Association. The story had received some publicity in southern Brittany via the efforts of Jean-Yves Le Lan and Jean Robic.

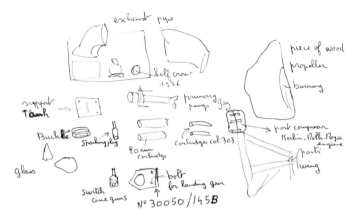

6.12 Metal wreckage recovered from the Kercavès
crash site. Diagram and Photo by Jean Robic.

This had captured the mood for providing some form of permanent public recognition for Russell. The gesture was a wholly unexpected development that raised the spirits with regard to the ongoing attempt to achieve recognition of the unmarked grave at Guidel.

In the summers of both 2007 and 2008, the 234 Squadron Annual Reunions took place at RAF Cranwell, at which the author met with two Spitfire pilots, Sqn Ldr Alan Frost and Fl/Lt David Ferguson, who had known and flown with the author's uncle.

6.13 RAF 234 Squadron Reunion – Three WWII Spitfire pilots and their wives. L to R, Liz Frost, Alan Frost, Ray Stebbings, Effie Stebbings, Dave Ferguson and Brigid Ferguson. Photo Richard Lyon.

Alan recounted to the author that Russell had been one of his pals in the squadron. Moreover, when Russell was given a 48-hour pass, he would often spend this leave with Alan's parents, who lived in the south of England. This was not that Russell did not wish to go home to Edinburgh, but if he had chosen to go to his Edinburgh home on such short leave he would have spent much of the 48 hours on the train travel alone.

Dave Ferguson also recounted to the author that he had been a trainee pilot in the southern states of America, and Russell taught him to fly. An Irishman, Dave was full of other stories, often scary, from his time learning to fly in the States and also in 234 Squadron.

At the 2007 Reunion Alan Frost indicated that George Sparrow, who was one of the eight Spitfire pilots (F/O G.F. Sparrow, Spitfire BM238) on the Rhubarb mission of 27 July 1944, lived close to the author. Contact was made in October 2007 with George's daughter Ruth, who explained that her elderly father was in a care home and so would be unable to talk with the author on the subject of the fateful mission. Photos were shared, one of which features at Photo 2.10 in Chapter 2. This shows a group of pilots in front of a half-timbered house, known as 'The Cookhouse'. The pilots are 'Ben' Lyon and Alan Frost in the back row, and Kjend Petersen, Bill Bennett, Johnny Johnston and Charlie Greenhalgh in the front row. The Cookhouse provided some hint of comfort to 234 Squadron pilots when they were posted to the temporary airfield with a metal strip runway at RAF Deanland in the lead-up to D-Day. Their tented accommodation was primitive. A further unidentified pilot, with his back to the camera in this photo, can only just be seen entering The Cookhouse.

George Sparrow died aged 93 on 17 April 2008. The author attended his funeral, held local to George's home near Cambridge. George had lived in a village near where the author had lived in the early 1970s, whose house he would have driven past twice daily on his journey to and from work. This is one aspect of the story where serendipity had not played its part with any connection then being made.

In March 2009 the author did manage to speak by telephone with another 234 Squadron pilot from the Rhubarb mission of 27 July 1944: Fl/Lt F.E. Dymond, Spitfire B L 810. Known as Jackson Dymond he kindly spoke with the author to indicate that the eight Spitfires split into two groups, Blue to attack the Kerlin-Bastard airfield and Red to look for targets further south over Lorient. Fred Elliot Dymond died aged 93 on 18 June 2013. The author attended Fl/Lt Dymond's funeral, held locally to his home near Chesterfield.

For the imminent roundabout inauguration, the author also set out for NE Scotland where he obtained a quantity of heather plants for the landscape planting around the Stele.

In July 2008 these Scottish heathers were delivered by the author to Plœmeur where the Stele was under construction. The author also met with those who had worked locally on the project, and with the principal eyewitness, Joseph Le Corroller. On this, the author's first visit, the hospitality of Jean-Yves Le Lan and Jean Robic was most heart warming.

This visit also included a trip to see the recently recovered and cleaned wreckage from Fl/Lt W. Walton's Spitfire BM200.

6.14, 6.15 Wreckage from Spitfire BM200, piloted by W. Walton, recovered, cleaned by a team of French Air Force veterans and on display at the Salle des Traditions de Lann-Bihoué. In 6.14, Jean Robic on right hand side; in 6.15, Jean Robic, Jean-Yves Le Lan and daughter back row right hand side. Photos Richard Lyon.

6.16
Invitation to the Stele
unveiling ceremony on
8 November 2008.
Collection Richard
Lyon.

In the summer of 2008, the author was also informed by the JCCC that the case material was being sent to the RAF Air Historical Branch at RAF Northolt. It was understood that one of the reasons for this was the heavy workload of the JCCC.

6.17, 6.18 Guard of Honour at the Stele unveiling, 8 November 2008. In 6.17, Guard of Honour under inspection by the Commanding Officer of Lann-Bihoué. In 6.18, L to R, Victor Tonnerre, Mayor of Larmor-Plage, Loïc Le Meur, Mayor of Plœmeur, and General Jean Fleury at the Stele unveiling, 8 November 2008. Photos David Webster.

On Saturday 8 November a Ceremony of Inauguration was held, commencing at 11.00 a.m. at the roundabout, which was presided over by the Commanding Officer of the large French air/naval base of Lann-Bihoué and M. Victor Tonnerre, the Mayor of Larmor-Plage. Despite a gloomy weather forecast, by 10 o'clock there were blue skies and sunshine. From early in the day a military Guard of Honour was in place at the roundabout and people started to arrive to take up their places for the ceremony. Between 300 and 400 persons were present and at 11.00 a.m. the ceremony commenced.

The occasion was attended by military and civic dignitaries from the area and from local veteran associations, a large contingent of local schoolchildren and their teachers, and representatives of the British Ambassador to France, the RAF, 234 Squadron and many others, and by nine members of the Lyon family. The most senior French military person present was General Jean Fleury, who commanded the French Air Force during the presidency of François Mitterrand. There were many other French military, air force and navy officers and ratings. In mid October the author had received the protocol documents prepared for the ceremony by the Commandant de la Marine à Lorient. With these was the invitation that the author, jointly with the Mayor of Larmor-Plage, be responsible for the unveiling of the Stele itself. He felt greatly honoured to be asked to do this.

A few weeks before the ceremony the author had indicated a wish to say a big thank you, on behalf of the family, to those responsible for the decision to create this rare individual memorial and who were making the ceremony happen. His name was now on the protocol document after that of the Mayor, who was also to give a speech.

On the protocol document he also spotted that there was going to be a strong attendance from local schoolchildren and their teachers so the author asked if two children, one boy and one girl, could be nominated to carry out the planting under his direction as 'head gardener'. That was one way, at least, for the author to keep his hands clean, and one way for the schoolchildren to go home with a stronger memory of the ceremony, if not also with muddy hands.

And so on the crisp, sunny Saturday morning of Remembrance Day Weekend the author found himself putting on his best suit and finding his way, with the rest of the family group, to the location of the new roundabout, which is at the village called Kercavès, just to the north of Larmor-Plage.

The author already knew some detail about the Stele that was being fabricated, having had a sneak preview or two while it was under construction. Jean Robic had delivered the propellor hub recovered from the crash site to the fabrication workshop and sketch drawings illustrating the structure had been sent for information. In July 2008, after the Scottish heather delivery had been made, the author also had an early sight of the Stele.

On arrival at the roundabout, the crowds were in place, with the Guard of Honour, official military and civic guests and schoolchildren all in position. Standing high and shrouded by the Union Jack and French Tricolour flags, above them all was the Stele. This was located on a piece of land adjacent to the roundabout itself, which gives access to the new housing development.

Most of the Scottish heather plants were already planted around the Stele base, with other plant species, and with gaps ready for the planting of the last few heather plants by the schoolchildren.

In the crowd the author also saw one or two faces familiar from his visit in July. Firstly Joseph Le Corroller, whose farmhouse was just a hundred metres away, and who was the first on the scene of the crash back on that July evening of 1944. A tall and rugged man, now in his late eighties, he stood out head and shoulders within the crowd.

The author also spotted Gérard Penobert, a retired French Air Force Mirage Jet pilot, amongst a large contingent of Air Force veterans. Gérard has been so entranced by the story that he has joined the tale of Russell into his new version of the story of *Le Petit Prince*, the well-known story by Antoine de Saint-Exupéry. Gérard also regularly sends new poems to the author in which Russell features. (See Appendix 8.)

After the arrival of the Lyon family, the crowd settled and the formal proceedings began with the Commanding Officer undertaking a formal inspection of the Guard of Honour and the other groups of military attendees. The Mayor of Larmor-Plage, M. Victor Tonnerre, then gave his speech.

6.19 The official party at the Stele unveiling. Front row, L to R, Commanding Officer of Lann-Bihoué; Victor Tonnerre, Mayor of Larmor-Plage; Loïc Le Meur, Mayor of Plœmeur; and General Jean Fleury. Second row, Alastair Lyon and Richard Lyon. Photo by the official photographer (name not known) for the Commune of Larmor-Plage, reproduced by kind permission of the City of Larmor-Plage.

6.20
Jean-Yves Le Lan reading
Russell's biography in French.
Photo Alain Terras.

This was followed by the reading of a biography of Russell in French by Jean-Yves Le Lan. The author's son Charles Lyon, aged 21, followed reading a translation of the same biography into English. By coincidence Charles' birthday is 27 July, the same date as the shooting down of his great uncle. As he was the same age as his Great Uncle Russell, when he lost his life, a murmur followed by a hush went around the crowd when Charles was introduced and this age comparison was made. Those present were thus moved by

the coincidence of the ages of the 21-year-old young man, Russell Lyon, who had given his life in WWII, and the 21-year-old young person now standing before them reading Russell's biography.

6.21, 6.22
Charles Lyon reading Russell's
biography in English.
Photo 6.21 by Alain Terras.
Photo 6.22 by David Webster.

Following the reading of Russell's biography, the author found himself ushered forward towards the microphone, with his prepared speech in French held ready to start.

This speech was, possibly, the first time since his French 'O' Level oral in the mid 1960s that the author had embarked upon saying anything approaching the length of this, in the French language.

6.23, 6.24 Richard Lyon thanking all for the occasion of the Stele creation and unveiling. Photos Jean-Yves Le Lan.

The author presented this in paragraphs first read in French, and then in English, so that all who were present would understand.

Following the speech that was on behalf of the Lyon family, the author then said a few words on behalf of the 234 Squadron Association that had been provided to him by Gp Capt Nigel Walpole. Again, the author delivered this first in French and then in English. After he had finished a trumpet sounded and he joined the Mayor to unveil the Stele.

6.25, 6.26 The unveiling of the Stele by the Mayor of Larmor-Plage, Victor Tonnerre, and Richard Lyon. Photos David Webster.

The author had learnt that the Mayor had run a small sail-making business. So the author was fairly confident that the arrangements for removal of the French flag and the Union Jack, which were draped over the Stele, would enable them to fall easily away. However, when the moment came the French flag fell away but the Union Jack stuck a little before the author managed to flick the top away from the highest point of the Stele.

The Stele stands on a large granite base and comprises the original Spitfire AR343 propeller hub, which had been excavated from the crash site, and on to this new metal images of the propeller blades have been attached. The whole Stele stands at around 3.6 m high. The base is a piece of granite brought from the Keroman U-boat base, where a layer of such granite was incorporated into the massive anti-blast roof structure, just a mile or two away to the south of the estuary.

There is a plate fixed on the Stele indicating Russell's name, his dates of birth and death, 234 RAF Squadron with whom he flew, and the place where his plane was shot down on 27 July 1944.

The laying of several official wreaths followed, by the Mayor of Larmor-Plage, by the commandant of the Lann-Bihoué Airbase, by the CWGC, and by the representative from the British Embassy in Paris. Lastly, on behalf of the whole Lyon family, Alastair Lyon, the elder brother of the author, placed a wreath. This, brought by Alastair from the UK, comprised a blue-and-white display of flowers in the form of St Andrew's Cross.

Following the laying of wreaths, the two nominated local schoolchildren stepped forward and the last two of the heather plants from the area of NE Scotland where Russell had his childhood holidays were skilfully planted.

This was then followed by one minute's silence, and then the French National Anthem, 'The Marseillaise', was played, followed by 'God Save the Queen'.

Salutes were given by the Commander to the Guard of Honour. The Lyon family left, accompanied by the official civic and military representatives, the ceremony finishing just a short while before midday. The Mayor of Larmor-Plage then hosted a civic reception at the Salle des Algues, in the centre of Larmor-Plage. Later that day the author and family members made another visit to the nearby crash site.

6.27
The Lyon family wreath.
Photo by Anne Lyon.

6.28 Children wreath laying. Photo by the official photographer (name not known) for the Commune of Larmor-Plage, reproduced by kind permission of the City of Larmor-Plage.

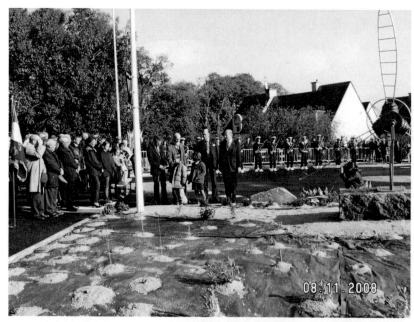

6.29, 6.30 Local children completing the planting of Scottish heathers around the Stele. Photo 6.29 by a photographer known only as Michel. Photo 6.30 by the official photographer (name not known) for the Commune of Larmor-Plage, reproduced by kind permission of the City of Larmor-Plage.

6.31 L to R, Sébastien Le Coupanec, Jean Robic, Victor Tonnerre, Jean-Yves Le Lan and Richard Lyon. Photo by the official photographer (name not known) for the Commune of Larmor-Plage, reproduced by kind permission of the City of Larmor-Plage.

6.32 L to R, David Webster, Russell Lyon, Richard Lyon, Anne Lyon, Charles Lyon, Victoria Windmill (née Lyon), Pamela Lyon and Alastair Lyon. Photo Mark Windmill, son-in-law of author.

6.33 Visit to the crash site. L to R, Richard Lyon, Anne Lyon, Victoria Windmill (née Lyon), Mark Windmill and Charles Lyon. Photo Jean-Yves Le Lan.

The author had felt very good as the days of the ceremony approached, a little nervous on the day itself, but everything went smoothly and after it had finished the author was able to relax a bit and look back at the remarkable chain of events that had led to him standing in this place, some sixty-four years and three and a half months after Russell's Spitfire had been shot down, in which Russell had lost his young life. He looks now to the memorial itself which, while representing an individual, is also seen by the French Local Authority as '*symbolique*' of many other lives lost in WWII in the locality. Talks have already been given to local school and adult audiences by the two researchers, Jean-Yves Le Lan and Jean Robic, in order that local people are aware of the significance of this gesture by their political masters.

Soon after the ceremony, another elderly person approached Jean-Yves Le Lan with his memories of the Spitfire being shot down in late July 1944. M. Joseph Kerdelhué recounted that he was 15 years old, then living in Kerdeff. He saw the eight planes arrive from the direction of Gâvres or from Port Louis. They were in line and headed for Lann-Bihoué. A plane was hit and then crashed very quickly; it fell in sixty seconds perhaps. He was 500m or so away from the crash towards Quehello-Congart, near the site of the new graveyard of Larmor-Plage. He took shelter in a sunken lane because shrapnel was falling everywhere around.

Gâvres is to the south of Port Louis, which is the 15th/16th-century citadel on the south of the estuary on which the city of Lorient is based. It would appear that the eight 234 Squadron Spitfires had all gone to the south of Lorient before circling back over Port Louis, when they split into two groups of four (Red and Blue), Blue to head for the air base of Kerlin-Bastard to the north, and Red for targets over Lorient.

This further memory from M. Joseph Kerdelhué is generally consistent with other preceding records and reports but, once again, it did not provide any evidence that would break through the impasse on the attempts to get recognition of the grave at Guidel.

The Lyon family are deeply grateful for all the hard work that Jean-Yves Le Lan and Jean Robic have done with their research on the subject and, with their spouses, opening their homes to provide overnight accommodation for nine Lyon visitors over the 2008 Remembrance Day Weekend. Arriving home later, the author and his family felt that the *entente cordiale* between the UK and France was alive and well.

The author regards the situation as a hugely unexpected and remarkable life event, but the task was still unfinished and his sights were then set upon success in the next part, to succeed in the more difficult task of persuading the MoD that it is **beyond all reasonable doubt** that the remains of F/O Russell Lyon were buried in the '*inconnu*' Grave 33 in Row 6 of 29 July 1944 at Guidel.

Chapter 7
Working towards Formal Identification of the Grave
2009–2014

During early 2009, communication was established by the author with the RAF Air Historical Branch at RAF Northolt. A number of questions were asked, and snippets of further information were provided.

On 3 March a response from the Head of the RAF Air Historical Branch was received containing good news and bad news. The good news was that the crash site itself was to be recognised as where Spitfire AR343 hit the ground on the evening of 27 July 1944. The bad news was that formal recognition of the grave at Guidel could not be given.

The responses included the comments:

- 'The panel could not establish beyond reasonable doubt that the grave is that of your uncle ...'
- '... principal reason given refers to the possibility that the occupant of the grave is a "wash-up victim" of an incident in the period of up to six months before 27 July 1944.'

Also ...

- 'Witness statements do not help very much.'

Following this disappointing response, a meeting was arranged for 17 April 2009 with the Head of the RAF Air Historical Branch (AHB) to discuss the matter further.

The AHB file material included the exhumation report of July 1946 which had indicated few human remains in the 29 July 1944 grave of the unknown casualty at Guidel. One explanation as to why this was the case, albeit difficult to prove or disprove, is that the US Quartermaster Corps who examined and transferred US casualties from Guidel in September 1945 also mistakenly exhumed the 'unknown' in Row 6, Grave 33.

Incidents of this kind of mistake are on the record; see page 69 of *Missing Believed Killed* by Stuart Hadaway, where it is written that the American Graves Registration Command mistakenly removed British casualties from a cemetery at Benediktbeuren. It is also recorded 'that it was common for the Americans to relocate all unidentified bodies to central cemeteries for processing and identification'.

Moreover, in the MREU post-WWII instruction document 'A Report on the RAF and Dominions Air Forces Missing Research and Enquiry Service for the period 1944–49' (AIR 20/0305) at page 56, this very problem is mentioned at 1.26XII where it says:

> Clothing – Everything, position, peculiarities. Note exactly where and how the clothing is found. If a tunic is found beside but not on the body, say so. Perhaps the body has already been exhumed by the American Graves Registration authorities, but the Germans might just as easily have put another man's tunic into the coffin ... etc. All peculiarities to be noted – decorations, mascots, pictures sewn under battledress labels, etc.

While this is a speculative theory that might explain the paucity of remains in the case of the unknown casualty in Grave 33, Row 6 at Guidel, it cannot be ruled out that this had happened.

During the meeting at the AHB, the author noticed handwriting in correspondence on the AHB files and recognised this as his grandfather's handwriting.

On file there were some 25 letters, from the period 1944–1949, written by the author's grandfather, Mr E.H. Lyon, to the Air Ministry and copies of the replies sent by the Air Ministry. The Head of the AHB kindly provided the author with copies of all this material or, in the cases where the original carbon copy was considered too fragile, full transcripts of the correspondence.

These covered the questions naturally being asked by the father of the missing pilot as to whether there was any development with regard to establishing what had happened in the search for his son, Russell, this missing casualty.

The most telling of the Air Ministry replies was dated 11 November 1949 and included:

> and to say that four unknown airmen rest in the Lorient (Kerentech) Cemetery, but investigations by the Research Services established that the crashes which resulted in their deaths occurred in 1941 and 1942. A careful check of Cemetery Lists in the Lorient area has disclosed no burial of an 'unknown' in 1944.

This statement was obviously incorrect as Grave 33 in Row 6 at Guidel was certainly on the record as an 'unknown' buried in 1944 and confirmed later by the CWGC headstone, Known unto God.

A further comment was then made by Joseph Le Corroller when he was told in April 2009 by Jean-Yves Le Lan that the Spitfire crash site had now been officially recognised, but that the approval for the recognition of the grave had not been given. Joseph's immediate response was to say, 'And yet the Germans said they had taken him to the cemetery.'

Further correspondence with the AHB occurred and a reply dated 2 July 2009 was received, but the stance taken did not move as they still considered that the evidence submitted was insufficient to allow them 'to conclude *beyond reasonable doubt* that Grave 33 contained the remains of F/O E.R. Lyon'.

Further comment included:

> … the only evidence linking the crash site with Guidel Grave 6/33 is the hearsay evidence of M. Corroller, i.e. what he recalls being told by other people, to wit the German guard and the gravedigger. Hearsay is that which is reported to, and not directly observed or experienced by, a witness. There is sadly no contemporary evidence to link the grave to the crash site.

And

> The cemetery register does not indicate where the body in the grave came from. We are left with the awkward fact that if it had been known that the body came from Kercavès then there would be the strong possibility that the date of death on the gravestone would have reflected that. Sadly we know that it does not.

The AHB's alternative theory, not being able to rule out the so-called wash-up casualty, was questioned further.

The AHB provided details of a number of RAF missing aircrew in the same region, from February 1944 to 29 July 1944, which included sixteen potential candidates:

- Seven crew from Stirling LJ462 of 75 (RNZAF) Squadron, lost without trace on a mine-laying operation to Saint-Nazaire on 13/14 March 1944.

- Two crew from Halifax HX314 of 424 Squadron crashed into the sea 28 km west of Lorient on 11 May 1944. (Five others recovered and buried at Guidel.)

- Five crew from Wellington MP 763 of 612 Squadron lost on an anti-submarine patrol on 12 March 1944. (One other washed ashore and buried at the Bay of Lampaul (west of Brest) before later burial at Guidel.) [The Bay of Lampaul is fairly close to the 'Baie des Trépassés', see below.]

- Two crew from Mosquito MM450 of 151 Squadron lost without trace on a night intruder sortie to Kerlin-Bastard airfield on 5/6 June 1944.

The dates of these missing casualties are at some distance (between seven and a half and twenty weeks) from the 29 July 1944 casualty burial at Guidel.

In August 2009 the author spent some time at the National Archives in Kew to see if he could find any more information that might help us argue the case further.

Among material that the author found was the original instruction material issued to the RAF MREU Search Units after WWII. These included the discipline to be adopted for exhumations, and for the recording of every detail, down to dental records and clothing material.

Among this material one instruction struck the author as being of relevance. In Air 20/9305 at 1.5 it is stated that:

> Search officers, when conducting enquiries and interrogations of local inhabitants and officials, **must recognise the ring of truth** and ignore garrulous gossip, but, on the other hand, to omit to question no individual [sic] who may be able to contribute information [author's emphasis].

What this said to the author was that we recognised the statement from the witness M. Joseph Le Corroller did indeed contain the 'ring of truth' referred to in the official instructions, albeit that this statement was made nearly seven decades after the fateful crash of 27 July 1944.

Those considering the case, however, could not argue that the witness statement from Joseph Le Corroller was made under any form of pressure from the pilot's family in the UK, as the date the statement was made in November 2003 preceded by over three years the date when the French researcher Jean-Yves Le Lan first made contact with the living kin of the pilot in March 2007.

Moreover, such a 'ring of truth' held more than the speculative comment, unsupported by evidence, that the occupant of Grave 33, Row 6 at Guidel might be a so-called wash-up victim.

A further point arising from the MREU search documentation, referred to on page 48, para 1.10, was that search officers were instructed with regard to publicity and enquiries: '*Local contacts should be made, in the following order:(1) Mayor (2) Gendarmarie (3) the Curé and the Cemetery Keeper (4) Local inhabitants.*'

Knowledge from those now closely associated with the Guidel Communal Cemetery was also obtained. M. Allain Mathurin, who was aged 17 in 1944, indicated that he was the old gardener and caretaker of the CWGC graves at Guidel. He was married to Paulette, the daughter of the gravedigger of 1944, M. Xavier Gouello, who had died in 1952. Mr. Mathurin explained that he did not attend the burial of 29 July 1944 because the Germans forbade anyone to approach the cemetery.

7.1
Allain Mathurin, 21 April 2009.
Photo Jean-Yves Le Lan.

Such small snippets of information were helpful to understanding the history, as far as that was possible, but they did not add anything conclusive to the efforts to gain positive identification of the grave.

Certainly, the AHB had data on the sixteen airmen missing in action whose planes were thought to have come down over the Bay of Biscay.

In addition the Guidel Communal Cemetery did contain a handful of casualties where the Old Register of WWII indicated the victims' remains were recovered from beach locations. But the Old Register record was inconsistent, with some known wash-up casualties being recorded as such and others not.

One avenue of potential information not yet researched was the possibility that the archives of the Red Cross might provide further information on the fate of the pilot of the Spitfire that had crashed at Kercavès on the evening of 27 July 1944. When the WWI site at Fromelles in northern France was found in May 2008, the press reports made reference to the voluminous Red Cross Totenlist records held in Switzerland. The Red Cross Totenlist is a system of reporting of casualties between warring parties that was in use from WWI onwards. In March 2009 an enquiry to the Red Cross in Geneva was made to see if any such record existed, arising from the events of 27 July 1944.

The Red Cross responded to confirm that they held no information on the fate of F/O E.R. Lyon, nor did they hold information on the capture of Fl/Lt W. Walton.

Information was held by the Red Cross on the Death Notification of F/O J.L. Coward that indicated that he was '*shot down on 22 July 1944, but with a burial place not yet stated (ICRC reference ACR 2GM GB/RB 48776). This information was communicated by the OKW on 4.1.1945.*'

Copies of the Red Cross source documents ACR 2GM GB/RB 48763–48781 and ACR 2GM GB/RB/I 662–663, containing this information, were received.

The former source document had much data on the fate of Canadian and English casualties communicated to the Red Cross in January 1945. Albeit with a degree of randomness atypical of the German meticulous record keeping, dating for the period from March 1944 to November 1944. Two questions arose from this information: (1) It was possible that the reported fate of F/O E.R. Lyon might have been mistakenly included by the German authorities as a Canadian (he was a flying instructor in Canada before his posting to 234 Squadron), and (2) it was also possible that any reporting could well have been delayed by weeks, or months, as the German forces in the area were in disorganised retreat into the Lorient Pocket. However, following these two lines of enquiry, further research proved unproductive.

Little progress was made for some 12 months or so but in June 2010 the author again attended the RAF 234 Squadron Annual Reunion. In conversation with the Commanding Officer after the formal dinner, a discussion took place on where the matter stood. The author spoke about the standard of proof being the highest legal standard – beyond all reasonable doubt – and questioned whether or not this should be a lower standard, for instance by preponderance of evidence. After all, his uncle was not a criminal but someone who had given his life for his country.

The matter was mulled over and later the author was asked to submit a paper arguing for such a change. The author understood that the higher standard had been in place since World War I.

The decision by the AHB of 3 March 2009, advising that recognition of the grave at Guidel could not be given, had been surprising and it left the recipients of this news with questions:

1. If F/O E.R. Lyon was not buried in Grave 33, Row 6 at Guidel, where had his mortal remains been buried by the German authorities?
2. Were they buried in another nearby cemetery as 'unknown'?
3. Were no remains recovered, contrary to the witness statement?
4. Or had the remains just disappeared in the 'fog of war', also contrary to the witness statement?

Question 1 has no reasonable answer.

Question 2 above could be explored, and so Jean-Yves Le Lan embarked upon a study of all cemeteries in the region. The result of this study is shown in Appendix 3, 'Commonwealth Cemeteries in Morbihan', as explained below.

For Question 3, there was no evidence to say that no remains were recovered.

For Question 4, there was no evidence to say that the remains had just disappeared.

A paper (with further input from Jean-Yves Le Lan) was submitted in September 2010, and this went before the Senior Lawyer in the RAF for his consideration. Included in this submission was Jean-Yves Le Lan's report on all burials in the CWGC cemeteries in the Morbihan Region, including all casualty details and including all 'unknowns'.

This also showed the pattern of burials at Guidel, and amongst these was another casualty from RAF 234 Squadron, F/O John Coward. Coward was shot down at Auray on 22 July but buried at Guidel, some thirty miles from Auray, on 24 July 1944 in Grave 32, Row 6.

The report proved that there was no CWGC grave in the region, other than Grave 33, Row 6 at Guidel, that could be linked to a burial of an RAF pilot after the evening of 27 July 1944.

The questions being put forward on the standard of evidence certainly captured the imagination of those in the Ministry of Defence who were asked to look over the subject.

At one stage the author was told that the matter had gone 'case exclusive'. This meant that F/O E.R. Lyon's name was taken out of the equation and the matter was being looked upon as a matter of principle only. The author was also informed that consultation was taking place among all Commonwealth countries and all EU countries to see the standards they have in place for such issues of identification of missing service casualties.

At the heart of the debate was the difference between the instructions given to the immediate post-war search units, see the quote earlier in this chapter regarding the 'ring of truth', and the resonance of the witness statements that do contain this 'ring of truth', and, against this, the fine legal point that the 2003–2009 witness statements did, in the view of the AHB, contain hearsay evidence.

Ultimately the RAF AHB had, in 2008, come to the decision that, regardless, the standard of proof was not being met and therefore insufficient evidence existed to link Russell Lyon to the burial at Grave 33, Row 6 in Guidel Communal Cemetery.

Moreover, the date of death and burial of the casualty given by the gravestone at Guidel on Saturday 29 July 1944 (at some 10 miles distance and less than forty-eight hours after the shooting down of Spitfire AR343 at 7.55 p.m. on the evening of Thursday 27 July 1944) do not exactly match. There is no reasonable explanation why the death date on the gravestone was marked as 29 July 1944, the same date as the burial of the casualty.

Many people have asked why, then, has there not been an exhumation and a DNA test on the contents of the grave at Guidel. The answer is quite simple. It is a general policy of the CWGC that they are opposed to any exhumations of existing war graves within their care for identification purposes unless it is absolutely necessary to do so. This is a wholly supportable stance based on the premise that once the combatant has been buried on foreign soil they should not be disturbed. This is firstly to protect the sanctity of burial and secondly, no precedent should be set that would create an open door for other families to exploit. A debate also exists regarding possible inscriptions that the CWGC may apply to a combatant's gravestone if the standard of proof of 'beyond all reasonable doubt' is not met. There are examples where the words 'believed to be' may be used. There are several examples in France. The CWGC criterion for this solution is 'where identification may be considered reasonable but not absolute'. Such grave identification decisions can be highly sensitive and in recent years a number of cases from both WWI and WWII have come forward.

In 2000, the responsibility for identification and naming changed from the CWGC to the Ministry of Defence. This followed a 1992 identification of a WWI grave being named for Lt John Kipling, of the Irish Guards, the son of Rudyard Kipling.

7.2
Joseph Rudyard Kipling
(1865–1936). https://
commons.wikimedia.org/wiki/
File:Rudyard_Kipling.jpg.

7.3
John Kipling (1897 – 1915).
Wikipedia, Pierter Kuiper.

My Boy Jack
by
Rudyard Kipling

'Have you news of my boy Jack?'
Not this tide.
'When d'you think that he'll come back?'
Not with this wind blowing, and this tide.
'Has anyone else had word of him?'
Not this tide.
For what is sunk will hardly swim.
Not with this wind blowing and this tide.
'Oh dear, what comfort can I find?'
None this tide,
Nor any tide.
Except he did not shame his kind-
Not even with that wind blowing, and that tide.
Then hold your head up all the more,
This tide,
And every tide;
Because he was the son you bore,
And gave to that wind blowing and that tide.

Rudyard Kipling's son is alluded to in this 1915 poem.

Lt. John Kipling was reported missing after the battle of Loos in September 1915. The imagery of this poem is maritime and generic and is written about a 'nautical' Jack at the time Rudyard Kipling was emotionally affected by the loss of his son John.

In this case a grave was reportedly identified for Lt John Kipling in 1992 but in 2002 this was put into question by military historians. In January 2016, however, further research, showed the original identification of the grave to be correct.

Rudyard Kipling and the Commonwealth War Graves Commission

Rudyard Kipling was closely involved when the Imperial War Graves Commission, constituted by Royal Charter, was founded by a British civil servant, Sir Fabian Ware, in 1917. It retained this name until 1960 when it was renamed the Commonwealth War Graves Commission.

After WWI Rudyard Kipling and the architect Edwin Lutyens were part of a study group developing recommendations for this new organisation and for war cemeteries to be founded over Europe and elsewhere to be preserved 'in perpetuity'.

With regard to the creation of permanent cemeteries abroad, the cultural origins influencing Kipling and Lutyens have been traced to the famous lines in Rupert Brooke's 1914 poem 'The Soldier':

'If I should die, think only this of me:
That there's some corner of a foreign field
That is forever England.'

Amongst Kipling's other contributions to the Commission was the selection of the phrase 'Their Name Liveth for Evermore' (Ecclesiasticus 44.14, King John Version). As mentioned earlier in this book he also proposed the phrases 'Known unto God' for the gravestones of unidentified servicemen and the inscription 'The Glorious Dead' on the Cenotaph in Whitehall, London.

There are many cases across the three UK Forces: the Army, the Royal Air Force and the Royal Navy, where a grave identification rests finely balanced one way or another. What might appear obvious to one point of view may be unacceptable to another.

As the year 2011 progressed, the author was conscious that those in the Ministry of Defence who had been charged with reviewing the standard of proof were continuing with their work without any further input being requested. The author had no idea whether debates were taking place nor who might be undertaking any review. He was not even sure where the dossier delivered to the MoD in September 2010 had ended up. All the author knew was that F/O E.R. Lyon's case and the challenge made had caused a review to take place.

Subsequently, the author understood that the RAF Defence Legal Services had been asked for advice on the standard of evidence being used, due to the author's feeling that the 'beyond all reasonable doubt' (BRD) policy seemed high. It was subsequently advised that the BRD was a high standard, with MoD Central Legal Services in agreement. Following this MoD Personnel Staff determined that BRD was an inappropriate standard and the policy for this case was revised to one at the higher end of 'balance of probabilities', more appropriate for a civil case. Moreover, where 'clear and convincing' could not be established for the purpose of full identification, then for a grave marked 'believed to be' the standard of 'balance of probabilities' would apply.

In September 2011 the author received a telephone call to confirm the review concluded that the standard of proof, as included in the:

> **Joint Services Practice Manual, 751 Volume 2 (Casualty & Compassionate Policy & Procedures)**
> **SECTION 10: Claims as to the Identity of Unknown Soldiers**

was changed from (see words in bold):

> ... the JCCC Historic Casualty Casework Team will consider subsequent claims as the casualty's identity, but will only authorise the CWGC to replace the headstone with a memorial

bearing an individual's name where the claim can be validated **beyond all reasonable doubt** using official records.

to:

... the JCCC Post Death Administration Team will consider subsequent claims as to the casualty's identity, but will only authorise the CWGC to replace the headstone with a memorial bearing an individual's name where the claim can be validated **using clear and convincing evidence** from official records.

The author and all those who had helped the case were exhilarated. A small change from four critical words to five critical words might now just give an opportunity for F/O Russell Lyon's name to go on to the gravestone at Guidel.

The next stage of the challenge opened up with a new problem. The author was told (again) that there were no official channels for reviews of previously heard cases to take place unless new evidence was forthcoming, but that steps were being taken to change this so that Russell's case could be heard again to the new standard of proof.

Time passed and another call told the author that a review was to take place and that he should prepare another dossier for submission. In discussion, the author was advised that the dossier should marshal and include as much as possible on some aspects, or rather arguments, refuting issues that had so far gone unchallenged.

This was probably the team's final opportunity. The main obstacles in preparing such arguments were that the team had to disprove the negative arguments in their path. Not an easy task when the principal events were seven decades ago. For instance, in the AHB 2009 rejection of the case the alternative theory was introduced that the grave casualty might be a so-called wash-up victim shot down over the sea, in the Bay of Biscay, later to be washed up on a beach and taken to Guidel for burial. Certainly there was a list produced by the AHB of some sixteen missing Air Force personnel lost over the sea in the six months preceding the burial date of 29 July 1944, but that was it; this theory was not supported by any evidence.

The argument from the AHB that the witness statements contained hearsay was also challenged and found to be a wrong interpretation of what was, or was not, admissible as hearsay evidence. Generally in civil proceedings hearsay evidence should not be excluded on the ground that it is hearsay. History of the law of recent decades concerning hearsay in civil proceedings was reformed substantially by the Civil Evidence Act 1995, and this was further modernised in the 2003 Criminal Justice Act.

The reforms resulted from belief in the legal world that there were common law cases that threw the rigidities of the then current hearsay rules into sharp relief. Under the 2003 Act a provision, sometimes referred to as the 'safety valve', allows any hearsay evidence, whether or not covered by another provision, to be admitted by the court if it is 'in the interests of justice' to do so.

The effects of Section 14 of the Criminal Justice Act 2003, 'Admissibility of hearsay evidence', sets out criteria in determining whether the interests of justice are met, though other considerations can be taken into account:

(1) In criminal proceedings a statement not made in oral evidence in the proceedings is admissible as evidence of any matter stated if, but only if:

(a) any provision of this Chapter or any other statutory provision makes it admissible,

(b) any rule of law preserved by section 118 makes it admissible,

(c) all parties to the proceedings agree to it being admissible, or

(d) the court is satisfied that it is in the interests of justice for it to be admissible.

(2) In deciding whether a statement not made in oral evidence should be admitted under subsection (1)(d), the court must have regard to the following factors (and to any others it considers relevant):

(a) how much probative value (that is, use in determining the case) the statement has (assuming it to be true) in relation to a matter in issue in the proceedings, or how valuable it is for the understanding of other evidence in the case;

(b) what other evidence has been, or can be, given on the matter or evidence mentioned in paragraph (a);

(c) how important the matter or evidence mentioned in paragraph (a) is in the context of the case as a whole;

(d) the circumstances in which the statement was made;

(e) how reliable the maker of the statement appears to be;

(f) how reliable the evidence of the making of the statement appears to be;

(g) whether oral evidence of the matter stated can be given and, if not, why it cannot;

(h) the amount of difficulty involved in challenging the statement;

(i) the extent to which that difficulty would be likely to prejudice the party facing it.

Source: The National Archives, www.legislation.gov.uk/ukpga/2003/44/section/114.

The five various independent witness statements obtained by the local French researchers, despite being taken from elderly people in their eighties, record some striking commonality, such as correctly knowing that F/O E.R. Lyon's plane was shot down by the Quatre-Chemins flak battery. Further, the knowledge from Joseph Le Corroller that the Germans had taken the body to be buried at Guidel, also confirmed by his encounter with the Guidel gravedigger on the morning of Saturday 29 July 1944, on the face of it, contained the 'ring of truth'. This and other factors provided no reason to doubt the truth of these recorded witness statements.

The Guidel Communal Cemetery burial record was inconsistent in this respect as occasionally entries recorded the location in which a casualty was found on a beach but in other cases, when the casualty was from an aircraft that was lost over the sea, the wash-up location was not included.

It was also noted that the AHB had not significantly disagreed with any evidence put forward but, having discounted the witness statements, the AHB introduces the apparently hypothetical wash-up victim theory without any evidence from RAF, German, French or MREU records to support this.

Moreover, the post-WWII MREU report of the grave exhumation records the coffin containing scraps of an RAF issue shirt and bone fragments, with the skull missing, a description far more consistent with a high-speed crash casualty than a wash-up casualty.

The contemporary cemetery record for the burial of 29 July 1944 says '*Anglais Inconnu*', a description that is precise. To be that precise would be a more difficult conclusion to reach for a wash-up casualty who had been in the sea for a long time (seven and a half weeks to twenty weeks; see above for the AHB's sixteen possible candidates) than it would be for the pilot of a Spitfire shot down nearby just two days before.

The wash-up theory was researched further in an effort to explore it and rule it out. By looking at the deaths recorded in the Commune of Guidel Death Register in the period of July 1944 the author checked if any wash-up victims were found on local beaches within the Commune that might subsequently have been buried in the Communal Cemetery on 29 July 1944, the date on the headstone over Grave 33, Row 6. In the weeks preceding 29 July 1944 there were no such deaths recorded in the Commune of Guidel Death Register.

Another aspect was also explored, relating to missing RAF personnel whose planes were lost in the Bay of Biscay in the six months or so preceding the end of July 1944 and whose remains, perchance, might have been washed up on a beach to be recovered and then buried at Guidel on 29 July 1944.

The author had read that to the south of Brest, north of the Pointe du Raz, there is a bay called the Baie des Trépassés (Bay of the Dead). This name was given because of the high number of drowned shipwreck victims from all over the eastern part of the Bay of Biscay, whose remains, over the centuries, were swept up the western coastline of France to be deposited on this remote beach area on the north-west tip of France.

This led to an investigation of the currents in the eastern part of the Bay of Biscay and their behaviour, and relating the data found to the chance of RAF casualties missing over the Bay of Biscay in the six months preceding the end of July 1944 being washed up on local beaches around the Guidel area.

Baie des Trépassés

7.4 Baie des Trépassés (France). Wikipédia, Fafner.

The waters along the western coastline of France are well known to have some of the strongest currents in Europe. The Baie des Trépassés location is some seventy miles distant overland from Guidel and is in the Finistère *département* in the extreme west of Brittany. This wild and windy part of France is likened to the Land's End area of the British Isles, being almost like the end of the world.

An old Breton legend recalls that the spirits of drowned victims get together at the Baie des Tréspassés and on All Soul's Day, 2 November, the spirits appear and can be heard over the whole bay, crying out in the white spray from the crests of the waves.

Expert comment on the chance of a wash-up occurring in late July 1944 came via an enquiry made to the Joint Operational Meteorology and Oceanography Centre (JOMOC), who looked at the issue and concluded:

> In summary the investigation suggests that body wash-up cannot be discounted and could have been possible under the right combination of set and drift conditions and on the balance of probabilities mentioned above, there is a 15% chance of this having occurred …

It was also noted that when balanced against the number of casualties lost at sea in the Bay of Biscay, wash-ups are a relatively rare occurrence. While the wash-up theory could not be ruled out, this expert opinion gave this alternative theory only a low 15 per cent chance.

Moreover, should a wash-up have actually occurred close to the period before the casualty burial of 29 July 1944 at Guidel, but in another Commune or even another region, then the author argued that in those days, as the Axis Forces were under heavy attack and in retreat back to the Atlantic Wall fortresses of Brest and Lorient, the question needing to be asked was: would the Axis Forces have taken the trouble to move the casualty remains to Guidel? More likely than not, a quick burial close to the coastline area of discovery of the casualty remains would have taken place, rather than a highly risky overland transfer to Guidel.

Just days before this burial on 29 July at Guidel, the remains of F/O John Coward had been moved, within the Morbihan Region, over a distance of twenty-nine miles from Auray to be buried at Guidel.

Against the low 15 per cent wash-up theory stood the more likely chance that the casualty of the Spitfire crash of 27 July 1944 at Kercavès would be buried at a distance of just nine miles away at Guidel. Attached to this scenario are the witness statements of Joseph Le Corroller with regard to (1) seeing the body of the pilot close to the wreckage on the evening of 27 July 1944 and (2) being in conversation with the gravedigger at Guidel on 29 July 1944, who had prepared a grave for the casualty.

A final thirteen-page case summary was prepared covering these and older issues and six bound copies were hand delivered to the Ministry of Defence on 3 October 2013. The author handed these copies over in a conference room on the 7th floor of the MoD in Whitehall and as he stood up from his seat to hand the copies across the table, he found himself looking out of the sash window with a view straight down Downing Street. His thoughts raced to wonder at how much we had so far achieved, but this was now our last chance and an opportunity that would not be repeated in his lifetime, if at all. Over the next few months the review then progressed. Again, the author was not made aware of any detail with regard to this. In mid summer 2014 the author enquired if any progress had been made and he was told by Rear Admiral Simon Williams, who was chairing the review, that a decision was imminent.

A few days later Admiral Williams telephoned the author to confirm that a positive decision had been reached such that the name of Ernest Russell Lyon could be put on the gravestone, albeit with the inscription 'Buried near this spot'.

A confirmatory letter was then received from the JCCC summarising the decision and with the following justifications:

a) 'The German authorities were using Guidel Cemetery as a "regional" cemetery for Allied dead recovered from land and sea, around the time of your Uncle's death.'

b) 'Eyewitness states that the remains recovered from the crash site accepted as being that of Spitfire AR343 were taken to Guidel Cemetery.'

c) 'Burials of Allied dead took place in Guidel Cemetery until 1st September 1944.'

d) 'Burials in Lorient-Kerentech, a nearby cemetery containing Allied dead, ceased in 1942.'

e) 'There are several possible candidates for the occupant of Grave 33 and it is now considered unlikely that a definitive case to confirm the occupant's identity can be made.'

It had taken some eleven years from the finding of the Spitfire AR343 crash site to reach this position. The good news was shared with the family and all those who had helped. Everyone agreed we really could not have expected any more.

Chapter 8

Grave Re-Dedication in October 2015

The letter from the JCCC explained the details of what would happen next with regard to the replacement of the gravestone. Firstly and most importantly, Russell's name would now appear on the gravestone. Secondly, contact details were provided to begin the process of arranging the Service of Re-Dedication at the graveside. It was also apparent that the JCCC was overloaded with work; they were in the process of hiring additional staff and it would be necessary to wait until spring 2015 before contacting them again about the service arrangements. Thirdly, came the information that the family would be able to compose an inscription limited to a maximum of four lines, each line with no more than twenty-five characters. Work on the inscription could begin and the author spent some time producing drafts for discussion and agreement with his two brothers.

The existing wording of 'Known unto God' (see Chapter 7, Rudyard Kipling) would no longer appear.

After discussion within the family, and with the CWGC, the following wording was agreed:

Always known unto God

Now resting here

'Ex Corde Caritas'

Remembered forever

The third line is the school motto of George Watson's College in Edinburgh, where Russell had spent a large proportion of his short life. Because of this it was felt appropriate to include this motto, with the strong message that it promotes. Since the discovery of the Spitfire wreckage the College had been kept informed of progress as the story developed. The College website records that the motto *Ex Corde Caritas* (Love from the Heart) is central to the values of the College as it seeks to sustain what is described as 'The Watson's Family'.

The months passed quickly again and in early 2015 a date was agreed with the JCCC for the Re-Dedication Service at Guidel. This was to be held on Monday 5 October 2015. The details of the service, the readings, wreath laying and so on were discussed with the JCCC. The service would also include the Act of Remembrance. A list of those who would be invited to attend from the UK, including some twenty-two family members of all ages and members of the RAF, including the 234 Squadron Association, was produced. Across the Channel in southern Brittany a similar list was put together. George Watson's College indicated that they would send representatives comprising two pupils and a member of staff. The author was most pleased to hear this and rather innocently asked if it might be possible for the pupils to be bagpipe players who could play a part in the proceedings. This request was made without the knowledge that the College had a pipe and drum band that had won many piping championships. It was good news when the College replied saying that of course this would be possible.

And so a large group all found themselves gathering at Guidel Cemetery on 5 October for the 10.00 a.m. service. The weather was not at all kind, with heavy rain throughout. One thing that many people notice with CWGC cemeteries is that they are maintained to the highest standards, and it was no different here at Guidel. There are around 110 UK and Commonwealth casualties buried at Guidel and one could sense that preparation and maintenance had occurred above the usual high standards. The position of Grave 33 in Row 6 is such that this grave is the first and nearest to the cemetery entrance. Russell's burial in 1944 was the last to occur here in WWII.

In addition to those formally invited to attend there was also a large attendance from the local population. Among these were a flag-bearing group of retired servicemen, and representatives from the local Red Cross organisation.

8.1
New gravestone over Grave 33, Row 6 in the CWGC section at Guidel Communal Cemetery. Lyon family collection.

8.2 Commencement of the Service of Re-Dedication at the graveside in the CWGC section of Guidel Communal Cemetery. Photo Jean-Yves Le Lan.

From the RAF, Air Marshal Dick Garwood, Air Vice Marshal Lindsay Irvine and the Secretary of the RAF 234 Squadron Association, Derek Colbourne, attended.

Also present was a large group of retired members of the French Air Force who lived locally, including a former Commander of the French Air Force, Général Jean Fleury.

8.3 French civil and military dignitaries. Photo Jean-Yves Le Lan.

8.4 Members of the Lyon family. Photo Jean-Yves Le Lan.

The two young bagpipers, Alistair Hutcheon and Andrew Spence, played 'Going Home', based on a Dvorak melody, as they led the family procession into the cemetery and to the graveside.

8.5 Alistair Hutcheon and Andrew Spence, bagpipers from
George Watson's College in Edinburgh. Photo Jean-Yves Le Lan.

The service was conducted by the Revd (Gp Capt) John Ellis, RAF (Deputy Chaplain in Chief), who also gave the first reading, John 15: 9–17.

8.6 The Revd (Gp Capt) John Ellis, RAF, conducting the service.
Photo Jean-Yves Le Lan.

The Second Reading, 'High Flight', was given by a representative of the Defence Attaché from the British Embassy in Paris.

High Flight
by
Pilot Officer Gillespie Magee

Oh! I have slipped the surly bonds of earth
And danced the skies on laughter-silvered wings;
Sunward I've climbed, and joined the tumbling mirth
Of sun-split clouds – and done a hundred things
You have not dreamed of – Wheeled and soared and swung
High in the sunlit silence. Hov'ring there
I've chased the shouting wind along, and flung
My eager craft through footless halls of air ...
Up, up the long, delirious, burning blue
I've topped the wind-swept heights with easy grace
Where never a lark or even eagle flew –
And, while with silent lifting mind I've trod
The high untrespassed sanctity of space,
Put out my hand, and touched the face of God.

Pilot Officer Gillespie Magee Jr, of 412 Squadron, RCAF, who was killed on 11 December 1941 in an accident over Lincolnshire.

The author was to give the third reading. Some time had been spent trying to find something appropriate and that touched upon Russell's sacrifice. A perfect answer was found in the poem ' When Freedom Bled' by Richard Scarr.

8.7
Richard Lyon reading
'When Freedom Bled' by
Richard Scarr.
Photo Jean-Yves Le Lan.

When Freedom Bled

by
Richard Scarr

When came the moment, came the men.
But they were made from special seed.
And so they flocked to heed the call.
For they were men of yesterday's breed.

Allied, they came from far and wide,
To fight in Freedom's name.
And valour was their watchword.
But their likes will never come again.

They were your Uncles and your Grandads
of every colour, culture, creed.
And they came because they could not bear,
to watch the cause for Freedom bleed.

They fought upon the battlefields.
On the sea and in the air.
There was barely a parent in their lands,
who could not say: 'My boy is there!'

Time and time they risked their lives.
Even knowing time was running out.
Yet still they ventured into hell.
That's what raw courage is all about.

They fought the scourge of tyranny
To keep us safe and free.
And many thousands gave their lives,
To protect the cause of liberty.

So spare a moment now and then,
In the midst of this and that.
To send a prayer of thanks to them.
And if you have one. Doff your hat.

Richard J. Scarr, Brighton, East Sussex, England

Following the Readings came the Act of Remembrance, during which the author's younger son, Charles Lyon, and his niece, Kate Lyon, both gave readings.

Wreath laying took place with several wreaths placed around the grave. Amongst the wreath layers we had chosen to include one of the author's grandchildren, Jack Lyon (9), and one of his younger brother Bob's grandchildren, Matilda Lyon (10). During the wreath laying the pipers played 'Highland Cathedral' (Michael Korb/ Ulrich Roever).

8.8 The RAF Bugler playing the Last Post. Photo Jean-Yves Le Lan.

8.9 Air Marshal (later Sir) Richard Garwood KBE CB DFC MA RAF. Photo Jean-Yves Le Lan.

8.10 Wreath laying by Jack Lyon and Matilda Lyon. Photo by Pascal Toureille for *Le Télégramme*. Reproduced by kind permission.

8.11 Air Marshal Sir Richard Garwood laying the wreath on
behalf of RAF 234 Squadron. Photo Jean-Yves Le Lan.

The Kojima Epitaph was read by Air Marshal (from January 2017, Sir) Dick Garwood KBE CB DFC MA RAF, without whom further progress on this story would have stalled way back in 2008. The service continued, the rain eased a little, and at the conclusion of the ceremony the family proceeded out of the cemetery to the pipers playing 'Scotland the Brave' (Trad.). A public reception with speeches was then hosted by the Mayor of Guidel.

Firstly, Jean-Yves Le Lan spoke on the history of the long fight to recognise Russell's grave. Secondly, the author spoke, acknowledging all of the work by many people that had taken place, especially the arrangements made for the ceremony, and not least to thank those who had volunteered to accommodate in their homes all of the Lyon family visitors to Guidel and Plœmeur. Thirdly, the Defence Attaché from the British Embassy in Paris spoke. Lastly, the Mayor of Guidel, François Aubertin, thanked everyone who had helped to make the ceremony proceed smoothly.

8.12 The Lyon family group at the civic reception hosted by the
Mayor of Guidel. Photo Jean-Yves Le Lan.

Following this public reception the Mayor of Guidel hosted a lunch
for the family and other guests, during which he announced that he
had organised two visits for the afternoon. The party would be divided
into two and each group would then be taken in turn to visit the Flore
Submarine Base at Lorient, housed in the former Keroman German
U-boat K1 bunker. The second visit would be to Jean Robic's farm,
adjacent to the Lann-Bihoué Air Base, known as Kerlin-Bastard,
during WWII. Jean has created a private museum of military artefacts
in old underground German concrete bunkers on his farm, which was
occupied by the Germans during WWII. In his museum, Jean has one
room dedicated to Russell Lyon, with much of the Spitfire wreckage
that was recovered in 2003–2005 on display. Jean had been involved
from the beginning of the story, having been responsible for the
Spitfire AR343 crash site excavations. A visit was also made to see the
roundabout Stele at Kercavès, unveiled in 2008, where the heather and
other planting had now matured.

The day concluded with the Lyon family entertaining the French
host families to dinner at a local restaurant, during which our excellent
pipers, Alistair and Andrew, entertained everyone with their favourite

8.13 Visit to the Stele at Kercavès. L to R, Dr Anne Lyon, Jack Lyon, Richard Lyon, Dr Alexander Lyon, Amelia Sutherland (née Lyon) and Charles Lyon. Photo Jean-Yves Le Lan.

piping tunes. Bagpiping in southern Brittany is well known. The city of Lorient annually hosts the Lorient Interceltic Festival, a large folk festival, held in the first week of August. As the Brittany region has Celtic origins, the local language, Breton, is closely related to Cornish and Welsh. This Festival started in 1971 with participating musicians now coming from all the 'Celtic' nations – Scotland, Ireland, Wales, the Isle of Man, Cornwall, Brittany and the Spanish regions of Asturias and Galicia. The friendliness of all these French people, who are closely associated with this story, to the Lyon family, and to the memory of the young Scotsman F/O Russell Lyon, is somehow reinforced by their common Celtic characteristics.

Chapter 9

Freedom of Information Request 2016

During the review by the MoD from 2011 onwards, the slow progress had left the author wondering what was causing the issue to take such a long time to be reviewed. On the one hand this suggested just how seriously the issue was being considered, but on the other hand the author was left wondering how strong the opposing arguments might be. And so in mid 2015 the author made a Freedom of Information request to the RAF AHB to see whether there was further information that might help answer this question.

This resulted in the author receiving, ten months later in April 2016, copies of six documents relating to the case, some of which provided new information and some clarification to him on the depth of the considerations that had taken place:

- Document 1) Case report of 2009.

- Document 2) Case report of 2011.

- Document 3) Case report of 2012 following change of standard of proof (many redactions).

- Document 4) Consideration for proposal of 'believed to be' grave marking at Guidel (many redactions).

- Document 5) Letter 5 December 2013 from the head of the RAF AHB, Mr Sebastian Cox, to Rear Admiral Simon Williams (several redactions).

- Document 6) Letter 19 December 2013 from Rear Admiral Simon Williams to the head of the RAF AHB, Mr Sebastian Cox (two redactions).

In summary, for the attempts at grave recognition the starting point is the inconclusive RAF MREU investigation of 1945, with a paucity of information from the exhumation resulting in (1) the inscription 'Known unto God' going onto the gravestone and (2) Russell Lyon's name being included, amongst some 20,400 other RAF casualties of WWII with no known grave, on the RAF Runnymede Memorial.

In late 2003 the French (Claude Hélias and others) submitted their request for grave recognition to the Beauvais Office of the CWGC. This was rejected due to insufficient evidence.

In October 2003 and January 2004 further requests were made, but these did not succeed.

In July 2004 a member of RAF 234 Squadron made an application for review but this was also rejected in October 2004.

This demonstrated that the case had been considered some five times, once immediately following WWII and four times after the discovery of the Spitfire crash site near Plœmeur, but before the French researchers were able to make contact with the Lyon family.

In May 2007 the author made his first application for grave recognition but this was rejected by the JCCC (to whom he had been referred by the CWGC and who had confirmed that the MoD would reopen the case) in June 2007. This mentioned that potential wash-up casualties could not be ruled out and concluded that the grave should remain marked as 'unknown'.

Later in 2007–2009, with more evidence appearing, the author's second application for review was made to the JCCC, but on this occasion the case was referred to the RAF AHB. These applications were rejected in January 2008, March 2009, May 2009 and July 2009 because of insufficient evidence, primarily as the hearsay evidence was considered inadmissible, together with the proposition of the alternative 'wash-up' theory.

Following the change in the standard of proof of September 2011, the next review took place. The new standard of proof under which the case was to be reviewed was now 'Clear and Convincing: a high level of burden of persuasion where it is substantially more likely than not that the matter is in fact true'. This review included visits to the AHB by Air Vice Marshal Irvine in September 2010 (before the September

2011 change) and by Air Marshal Garwood (President of the 234 Squadron Association) in October 2011.

Documents 3 and 4, mentioned above, relate to this period, with Document 4 summarising considerations for the categories 'Believed to have been buried elsewhere in this cemetery' (CWGC Type B Headstone), 'Buried near this spot' (CWGC Type C Headstone) or 'Believed to be in this grave' (CWGC Type D Headstone), with evidence and arguments put for and against.

For these three options the case for a Type B Headstone concluded that on the balance of probabilities the remains of F/O Lyon were buried at Guidel.

The case for a Type C Headstone could be considered.

The case for a Type D Headstone remained circumstantial.

Document 4 of 23 July 2014 concludes with the Recommendation: 'It is recommended that "Buried near this spot" (Type C) is accepted for F/O E.R. Lyon and a headstone be placed accordingly in Guidel.'

The two last documents are an exchange of letters between Mr Sebastian Cox, the Head of the RAF AHB, and Rear Admiral Simon Williams, Assistant Chief of the Defence Staff (Personnel & Training), who was conducting the review and who was also the Defence Services Secretary.

Between the redactions in the two letters, which often make for difficult interpretation of the whole, the writers speak about the drafts of decisions about to be made; the policies of the MoD, the RAF and the CWGC for such Historic Casualty Casework; the protocols involved; essential criteria to be met for the Types B–D Headstones, the reliance or otherwise on date evidence alone; the risk of precedents being set; the role of the expert witness; the role of the AHB itself; department workloads; and the primacy of the Joint Services Practice Manual.

Interestingly, Document 6 also makes reference to a letter from the CWGC to Rear Admiral Simon Williams' predecessor making it clear that the CWGC 'would be content with a "Believed to Be" (Headstone Type D) assessment in this particular case'.

To see these documents was a relief. Moreover, they demonstrate just how tricky it is to come to decisions in such cases. On the one hand the Service Authority has to abide by the book in their behaviour, but on the other hand the Applicant, most likely (as in this case) a member of the casualty's family, can be driven by emotion as much as by the facts that appear before their less expert eye.

Early in the author's involvement with the case there were occasions when others with whom the story was shared, including high-ranking military personnel, would say that the case was a 'no brainer'. The fact that the case came to light some fifty-eight years after the end of WWII and then took a further eleven years to resolve might suggest that this description was an oversimplification, as there were strong issues of principle on both sides of the argument.

This case, known in the files as ID Case No. 28 – F/O E.R. Lyon, has certainly been a difficult one to bring to a conclusion with which all are content.

Having been closely involved with the case since 2006, and finally having seen this last set of documents made available via the Freedom of Information request, the author would just like to say that the Lyon family and their supporters were satisfied with the conclusion reached by the authorities.

Chapter 10
Conclusion

The 21st-century phase of this story about the young Spitfire Pilot Russell Lyon could not, for the author, have been at all predictable.

If somebody had questioned the author, in or before 2005, on his views or knowledge on the subject of those service personnel who had gone missing in action with no known grave, the author would have appeared to look a little blankly back at them. That is no longer the case.

When the French researchers first made contact with the Lyon family in March 2007, the author little knew what lay ahead of him once he chose to try and get official recognition for the grave at Guidel. In the eight years that followed much occurred that could not have been predicted. The extensive research required was made a little easier by the fact that in 2008 he took retirement, so his time and commitment to the case was available and less constrained by other issues.

Looking back at the events, the author feels that progress was often the result of pure serendipity.

As this story began in around 2001, it proceeded and was fuelled by moments of happenstance and of serendipity. As it concluded fifteen years later, there was huge satisfaction at what had been achieved. One might compare it almost with the Rhubarb mission definition, setting off with such an ill-defined target and not knowing what would happen on the way.

The placing of the memorial on the Scottish family website in late 2006 was one example, followed by the diligence of Jean-Yves Le Lan in spotting this a few months later and making contact with the author. Without the Internet this connection would, in all likelihood, never have been made.

Although time was on the author's side in this one respect, time was not on his side in another respect. With the efforts taking place to try and reconstruct the events of 27 July 1944 onwards, the six or seven decades that had followed had naturally made matters more difficult. For instance, the witnesses were elderly persons and despite their memories being sharp their recollections of July 1944 would not go on indefinitely. The principal eyewitness, Joseph Le Corroller, who was of a similar age to F/O E.R. Lyon at the time of the crash in late July 1944, lived to see the roundabout near his farmhouse named after F/O E.R. Lyon in 2008, but sadly died in his mid eighties, before the formal grave recognition was achieved in 2014. Both the author and his elder brother were pleased to have met this elderly gentleman between 2007 and 2008, but fate could easily have taken away not only that possibility, but also the possibility of Joseph making his earlier witness statements.

Contact with RAF 234 Squadron by the author was another area that might have been less productive were it not for the presence of Air Marshal Sir Richard Garwood, who encouraged and provided support to the author to keep on pursuing his objectives. This contact also enabled the author to meet and speak with elderly Spitfire pilots who had known and flown with F/O E.R. Lyon, something he would not have dreamed possible a few years before.

The author also believes that the time was right for the challenge and review that took place resulting in the change of the Ministry of Defence standard of proof required for the identification of casualties missing in action. It was to the good fortune of this case that the challenge was made without the need to instigate an expensive legal case; rather, it struck those in authority charged with looking at the issue that the UK policies were out of line compared with other countries. Developed in a previous era and unchallenged for decades, the policy appeared to some as not being in keeping with the current age.

For the author the journey has been a little like the description one of the veteran Spitfire pilots gave to him at a 234 Squadron Reunion. He said that you did not so much get into the iconic Spitfire and fly it; rather you got into the cockpit and took off with the Spitfire and its powerful Merlin engine strapped onto your back.

The story received attention from the press, radio and TV media, which led to people from across the country making contact with the author, some who had known F/O Russell Lyon in his early life in Edinburgh, others who had similar stories to tell and to share.

In addition to being a family history project, the story has become a cause around which the Lyon family could unite. Also friendships with others, those associated with RAF 234 Squadron, and with the families of the French researchers, have developed.

The task was challenging throughout, often with the need to disprove what was seen as the negative or opposite position backed by scanty or even no evidence.

In this philosophic respect there is an analogy called, coincidentally, 'Russell's Teapot', named after the philosopher Bertrand Russell (1872–1970) who formulated this metaphor. Put simply, Bertrand Russell postulated that there was a teapot orbiting the sun somewhere between the orbits of the planets Earth and Mars, knowing that this was virtually impossible to disprove. The philosophic debate on this conundrum concluded that the philosophic burden of proof rests with the person making far-fetched claims rather than transferring the burden of disproof to others.

The falsifiable or testability aspect in Russell Lyon's case was thus tested by the need to weaken or disprove the alternative wash-up victim theory introduced as a reason to reject the case. In this case that alternative wash-up victim theory was reduced scientifically to a 15 per cent chance of being true.

The analogy of Russell's Teapot, conceived by Bertrand Russell in 1952, has often been used by philosophers, including Betrand Russell himself in 1958, in debates concerning the existence, or otherwise, of God.

Kipling's suggestion for the use of the words 'Known unto God' for the graves of unknown servicemen resounded strongly over Grave 33, Row 6 in the Commonwealth War Graves section in the Guidel Communal Cemetery from the early 1950s onwards. It still resounds strongly over many other similarly unidentified war graves.

Now that a change of wording has occurred on the gravestone following the decisions of 2014, the grave casualty is no longer only 'Known unto God', but is now known both to God and man.

Russell Lyon's father, Ernest Lyon, was a member of the Plymouth Brethren Christian Church in Edinburgh, a fairly strict, low and non-conformist evangelical movement originating from within Anglicism in the 1820s. With its strong emphasis on the importance of family life and faith through the Bible, one wonders what reaction there would have been from Russell's father and stepmother when he broke the news to them in late 1940/early 1941, just past his eighteenth birthday, that he had volunteered to join the Royal Air Force.

In the book *Dragon Rampant: the Story of No. 234 Fighter Squadron*, at page 106, there is reference (using Russell's nickname Ben) to 'Ben's Calvinist family had disowned him when he went to war, and with nowhere to go for his infrequent leaves, Alan Frost often invited him to his home'.

The author cannot say whether or not he was disowned and would prefer to think that when leave was granted to Russell, he preferred not to use much of his short leave sitting on a train to Edinburgh and

10.1 F/O Alan Frost *c*.1944. Frost collection.

back, but rather accepting the kind hospitality of the Frost family. In support of this the author is pleased to be able to quote a letter, shown below, which dispels any suggestion of Russell being disowned by his family, as he is clearly heading home, on seven days' leave, to Edinburgh from RAF Hutton Cranswick via Newcastle.

In the family archive there is only one letter written by Russell, to the author's mother, May, dated 6 December 1943, written at RAF Hutton Cranswick, which says:

Dear May,

I am afraid this is going to be a very short note as I am very cold and very tired and have already written four letters this evening and am feeling rather browned off with writing. Anyway I hope to see you soon and I can give you all my news then.

I am going home on leave for seven glorious days starting on Tuesday 14th December and I expect to be passing through Newcastle in the morning or early afternoon so if you can get to Newcastle I should like to see you for a few hours. At the moment I am not sure what time I will be arriving but I shall drop you a line before Tuesday to let you know. If you will write and tell me if you can make it, and if so where to meet you. Well that is all for now sister dear so cheerio and

love from Russell.

P.S. By the way, I might even have a silk stocking with me so remember to be ever so sweet to me.

The author's father, Stanley, then a 2nd Lieutenant, Royal Engineers, had married May in August 1940, so this letter from Russell to his sister-in-law, May, is written with a close familiarity. As shown in the 'Another Ben Lyon' insert box in Chapter 2, in WWII Stanley Lyon served with the Tyne Electrical Engineers in places such as Basra in Iraq, and in Palestine. After WWII he was de-mobbed with the rank of Major.

10.2
Wedding photo of Stanley and May Lyon, Whitley Bay,
Northumberland, 2 August 1940.
Lyon family collection.

The actions of Russell's father after WWII in his lengthy correspondence with the Air Ministry do not suggest, either, that the family had disowned him.

Achieving a successful end to this case by the author alone would have been well nigh impossible. Without the help of the French researchers and of Air Marshal Sir Dick Garwood, this 'flight' would have never left the ground.

During the research, at one stage the author was told that there were perhaps some fifty or so similar cases in which the graves of missing services personnel were being investigated further. The author hopes that the September 2011 change to the Ministry of Defence standard of proof brought about during Russell Lyon's case will help other families and researchers to bring some conclusion to these other cases. While most will not receive a great deal of publicity, the author has read about two high-profile cases, each coming to a conclusion.

A month after the ceremony of October 2015, a report appeared in the press regarding a visit by HM The Queen to the Joint Compassionate and Casualty Centre at RAF Innsworth, together with the story of a new CWGC headstone with the wording 'Buried near this spot' being placed at the Quarry Cemetery, Vermelles, commemorating a WWI casualty of the Battle of Loos in 1915. The casualty was named Captain Fergus Bowes-Lyon, the elder brother of the late Queen Elizabeth the Queen Mother, who was previously recorded amongst the names of the missing on the Loos Memorial.

Later, in January 2016 the author read in the press another similar story where the CWGC were reported as 'welcoming the latest research which supports the identification of the grave of Lieutenant John Kipling', son of Rudyard Kipling, another casualty of the Battle of Loos in 1915.

The author hopes that other families from amongst the fifty or so other cases will achieve a similar degree of satisfaction as he and his family have experienced.

Following the conclusion of the ID Case No. 28 – F/O E.R. Lyon, the Lyon family were most thankful for all the time and effort that had been put into the official reviews, not just by those in positions of authority charged with making the decisions, but also to all those who gave voluntarily and freely of their time and energy to help the family reach this unpredictable and unexpected but pleasing conclusion.

Appendix 1
Speeches Given 8 November 2008

Speech by Richard Lyon

Monsieur le Commandant de la base de Lann-Bihoué, Monsieur le Maire, Mesdames et messieurs les élus, Messieurs les officiers généraux, Messieurs les anciens combattants, Les représentants honorables du Royaume-Uni, Mesdames, messieurs, toute ma famille, et chers amis.

Pour la bonne compréhension de tous, je vais parler en français et en anglais, avec pour chaque paragraphe en premier le français et ensuite en deuxième l'anglais.

For the benefit of all I am going to speak both in French and in English, with each paragraph spoken first in French and then secondly in English.

En Premier, je vais parler pour la famille Lyon.

Firstly I will speak for the Lyon family

De la part de la famille Lyon, je dois remercier sincèrement tous ceux qui sont présents ici, aujourd'hui, et qui sont venus pour honorer la mémoire de mon oncle, le lieutenant de la Royal Air Force, Russell Lyon.

On behalf of the Lyon family I must say a heartfelt thank you to all of you here today who have come to honour the memory of my uncle, Flying Officer Russell Lyon.

Mon frère aîné, Alastair, mon jeune frère, Bob, moi-même, et tous les membres de notre famille avons été très touchés par la décision de la municipalité de Larmor-Plage d'honorer mon oncle et d'avoir organisé cette cérémonie aujourd'hui.

135

My elder brother, Alastair, my younger brother, Bob, and I, and our families have been very very moved by the decision of the Local Authority at Larmor-Plage to honour my uncle in this way, and who have organised this ceremony today.

Je vous transmets aussi, la reconnaissance et les remerciements, à vous tous, de la part de notre jeune frère Bob, et des autres membres de la famille qui ne sont pas présents, aujourd'hui, à Larmor-Plage.

We bring the best wishes and thanks to you all from our younger brother, Bob, and other family members who cannot be with us here in Larmor-Plage today.

Russell est mort, en ce lieu de Kercavès, en juillet mille neuf cent quarante quatre. Mes frères et moi-même, sommes nés quelques années après son décès; mais, notre génération a bénéficié de la liberté pour laquelle Russell et beaucoup d'autres ont lutté et perdu la vie.

We were all born a few years after the death of Russell at this place in July 1944. Our generation has benefited from the freedom that Russell and many others fought for.

Nous sommes conscients que ce mémorial individuel est aussi représentatif des centaines et des milliers de militaires et de civils qui ont donné leur vie au cours de la deuxième guerre mondiale pour offrir un monde meilleur à ceux qui ont survécu à ce conflit.

We are conscious that this individual memorial is also representative of the hundreds and thousands of other service personnel and civilians who gave their lives in World War II to bring a better world to those who survived that conflict.

Merci, vivement, pour tout ce que vous avez fait pour que cette cérémonie ait lieu aujourd'hui et pour votre accueil.

Thank you deeply for everything that you have done to enable today's ceremony to happen and for the hospitality that we are being given.

Deuxièmement, je vais vous dire quelques mots de la part du colonel Nigel Walpole de l'escadron deux cent trente quatre, qui est un escadron dissous de la Royal Air Force.

Secondly, I am going to say a few words on behalf of Group Captain Nigel Walpole, of 234 Squadron, which is a disbanded Royal Air Force Squadron.

De la part de l'Escadron deux cent trente quatre, de la Royal Air Force, le colonel Walpole souhaite remercier Monsieur Victor Tonnerre et tous ceux qui ont travaillé si durement pour honorer le Lieutenant Russell Lyon, le travail réalisé ici pour lui rendre cet hommage est magnifique.

On behalf of No. 234 (Fighter) Squadron, Royal Air Force, Group Captain Walpole wishes to thank Monsieur Victor Tonnerre, and all who have worked so hard to honour Flying Officer Russell Lyon, work which has led to this splendid tribute to him here.

Nous sommes fiers de Russell et des nombreux jeunes hommes qui, comme lui, ont donné leurs vies tout au long des années sombres de mille neuf cent trente neuf à mille neuf cent quarante cinq et votre geste souligne aujourd'hui encore une fois le respect permanent que nous partageons pour la cause de la liberté.

Merci à vous tous.

We are grateful to and proud of Russell, and the many young men like him who gave their lives throughout the dark years of 1939–45, and your gesture today underlines once more the enduring respect we share for the cause of freedom. Thank you all.

Richard Lyon
8 November 2008

Speech by Jean-Yves Le Lan

Ernest Russell Lyon

Je vais vous présenter une biographie sommaire d'Ernest Russell Lyon pour que vous puissiez connaître un peu de la vie de la personne que nous honorons aujourd'hui.

Ernest Russell Lyon est né le 19 décembre 1922 à Colinton, c'est une paroisse de la banlieue d'Edimbourg en Ecosse, ses parents étaient Ernest Hutcheon Lyon et Pealling Elizabeth Wright.

Dans la famille, il était prénommé Russell. Il fit ses études à l'école George Heriot et à l'école George Watson d'Edimbourg. C'était un garçon joyeux qui aimait plaisanter.

A l'école George Watson, il a obtenu la médaille de bronze pour la natation en quatrième année et au moment où il était en sixième année, il était dans l'équipe première de rugby à XV. Il étudia l'anglais, le français, la physique et la chimie en sixième année. Il a été aussi un chef de patrouille dans les scouts et a également fait une formation militaire à cette époque. Il jouait au tennis et au cricket.

Russell était célibataire.

Il rejoignit la Royal Air Force comme volontaire à l'âge de 18 ans. Après une formation aux États-Unis et au Canada en 1941- 42, il entra dans l'escadron 234 de la Royal Air Force, en 1943. Il avait le grade de lieutenant. Il y fut surnommé « Ben » d'après le nom de l'acteur d'Hollywood Ben Lyon.

Il vola en soutien le jour « J » pour le débarquement de Normandie. Il effectua alors des sorties d'escorte, pour les avions remorqueurs et les planeurs, et a fourni également une couverture aérienne sur les plages du débarquement de Gold et d'Omaha.

Après, il fut basé à Predannack, la base aérienne de la péninsule du cap Lizard au sud-ouest de la Grande-Bretagne.

Il effectua alors des missions de harcèlement de l'ennemi et en particulier le 27 juillet 1944, il décolla avec sept autres Spitfire pour attaquer la base de Kerlin Bastard (Lann-Bihoué actuellement). Il fut abattu par la défense anti-aérienne allemande des Quatre-Chemins à Larmor-Plage et son avion tomba en flamme près de Kercavès au lieu-dit maison rouge. Il perdit la vie dans le crash. L'épave de l'avion sera retrouvée soixante années après le crash et vous pouvez voir ici sur cette très belle stèle, réalisée par les Services techniques de la ville de Larmor-Plage, le moyeu de l'hélice de l'avion de Russell.

Ernest Russell Lyon n'a pas de tombe connue et son nom est inscrit avec les 20,400 autres personnels de la RAF sur le mémorial de Runnymede en Grande-Bretagne. Son nom est également sur le monument de la guerre à l'école George Watson à Édimbourg et est aussi rappelé sur la tombe familiale au cimetière de Colinton.

Jean-Yves Le Lan

Speech by Charles Lyon

Ernest Russell Lyon

I will present a brief biography of Ernest Russell Lyon for you to know a bit about the life of the person we honour today.

Ernest Russell Lyon was born on 19 December 1922 in Colinton, a parish in the outskirts of Edinburgh in Scotland. His parents were Ernest Hutcheon Lyon and Elizabeth Wright Pealling. In the family, he was named Russell. He was educated at George Heriot's School and George Watson's School of Edinburgh. He was a happy boy who loved to joke.

At George Watson's School, he got the bronze medal for swimming in fourth year and by the time he was in sixth year he was in the rugby First XV. He learnt English, French, physics and chemistry in sixth year, was a patrol leader in the Scouts and was also in the Army Training Corps and played tennis and cricket.

Russell was not married.

He joined the Royal Air Force as a volunteer at age 18. After training in the United States and Canada in 1941–42, he entered the 234 Squadron of the Royal Air Force in 1943. He was a Flying Officer. He was nicknamed 'Ben' after the Hollywood actor Ben Lyon.

He flew in support of D-Day for the Normandy landings and he flew on sorties including escorting the tugs and gliders, and also providing air cover over Gold and Omaha beaches.

After D-Day he was based at RAF Predannack on the Lizard Peninsula in the South-West of the United Kingdom.

He then flew on missions of harassment of the enemy and in particular on 27 July 1944, he departed with seven other Spitfires to attack the airport of Kerlin-Bastard (Lann-Bihoué now). He was shot down by the German anti-aircraft defence at Quatre-Chemins near Larmor-Plage and his plane fell in flames near Kercavès at a place called Maison-Rouge. He died in the crash. The wreckage of the aircraft was found sixty years after the crash, and you can see here on this beautiful stone, built by the Technical Services of the city Larmor-Plage, the hub of the propeller of Russell's plane.

Ernest Russell Lyon has no known grave and his name is inscribed with 20,400 other missing personnel of the RAF on the Runnymede Memorial in United Kingdom.

His name is also on the War Memorial at George Watson's School in Edinburgh and is also recalled on the family tomb in Colinton Cemetery.

Charles Lyon

Appendix 2
Speeches Given 5 October 2015

Speech by Richard Lyon

I would like to say thank you to a number of people for today and the events that have led to the Re-dedication here in Guidel this morning.

Je voudrais dire le merci à un certain nombre de personnes pour aujourd'hui et aux événements qui ont causé la Redédicace ici dans Guidel ce matin.

Firstly, may I thank the Mayor of Guidel and his colleagues for the goodwill, hospitality and welcome given to the Lyon family by the people of Guidel.

Premièrement, peux je remercier le Maire de Guidel et ses collègues pour la bonne volonté, l'hospitalité et accueillir donné à la famille Lyon par les gens de Guidel.

We are a large group of over twenty people of all ages. I speak for us all in saying we are all most grateful for the hospitality that has been forthcoming for this short visit to southern Brittany.

Nous sommes un grand groupe de plus de 20 personnes de tous les âges. Je parle pour nous tous dans le dicton nous sommes tous les plus reconnaissants à l'hospitalité qui a été prochaine pour cette visite courte dans Bretagne du sud.

Secondly, I thank Tracey Bowers and her team from the Ministry of Defence–Defence Business Services Joint Casualty and Compassionate Centre at RAF Innsworth. The organisation and attention to detail that I have seen over the last few months has been excellent.

Deuxièmement, je remercie Tracey Bowers et son équipe de l'Accidenté d'Articulation de Services d'Affaires de Défense de

Ministère de la Défense et du Centre Compatissant à RAF Innsworth. L'organisation et l'attention pour l'exposer en détail que j'ai vu pendant quelques mois derniers ont été excellents.

A thank you is also due to The Revd (Gp Capt) John Ellis for his role in conducting the service, and to the bugler.

Un merci est aussi en raison du Revd (Gp Capt) John Ellis pour son rôle dans la conduction du service et au clairon.

Of course, I also need to thank our two bagpipers, Alastair Hutcheon and Andrew Spence, of George Watson's College in Edinburgh. Your role has added a very poignant touch to the morning.

Évidemment je dois aussi remercier nos deux cornemusiers, Alastair Hutcheon et Andrew Spence, du Collège de George Watson à Édimbourg. Votre rôle a ajouté un contact très poignant au matin.

The day should not pass without a mention of the role of Air Marshal Dick Garwood and his colleague Air Vice Marshal Lindsay Irvine over the last few years with regard to the formal recognition of the grave beside which we all stood this morning. I use this public occasion to say a huge thank you for all the freely given guidance and assistance through the bureaucratic web.

Le jour ne doit pas passer sans une mention du rôle de Air Marshal Dick Garwood et son collègue Air Vice Marshal Lindsay Irvine au cours de ces dernières années en ce qui concerne la reconnaissance formelle de la tombe à côté de laquelle nous avons tous atteint ce matin. J'utilise cette occasion publique pour dire un grand Merci pour tous les conseils donné librement et assistance à travers le web bureaucratique.

And then I come to our local researchers without whom we would not be gathering here today, Jean Robic, Jean-Yves Le Lan and Claude Hélias. May I also publicly say that their efforts have been absolutely magnificent in setting the identification case off on a strong start, some 14 years ago, and for their ongoing help over the years.

A puis je venir à nos chercheurs locaux sans lesquels nous n'aurait pas réunis ici aujourd'hui, Jean Robic, Jean-Yves Le Lan et Claude Hélias. Je dirai aussi publiquement que leurs efforts ont été absolument magnifiques en déclenchant le cas de l'identification sur un bon départ, quelque 14 ans auparavant et pour leur aide en cours au fil des ans.

And so I cannot finish without a mention of why we are here, for our Uncle Russell Lyon. With my two brothers, none of us knew him personally, as we were all born after the end of WWII. Well, I think that I can say that I know him now, and we will hold his memory for the rest of our lives.

Et donc je ne peux pas terminer sans une mention de pourquoi nous sommes ici, pour notre oncle Russell Lyon. Avec mes deux frères aucun d'entre nous ne connaissaient personnellement, car nous sommes tous nés après la fin de la 2nde GM. Eh bien, je pense que je peux dire que je le connais maintenant, et nous procéderons à sa mémoire pour le reste de notre vie.

On the RAF Runnymede Memorial there are some 20,456 names of RAF servicemen who lost their lives in WWII and who have no known grave. Russell's name will, in due course, now be removed from this memorial, but I am left with the thought that there are still over some 20,450 casualties who do not have the good fortune that has shone on Russell's case.

Sur le monument de Runnymede RAF il y a quelques 20 456 noms des militaires de la RAF qui ont perdu leur vie dans WWII et qui n'ont pas de sépulture connue. Nom de Russell, en temps voulu, sont supprimé de ce mémorial, mais je suis parti avec l'idée qu'il existe encore à plus de quelques 20 450 blessés qui n'ont pas la chance qui a brillé sur le cas de Russell.

The Lyon family are all most grateful for the events of today and to all those who have brought this about.

La famille de Lyon est tous très reconnaissante pour les événements d'aujourd'hui et à tous ceux qui ont permis cela.

Richard Lyon

5 October 2015

Cérémonie du 5 octobre 2015

Aujourd'hui, nous nous sommes retrouvés pour la cérémonie de reconnaissance officielle du lieu de sépulture d'Ernest Russell Lyon appelé Russell dans sa famille. Pour aboutir à ce résultat, il y eut de nombreuses et longues démarches mais ce fut aussi une aventure humaine qui a vu de nombreux acteurs collaborer pour arriver à ce que voulait le père de Russell : retrouver le lieu où avait été inhumé son fils après le crash de son avion en France le 27 juillet 1944.

Le début de la démarche a été initié par Jean Robic le 12 septembre 2003. Grâce à des informations communiquées par Joseph Le Coroller, un agriculteur de Larmor-Plage, près de soixante ans après le crash, Jean Robic entreprit, avec l'aide de Sébastien Le Coupanec et d'Alain Gargam, des fouilles sur le lieu de l'épave de l'avion.

Claude Hélias, du Conservatoire Aéronautique de Cornouaille, alerté par Jean Robic a alors monté un dossier pour obtenir la reconnaissance à la fois du lieu du crash et d'une tombe d'un inconnu située dans le cimetière du Commonwealth à Guidel comme étant celle de Russell. Cette demande fut rejetée par la commission des tombes de guerre du Commonwealth. Le dossier étant bloqué, la seule façon à cette époque de relancer la procédure était de retrouver la famille.

Jean Robic m'ayant parlé de cette affaire, je m'y suis intéressé dans le but de rédiger un article dans les Cahiers du Pays de Plœmeur, revue du Comité d'histoire du Pays de Plœmeur. Pendant de nombreux mois, j'ai cherché sur Internet la famille mais sans succès. Ce ne fut que le 1er avril 2007 sur le forum TalkingScot – forum de généalogie écossaise – que j'ai trouvé une personne qui s'intéressait à Russell. Mais je n'avais que son pseudonyme qui était Puffin (macareux en français). Je réussis toutefois à découvrir que c'était un architecte qui habitait Cambridge. J'ai donc poursuivi la démarche et trouvé un architecte à Cambridge qui s'appelait Lyon. Je lui ai écrit et effectivement, c'était bien un parent du pilote: un neveu nommé Richard Lyon.

A partir de ce moment, Richard, ici présent, a pris le relais avec le soutien de ses frères Alastair et Bob, présents aussi aujourd'hui, et s'est donné comme challenge de faire reconnaître par les autorités britanniques le site du crash et la tombe. De nombreux échanges ont alors eu lieu entre l'équipe française et la famille. Des échanges par écrit mais aussi des échanges sur le terrain. Alastair et Richard sont venus dans la région en 2007 et en 2008 pour se faire une opinion précise des faits : visite du lieu du crash, rencontre avec Joseph Le Coroller, visite des restes de l'avion et du cimetière de Guidel.

Richard a alors monté un nouveau dossier, qui lui aussi a été rejeté, mais qui donnait des précisions sur ce qu'attendait le ministère britannique.

De nouvelles recherches d'informations furent lancées dans les archives en France et en Allemagne mais aussi avec l'aide de la presse à partir de nouveaux témoignages. Ces recherches furent un succès et permirent de remonter un nouveau dossier qui aboutit à la reconnaissance officielle par les autorités britanniques du lieu de crash à proximité du village de Kercavès en Larmor-Plage mais hélas qui n'aboutissait pas encore à la reconnaissance de la tombe.

Un peu en avance de phase par rapport à cette décision car du côté français, il n'y avait aucun doute, le 8 novembre 2008, une stèle a été érigée à la mémoire de Russell sur un rond-point à Kercavès grâce à la municipalité de Larmor-Plage.

Nous n'étions pas encore arrivés à l'aboutissement, il a donc fallu poursuivre la démarche. De nouvelles recherches furent lancées dans les archives: dans celles de la gendarmerie française et dans celles de la Croix Rouge à Genève mais sans donner d'élément. Richard Lyon entreprit alors, avec l'aide de l'association de l'escadron 234 dont faisait parti Russell, de faire modifier les critères des lois britanniques pour juger de tels cas. Il réussit à faire modifier la loi et surtout la norme de la preuve nécessaire pour de telles affaires. Elle passa de « au-delà de tout doute raisonnable » à « preuves claires et convaincantes ».

Après cette modification de la loi, il fut donc demandé par Richard Lyon de revoir le jugement mais comme l'affaire avait été déjà jugée et qu'il n'y avait pas de possibilité d'appel dans la procédure nous étions dans l'impasse. La famille demanda alors la mise en place d'une procédure d'appel ce qui fut fait pour les trois armes : la Royal Air Force, l'Army et la Royal Navy.

Toutes ces démarches furent très longues et ce ne fut seulement que le 23 juillet 2014, qu'une réunion eut lieu au Ministère de la défense britannique pour statuer sur le cas de Russell. A cette réunion, il fut conclu qu'il n'y a pas de preuve pour affirmer que le corps de Russell soit dans la tombe 33 de la ligne 6 du cimetière de Guidel mais qu'il est raisonnable de supposer qu'il avait été inhumé dans une des tombes de ce cimetière. Comme le ministère et la commission des tombes de guerre du Commonwealth ne permettent pas l'exhumation des corps pour réaliser une identification ADN, il a été décidé de remplacer la pierre tombale de l'inconnu de la tombe 33 par un mémorial en l'honneur de Russell avec la mention « enterré près de cet endroit ».

La famille a été prévenue de cette décision par courrier du ministère de la défense britannique daté du 7 août 2014 soit 11 ans après l'extraction du moteur par Jean Robic.

Nous sommes donc aujourd'hui tous réunis pour honorer la mémoire de Russell. J'ai bien sûr une pensée pour lui qui n'est plus un inconnu pour nous. Je me dois de remercier toutes les institutions britanniques et françaises, les acteurs locaux et bien sûr la famille de Russell qui ont permis de lui rendre son histoire et son identité. A travers le cas de Russell, nous avons toujours eu une pensée pour ces nombreux aviateurs qui ont perdu la vie en luttant contre l'occupant et en permettant ainsi la libération de la France. Merci à eux.

Jean-Yves Le Lan

Appendix 3

Commonwealth Military Cemeteries in Morbihan

Introduction by Richard Lyon

In Chapter 7 reference is made to 'A paper (with further input from Jean-Yves Le Lan) was submitted in September 2010, and this went before the Senior Lawyer in the RAF for his consideration. One new paper, prepared by Jean-Yves Le Lan, was a report on all the CWGC Cemeteries in the Region including all casualty details and including all "unknowns".'

This latter short reference to a new paper is to the research work titled '**Commonwealth military cemeteries in Morbihan'** prepared by Jean-Yves Le Lan in 2009/2010.

The need for this study was prompted by the belief that exploration was needed to rule out all other options with regard to other potential burial locations, by the German authorities, of the remains of the pilot after the crash at Kercavès, on the evening of 27 July 1944, of Spitfire AR 343, piloted by F/O E.R. Lyon; i.e. if the unidentified grave at Guidel was not his last resting place where did the Germans bury his remains?

On the CWGC website online searches could be made for <u>named</u> grave casualties in the various Commonwealth War Grave Cemeteries in the region, but it was not possible to search online for details of any <u>unknown</u> casualty, to find, for instance, a date of death from the headstone, and from which a conclusion might be drawn.

The CWGC website for Guidel provided the information that there were 108 identified casualties, amongst a total of 117 casualties buried in that cemetery. Full details for all the identified casualties is provided, but no information on unidentified casualties is provided. (Following recognition of the F/O E.R. Lyon grave at Guidel the CWGC website now records a total of 109 identified casualties).

That proved to be a 'brick wall' in terms of anyone trying to find potential burial information on a missing and unidentified casualty. The only way to find information on any missing and unidentified casualties would be to undertake an on-the-ground search in each CWGC cemetery in the Morbihan area.

Jean-Yves Le Lan embarked on this study and the results of this follow in the document titled 'Commonwealth military cemeteries in Morbihan'. The original of the study is in French. This English version has been translated from French into English by Richard Lyon.

In Chapter 10 the analogy of 'Russell's Teapot' is mentioned. The need for this study of CWGC cemeteries in Morbihan also has a resonance with this philosophical conundrum: i.e. are there any other graves of missing RAF personnel in the Morbihan Region that might be connected with F/O E.R. Lyon? Once again, as researchers the team was being asked to prove a negative. Thankfully, in the case of this question that answer could be provided, but only by this extensive on-the-ground search and report.

This extensive study revealed that no other potential burial location in the CWGC Morbihan area cemeteries was possible other than Row 6, Grave 33 at Guidel, dated 29 July 1944 and marked 'Unknown Airman'.

The study is included here firstly as it formed an important part of the submission seeking the grave recognition and secondly, the information contained within it may be of help to other researchers seeking more information on unidentified CWGC graves in the Morbihan Region.

Richard Lyon

Commonwealth Military Cemeteries in Morbihan, by Jean-Yves Le Lan

In Morbihan, we find Commonwealth graves in fourteen cemeteries. Four are around Lorient (Guidel, Lorient-Kerentrech, Lanester and Gâvres) and include mainly airmen who perished during the attacks on the submarine base and the arsenal of Lorient, and eight others are scattered in the south of the *département* (Vannes-Boismoreau, Plougoumelen, Quiberon, Sarzeau, La Trinité-sur-Mer, L Île aux Moines, Pénestin and Le Palais) and two in the interior of the land, one near Pontivy à Réguiny and one near to Scaër à Guiscriff.

The graves of the soldiers in these Commonwealth cemeteries are mainly for Englishmen of the Royal Air Force, but there are also Canadians of the Royal Canadian Air Force, New Zealanders of the Royal New Zealand Air Force, Australians of the Royal Australian Air Force, and Poles of the Polish Air Force incorporated into the RAF. Two soldiers of the Royal Navy also have their graves in the cemetery of Guidel, three soldiers – a stranger at Lorient-Kerentrech, a soldier from the Royal Regiment of Liverpool to Sarzeau and a man of the Royal Artillery at Guiscriff – and a officer of the merchant marine in the cemetery at Le Palais. All the graves are from the Second World War with the exception of Le Palais, which is from the First World War.

During the war the men were buried summarily and a wooden cross was placed on the grave. After the war, the Allied countries raised the question of the repatriation of the bodies of their soldiers. Of course, it was economically and technically impossible to repatriate the bodies of the soldiers killed on French soil.

The United States decided to exhume the bodies of their soldiers to group them in American military cemeteries located in France (with perpetual concession). This is how the majority of the Americans (thirty-seven soldiers) buried in the cemetery of Guidel were transferred to the Cemetery of Saint-James[1] close to Mont-Saint-Michel, others to Colleville-sur-Mer in Normandy above Omaha Beach, and one to Neupré in Belgium.

---

1   Saint-James is located in the *département* of Manche, to the south of Avranches and Mont Saint-Michel.

On the other hand, the Commonwealth countries chose not to move the bodies of their soldiers and left them in communal cemeteries where they were first buried. In these cases, at the entry to each of these cemeteries is marked 'Commonwealth War Graves – Tombes de Guerre du Commonwealth'.

American Cemetery of Saint-James

A3.1 American Cemetery at St. James.
Copyright Association – Les fleurs de mémoire.

This cemetery, with an area of 12 hectares, was built on the site of a temporary cemetery established shortly after the liberation of the region, by the 8th U.S. Infantry Division, on 2 August 1944. After the war, the remains of American soldiers who died in combat and whose families had requested burial abroad, were transferred from the temporary cemeteries to fourteen permanent cemeteries. The use of the land was granted in perpetuity to the US Government by the French government in recognition of the sacrifices made.

Most of the soldiers buried in this cemetery died during the liberation of Brittany, the breakthrough of Avranches and the violent fighting around Saint-Lô and Mortain.

The cemetery contains the remains of 4,410 soldiers who had been killed in the north-west region of France. They represent 43 % of the burials originally in the region. The 4,408 tombs are divided into 16 squares, arranged in concentric rows compared to the central lawn. The dead who gave their lives for their homeland, come from all the States of the Union, the District of Columbia, Hawaii, Alaska but also Canada.

Ninety-five steles bear the inscription 'Unknown soldier', and contain the remains of soldiers who could not be formally identified.

Source: Website of the association 'The flowers of memory', accessed 9 December 2007: address: http://fleursdelamemoire.free.fr/

The Commonwealth War Graves Commission

The Commonwealth War Graves Commission (CWGC) was established by Royal Charter in 1917. It is a non-profit organisation which was founded by Sir Fabian Ware. Its vocation is to pay tribute to the 1,700,000 men and women of the armed forces of the Commonwealth who died in the two world wars.

Since its inception, the Commission has built 2,500 military cemeteries and has erected the headstones over each grave. In cases where the remains are missing, the names of the dead are written on permanent memorials. More than a million victims are now commemorated at military and civilian sites in some 150 countries.[2]

The first members of the Commonwealth are Australia, Canada, New Zealand and the United Kingdom, but many more countries joined after the 1939–45 war. Queen Elizabeth II is head of the Commonwealth and the president of the CWGC is Prince Edward, Duke of Kent.

The largest cemeteries are in France and Belgium and were built after the First World War. But there are also cemeteries in the Middle East and in Iraq as a result of the battles against the Ottoman Empire during that war. There are also cemeteries in North Africa, in the Far

2   Website of the Commonwealth War Graves Commission, accessed 9 December 2007: http://www. cwgc.org/.

A3.2 Plate at the entrance to the cemetery of Gâvres indicating that there are graves of the Commonwealth. Photo J.-Y. Le Lan.

A3.3. Grave of an airman from the United Kingdom at Guidel. Photo J.-Y. Le Lan.

East and in Italy with regard to the Second World War. The largest CWGC cemetery is located north of Ypres, the Tyne Cot cemetery, which contains 12,000 graves. The smallest cemetery is on Skyros in Greece where there is just one grave, that of the poet Rupert Brooke. Three memorials have been built to commemorate the unidentified soldiers. The largest of them is the Thiepval Memorial which is 45 metres high, showing the names of 72,000 soldiers missing during the battle of the Somme.

The principles of the Commission are that every casualty must be celebrated by his name on the headstone or a memorial, that the tombstones and monuments are permanent, the headstones are identical, and that no distinction is made by reason of rank, race or beliefs.

Every cemetery is ordered in rows of white headstones. Unlike the French and German graves, which are planned as rectangles whose upper edge is in an arc, and no crosses, each stone is marked with a cross or a symbol of the religious denomination of the grave occupant unless the CWGC does not know the religion of the casualty. If the casualty had no religion, no religious symbol is engraved on the stone. At the top of the stone, is a military badge representing the country of the casualty. The stones are engraved with service number, rank, initials of first names, surname, the name of the part of the Army, Air Force or Navy of the casualty, the date of death, age and at the bottom of the tombstone an inscription, generally written by the family. The insignia of the United Kingdom, Canada and Australia are composed of an Eagle taking flight topped by a Crown and in Latin the motto of the RAF: '*PER ARDUA AD ASTRA*' which is translated as 'Through Adversity to the Stars'. For Canada, there is also a ribbon, with the words 'Royal Canadian Air Force', and for Australia, a circle marked 'Royal Australian Air Force'. The badge of New Zealand consists of the fern, emblem of New Zealand, and the words 'NEW ZEALAND'. For Poland, it is the Polish Eagle in a coat of arms.

A3.4 Badge of a member of
United Kingdom forces.
Photo J.-Y. Le Lan.

A3.5 Badge of a member of
Canadian forces.
Photo J.-Y. Le Lan.

A3.7 Badge of a member of
New Zealand forces.
Photo J.-Y. Le Lan.

A3.6 Badge of a member of
Australian forces.
Photo J.-Y. Le Lan.

A3.8 Badge of a member of
Polish forces.
Photo J.-Y. Le Lan.

Below are a few examples of inscriptions on headstones:

- Headstone of C.S. Bell at Guidel: 'Deep in my heart a memory is kept of one I loved and will never forget' (*Au plus profond de mon cœur est gardé le souvenir d'un être cher que je n'oublierai jamais*).

- Headstone of E. Burton at Guidel: 'A secret longing a silent tear for ever a beautiful memory of one we loved so dear' (*Un secret désir de larme silencieuse pour conserver à jamais un beau souvenir de celui que nous avons beaucoup aimé*).

- Headstone of J.C.W. Stevens at Guidel: 'Beautiful memories of our darling boy, John loved and longed for Mum and Dad' (*Beaux souvenirs de notre petit garçon chéri – Jean aimé et désiré pour Maman et Papa*).

- Headstone of H.D. Lewis at Guidel: 'One of the best' (*Un des meilleurs*).

- Headstone of A.R. Parker at Guidel: 'In memory of my son whom I loved – his love and smile will ever linger Father' (*En souvenir de mon fils que j'ai aimé – son amour et son sourire resteront à jamais Père*).

- Headstone of C.F. Abraham at Guidel: 'Time passes but memories cling' (*Le temps passe mais les souvenirs restent*).

The graves of unidentified soldiers show the little information that could be found from the battlefield: 'A Soldier of the Great War' (*Un soldat de la Grande Guerre*) or 'A Soldier of the Second World War' (*Un soldat de la Seconde Guerre mondiale*) or 'Known unto God' (*Seulement connu de Dieu*), the phrase proposed by Rudyard Kipling.[3] In these Commonwealth cemeteries there are also graves of the Polish crews, who fought alongside Allies, who died in the region. Their headstones have a different shape.

---

3   Wikipedia accessed 11 December 2007: https://en.wikipedia.org/wiki/Commonwealth_War_Graves_Commission.

Brief History of Polish Air Squadrons

In May 1939, a mutual assistance agreement was signed between Britain and Poland, angering Hitler. On 1 September, Germany attacked Poland, and World War II began.

Poland was defeated in three weeks. In the spring of 1940, France – another ally of Poland and also of England, as well as being a strong military force at the time – was beaten in four weeks. The Polish Army, partly routed in France, is evacuated to Britain in September. The Polish Air Force becomes an integral part of the RAF. Pilots began their training at Redhill (approximately 40 miles south of London), while the Navigators and the Gunners were taught, first at Eastchurch, then at Hucknall near Nottingham.

The first group to be formed, on 1 July, 1940, was 300 Squadron (as told to 'Masovian'). The 300 Squadron is composed of ten crews of bombers with 180 people for maintenance and stewardship. It is equipped with the Fairey Battle, a light bomber crewed with three men. Its first Commander, advised by the commanding officer K.P. Lewis of the RAF, was Commander W. Makowski. Other squadrons were organised and formed Squadrons also in the '300' series.[4]

---

4   Ratuszynski, Wilhelm, Internet site http://www.geocities.com/skrzydla/ consulted 14 December 2007.

Commonwealth Cemeteries in the Lorient Region

In the Lorient Region, there are four cemeteries where the Commonwealth soldiers who died during the war 39–45 are buried. These four cemeteries are Guidel, Lorient-Kerentrech, Lanester and Gâvres. In these cemeteries are buried mainly pilots or flight crews who participated in the attacks and bombardments of the German facilities of Lorient. These four cemeteries represent a large part of the military of the Commonwealth buried in the *département* and most casualties are in Guidel and Lorient-Kerentrech. The combatants who were buried in these four cemeteries are listed cemetery by cemetery in Annexes I to V.

Reflections on the Cemeteries in the Lorient Region

From the above lists, we conducted an analysis to determine the period where most casualties occcurred, details on most casualties and the types of aircraft shot down by the German anti-aircraft defence.

In Annexe VI, we identified by date and by cemetery buried casualties. We recorded a total of one hundred and sixty-eight headstones. From analysis of the tables, it appears that the main place of burial is Guidel (117 graves) followed by Lorient (39 graves). Four cemeteries were used from 1940 to late 1942, mainly Lorient-Kerentrech in 1942, as places of burial depended on the location of the plane crash. But in January 1943, only the Guidel cemetery was used as a burial ground with the exception of three cases whose interment took place at Gâvres. We also notice that the number of burials (80) is very important during the months of January and February 1943. Those then killed reflect the intense bombing of German military installations from the beginning of the year 1943. Indeed, during the raids of 14, 15, 23, 26 and 29 January; 4, 7, 13 and 16 February; 6 March; 16 April; and 17 May 1943, the city of Lorient and the arsenal are reduced to ashes by the Allies.[5]

It is also possible to examine the types of aircraft in which these men have been killed. In Table 1 of Annexe VII, the number of aircraft shot down by type are identified by each cemetery. This summary

---

5   Estienne, René, 'Lorient and the Second World War', article previously found on the website of the Defence Service History.

analyses the total number of aircraft following the established order for the number of deaths by cemetery with the exception of Gâvres, because casualties buried in this cemetery are from three different crews of aircraft found on the coast due to being shot down over the sea and are related to a crash on the land around Gâvres.

The analysis of this table quickly allows us to see that the type of plane that has been shot down most often is the Wellington, ahead of the Hampden, the Halifax, the Lancaster and then the Typhoon.

Now, if we place the number of aircraft with higher priority than the number of casualties buried in each cemetery by aircraft type, we find a similar but stronger order (see Table 2, Annexe VII). However, it should be noted that this assessment of human losses, as for the planes, is only a partial view of events because it does not consider the men who died where their plane was shot down over the sea and whose remains have not been recovered. Nor are American crew losses taken into account.

We notice that it is the crews of the Wellington bombers who paid the heaviest price during the bombing of the Lorient Region because there were 81 men who embarked on this type of aircraft who have been buried in different cemeteries of the Lorient Region. Then we find the Halifax (24 men), followed by the Lancaster crews (17) and the Hampden (13).

Guidel Cemetery

Guidel cemetery is located in the village, on the left-hand side of the road out of Guidel, on the road leading to a place called Les Cinq Chemins. The military area of the cemetery is located immediately to the left of the entrance to the cemetery. The tombstones are arranged on a lawn facing a large cross of sacrifice in white stone with two swords, mounted on an octagonal base.

A3.9 Overview of the graves in the cemetery at Guidel.
Photo J.-Y. Le Lan.

A3.10 The cross of sacrifice at the entrance of the cemetery at Guidel. Photo J.-Y. Le Lan.

There are five rows of graves with blank spaces between some tombs corresponding to the places where the casualties from the American military were transferred after WWII to St. James. Rows include thirty-three tombs for row No. 6, twenty-six for row No. 5, twenty-eight for row No. 4, twenty-two for row No. 3 and eight for the last numbered Row 2 (there is no row No. 1), making a total of one hundred and seventeen graves.

The details of the men buried in Guidel is given in Annexe I. There are a hundred and eight soldiers whose identity is known, including one member of the Polish forces, and nine 'unknowns', all members of the countries of the Commonwealth (United Kingdom, Canada, Australia, New Zealand).

Guidel cemetery contains some graves from the years 1941 and 1942, but the vast majority are from the year 1943 and a few for the year 1944. The most likely reason is that after 1942 Lorient became very unsafe for burial ceremonies; the Germans chose this cemetery which was further away from the heavily bombarded area.

Thirteen military casualties who were buried temporarily further away from Guidel in Finistère (Cléder (2), Garlan (8), Plogoff (1) and Lampaul-Plouarzel (2)), and three in Morbihan (Étel (1), Plouhinec (1) and Saint-Philibert (1)), were all transferred to Guidel after the war[6] (details in Annexe II). These tombs have been highlighted in yellow in the table in Annexe VI but they do not fundamentally alter the previous analysis because the majority of these victims are from the aircraft that were shot down during the missions over Lorient. In particular, the crew of six men from the Wellington of 420 Squadron of the RCAF were buried in Garlan after losing their lives on the return from a bombing raid over Lorient on 13 February 1943, as well as other airmen buried in Morbihan.

---

6   Information given by Mme Colette Vandeville of the Commonwealth War Graves Commission at Beaurains.

German Burial Ceremonies

According to the testimony of Henri Hado, who was present at the age of nine at burials of foreign military casualties in Guidel Cemetery during the 1939–45 war, the Germans proceeded with respect. The casualties were placed in coffins by the Germans, and a ceremony was held in the presence of an armed German military detachment, who fired a salvo of rifles over the grave. There were no local French people present, apart from the gravedigger.

A3.11 The cemetery at Guidel in January 1944. Graves are covered with sand of kaolin and identified with a simple wooden cross. Photo published with the permission of François Coëffic.

An article by the *Nouvelliste du Morbihan,* dated 25 December 1940, recounts funerals at the cemetery of the Lanester Corpont for the crew of the Beaufort L4474 bomber shot down on 20 December. This article confirms the words of Henri Hado in respect of the German Army for Allied soldiers killed in combat. This is what is recorded: 'Their remains had been buried in two coffins supervised by a section of German soldiers under the guidance of an officer. [...] At the cemetery, the German officer delegated to officiate at the funeral, spoke over the freshly dug grave. Movingly, he honoured the English airmen who had fallen in the line of duty. Then, following the practice of the German army, a triple barrage was fired at the edges of the grave where the British airmen had been laid to rest.'

Lorient-Kerentrech Cemetery

The military section of the Lorient-Kerentrech cemetery is located at the bottom of the cemetery to the left of the main aisle to the sixty-two area. As at Guidel, the headstones are arranged on a lawn and in six rows. The first row (marked A) includes eight graves, the second (B) seven graves, the third (C) seven graves, the fourth (D) seven graves, the fifth (E) six graves and the last (F) four graves, for a total of thirty-nine graves. Of these thirty-nine graves, there are thirty for predominantly airmen of the Commonwealth, with five not identified, and nine from the Polish military. All of the graves are dated for the year 1942 with the exception of one, for the New Zealand pilot Dennis Herrick who died on 30 June 1941. The details of the military buried at Lorient-Kerentrech is given in Annexe III.

A3.12 Commonwealth war graves at Lorient-Kerentrech.
Photo J.-Y. Le Lan.

Lanester Cemetery

The military section of Lanester cemetery (Corpont) is located opposite the main entrance and to the left of this area. It contains seven graves as shown in the casualty list in Annexe IV. These seven soldiers died in two groups. Three who belonged to 50 Squadron of the Royal Air Force and died on 20 December 1940 and four from 217 Squadron of the Royal Air Force who died on 28 December 1940. Their graves are in two rows (Row 1 with three graves and Row 2 with four graves), each row being laid in a gravel space separated by a few metres from a lawn and a sculpted bush.

A3.13 Commonwealth war graves at Lanester.
Photo J.-Y. Le Lan.

Gâvres Cemetery

The military graves of Gâvres are integrated with the other graves in the cemetery and are not, as in previous cemeteries, in an isolated military area. There are five tombstones placed amidst an area of white gravel, a group of two and three isolated graves. These graves are for three members of the RAF, for a Canadian and for a Pole. The details of these graves is given in Annexe V. We can notice that the Pole buried at Gâvres was part of the same aircraft crew as the Pole who is buried at Guidel. These five graves are military personnel who died, two in 1941 and three in 1943. These three burials in 1943 at Gâvres are inconsistent with the fact that the centralisation of the burials was at that time in Guidel. The explanation is that these three soldiers died in the crash of their plane at sea and their bodies were found at sea or on the coast of Gâvres and so are buried in the nearest cemetery.[7]

A3.14 Commonwealth war graves at Gâvres.
Photo J.-Y. Le Lan.

Other Commonwealth Military Cemeteries in Morbihan

In addition to four cemeteries in the Region of Lorient, there are ten other Commonwealth grave sites in the Morbihan Region. Eight are located in the south of the *département* (Vannes-Boismoireau, Plougoumelen, Quiberon, Sarzeau, a La Trinité-sur-Mer, L'Île aux Moines, Pénestin and Le Palais) and two others inland, one near to Pontivy à Réguiny, and one near to Scaër à Guiscriff. In all of these places, we find thirty tombs of airmen mainly from countries who are members of the Commonwealth killed during the Second World War with, however, two graves of casualties from the Army, a grave of a

---

7   Testimony of Jean-Pierre Jégo, 14 December 2007. His grandmother, Stéphanie Padellec, was the gravedigger during this troubled period in Gâvres.

Polish airman and a grave of a British Merchant Navy officer. We did not include the victims of the aircraft crashes in the previous study because we do not have detail of these crashes or overall information on the purpose of their mission. It is likely that the majority of the missions were connected with the bombing of the Lorient submarine base from 1940 to 1942 but for August 1944 the objectives would have been different, perhaps for dropping of mines or equipment for the troops on the ground. Details of burials by cemetery is given in Annexe VIII.

Reflections on Other Cemeteries in Morbihan

In Annexe IX, we conducted the same analysis as for the Lorient Region. In the census by date and by cemetery (Table 1 of Annexe IX), it is not a characteristic period and this is normal as all of these crashes are isolated cases. It must be noted, however, that no burial occurred in 1943 in other places in the Morbihan *département* while it is the period where there were the most victims in the Lorient Region.

In regard to the type of aircraft having suffered the largest losses, we also note that it is the Wellington that bears the largest loss, whether for aircraft losses or for human casualties (Tables 2 and 3 of Annexe IX).

Vannes-Boismoreau Cemetery

In the Vannes-Boismoireau cemetery, there are nine graves of British airmen but only seven headstones. The graves are arranged in a rectangle of gravel with a border in concrete in front of a space planted with heathers. They are located at the end of a narrow path beside the wall, to the right of the entrance by the office of the concierge.

These tombs include the crews of two planes; a Hampden fell over Pluneret on 22 November 1940 and a Wellington fell at Grand-Champ on 8 November 1942.

The aircraft which crashed at Pluneret, at a place called La Croix Percée, was on a mission to attack the submarine base at Lorient then under construction. It was the first aircraft shot down by the Germans. The four airmen were buried in a field near the crash site, wrapped in a French flag. Their identity was discovered on a paper put in a bottle near the bodies during the transfer to the cemetery of Vannes in 1945.

Their graves are collective, because there are only two headstones for these four men.

A3.15
Boismoreau à
Vannes cemetery,
the seven
tombstones.
Photo J.-Y. Le Lan.

Plougoumelen Cemetery

At Plougoumelen, there is a Stirling crew buried at the cemetery of this Commune. They were shot down on 6 August 1944. In this six-man crew, there were two New Zealanders, two Canadians, one Australian and a Briton. The six headstones are arranged in a rectangle of gravel with a concrete border. They are located north-east of the entry against the wall (to the right of the central pathway).

A3.16
The six war graves at
Plougoumelen.
Photo J.-Y. Le Lan.

Quiberon Cemetery

In the cemetery of Quiberon, there are six graves of airmen whose planes crashed into the sea off the coast of Quiberon. Three British airmen of the crew of a Beaufort shot down on 2 December 1941, and an Australian (4 August 1942) and a Pole (23 September 1942) from two different Wellington bombers. There is also the grave of an Australian, unidentified, who was transferred from the graveyard of the church at Houat to the communal Quiberon cemetery. The two groups of graves are in rectangles of gravel to the left of the main alley behind the ossuary, among the other graves. The first group includes the Australians and the Pole and the second group the three British.

A3.17
Quiberon cemetery,
first group of
three war graves.
Photo J.-Y. Le Lan.

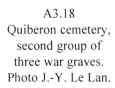

A3.18
Quiberon cemetery,
second group of
three war graves.
Photo J.-Y. Le Lan.

A3.19
Quiberon cemetery,
detail of the war grave
of Sergeant W. Furzey.
Photo J.-Y. Le Lan.

Cemeteries at Sarzeau, on L'Île aux Moines, at La Trinité-sur-Mer, at Pénestin, at Le Palais, at Réguiny and at Guiscriff

In the cemetery of Sarzeau, there are two graves, one of a soldier of the Royal Regiment of Liverpool, the other an airman from a Canadian crew of a Wellington that fell on 16 November 1942.

A3.20 The two war graves at L'Ile aux Moines facing the
sea and near the very beautiful small church of the island.
Photo J.-Y. Le Lan.

On L'Île aux Moines, there are two British Royal Air Force airmen who are buried here. They were aboard a Mosquito that crashed on 14 August 1944.

Five isolated burials are found in the *département*. Three graves of airmen at La Trinité-sur-Mer, Pénestin and Réguiny, and one of a soldier at Guiscriff and a burial of an officer of the Merchant Navy at Le Palais. At La Trinité-sur-Mer and at Réguiny, these men were British airmen: respectively, one from a Beaufort that crashed on 17 December 1940 and the other from a Spitfire shot down on 28 July 1944. At Pénestin the buried casualty was a Sergeant Observer, killed on 26 June 1942.

The grave located in the cemetery of Guiscriff is that of a Major from the Royal Artillery killed on 29 July, 1944 and the casualty at Le Palais was a first officer from the Merchant Navy killed on 27 March 1917 aboard the SS *Thracia*.[8]

Conclusion

This census of the Commonwealth war graves in Morbihan allowed us to list a total of one hundred and ninety graves, mainly airmen who participated in attacks against the Lorient submarine base during the Second World War. These graves are scattered in fourteen cemeteries but the vast majority are at Guidel and Lorient-Kerentech. In these cemeteries, there are also the bodies of Polish airmen serving in the Royal Air Force. The type of aircraft suffering the highest losses is the Wellington bomber, with a crew of five or six men. These places of burial are perfectly maintained by the CWGC. The French branch of the CWGC, located at Beaurains, south of Arras, is in charge, in France, of some three thousand cemeteries and twenty-two memorials and with job maintenance for about four hundred and twenty-five people, the majority of whom are gardeners.

Jean-Yves Le Lan

---

8   The SS *Thracia* had left Bilbao for Glasgow, with a load of iron ore, in a convoy of eight ships that had sailed on 27 March 1917. On the 18-hour journey to Belle Île, it was torpedoed on the night of 27/28 March and sank in less than a minute. The torpedo was fired by the UC69 submarine that was commanded at the time by Erwin Wassner.

Bibliography

Internet Site of the Commonwealth War Graves Commission consulted 20th January 2009: http://www.cwgc.org/

Internet site of l'Association Bretonne du Souvenir Aérien consulted 20th January 2009: http://www.absa39–45.asso.fr/

Bohn, Roland, *Raids aériens sur la Bretagne durant la seconde guerre mondiale*, Imprimerie Régionale à Bannalec, tome I, 1997, tome II, 1998.

Acknowledgments

I would like to thank the following people who have helped me with this study:

Madame Colette Vandeville of the CWGC at Beaurains for all the information she has given to me to carry out this study.

Mr Yves Pezennec for information on the American graves in the cemetery of Guidel.

Annexe I

List of Military Burials at Guidel Cemetery

No.	Surname and Christian name(s)	Rank	Service Number	Air Force and Regiment	Date of Death	Age	Headstone Marker
1	ABRAHAM, CHARLES FREDERICK	Sergeant (Flt Engr)	1035724	Royal Air Force Volunteer Reserve – 61 Sqn	07/02/1943	29	Row 4 Grave 21
2	ADAM, JAMES DICK	Sergeant (Air Gnr)	655432	Royal Air Force – 408 (RCAF) Sqn	29/01/1943	26	Row 3 Grave 5
3	AMY, HARRY THOMAS	Flight Lieutenant (Nav)	C/2233	Royal Canadian Air Force – 424 Sqn	11/05/1944	Not known	Row 6 Grave 16
4	BAKER, RONALD VALENTINE	Sergeant (W/Op/ Air Gnr)	1286156	Royal Air Force Volunteer Reserve – 199 Sqn	07/02/1943	21	Row 3 Grave 18
5	BARTON, WILLIAM KENNETH	Sergeant (W/Op/ Air Gnr)	1177728	Royal Air Force Volunteer Reserve – 408 (RCAF) Sqn	29.01.1943	Not known	Row 3 Grave 9
6	BEESLEY, PETER LESLIE	Flying Officer (Pilot)	47763	Royal Air Force – 158 Sqn	07/02/1943	23	Row 4 Grave 6
7	BELL, CLAUDE STEPHEN	Sergeant (W/Op/ Air Gnr)	1270241	Royal Air Force Volunteer Reserve – 199 Sqn	14/06/1943	35	Row 5 Graves 45–46 (26)

No.	Surname and Christian name(s)	Rank	Service Number	Air Force and Regiment	Date of Death	Age	Headstone Marker
8	BELL, JOHN MORLING	Flying Officer (Nav)	121435	Royal Air Force Volunteer Reserve – 199 Sqn	13/02/1943	Not known	Row 5 Grave 4
9	BOWLEY, KENNETH	Sergeant (Air Gnr)	968910	Royal Air Force Volunteer Reserve – 158 Sqn	07/02/1943	Not known	Row 4
10	BRACKENRIDGE, DOUGLAS MATTHEW	Sergeant (Flt Engr)	R/79608	Royal Canadian Air Force – 408 Sqn	07/02/1943	21	Row 4 Grave 2
11	BRINDLE, ERIC	Sergeant (Nav)	657693	Royal Air Force Volunteer Reserve – 158 Sqn	07/02/1943	23	Row 4 Grave 9
12	BRINKWORTH, ROWLAND GEORGE	Pilot Officer (Air Gnr)	132736	Royal Air Force Volunteer Reserve – 408 (RCAF) Sqn	29/01/1943	28	Row 3 Grave 10
13	BURGESS, ALFRED BRIAN	Sergeant (Air Bomber)	1230174	Royal Air Force Volunteer Reserve – 166 Sqn	07/02/1943	19	Row 4 Grave 19
14	BURTON, EDWARD	Sergeant (Nav)	1576202	Royal Air Force Volunteer Reserve – 199 Sqn	14/06/1943	22	Row 5 Graves 45–46 (25)
15	BYGRAVE, LEONARD	Sergeant (Nav/Bomber)	933155	Royal Air Force Volunteer Reserve – 158 Sqn	07/02/1943	21	Row 4 Grave 3
16	CARDWELL, DOUGLAS ERIC	Sergeant (Flt Engr)	567350	Royal Air Force – 103 Sqn	16/02/1943	23	Row 5 Grave 16

Annexe I

No.	Surname and Christian name(s)	Rank	Service Number	Air Force and Regiment	Date of Death	Age	Headstone Marker
17	CARR, FREDERICK GEORGE	Sergeant (W/Op)	933802	Royal Air Force Volunteer Reserve – 158 Sqn	07/02/1943	24	Row 4 Grave 4
18	CAVADINO, FRANCIS ANTHONY	Sergeant (Flt Engr)	573801	Royal Air Force – 408 (RCAF) Sqn	29/01/1943	19	Row 3 Grave 7
19	CHAPMAN, FREDERICK RUSSELL FORBES	Flying Officer (Nav)	127265	Royal Air Force Volunteer Reserve – 420 (RCAF) Sqn	13/02/1943	32	Row 6 Grave 19
20	CHARLSWORTH, EDGAR RICHARD	Pilot Officer (Nav)	128692	Royal Air Force Volunteer Reserve – 427 (RCAF) Sqn	15/01/1943	32	Row 2 Graves 15–18 (5)
21	CLEMENTS, MAURICE FREEMAN	Sergeant (Pilot)	1242362	Royal Air Force Volunteer Reserve – 166 Sqn	07/02/1943	22	Row 4 Grave 5
22	COWARD, JOHN LIVERSEDGE	Flying Officer (Pilot)	156307	Royal Air Force Volunteer Reserve – 234 Sqn	22/07/1944	29	Row 6 Grave 32
23	COWIE, ARTHUR	Flight Lieutenant (Air Gnr)	45949	Royal Air Force – 199 Sqn	13/02/1943	25	Row 5 Grave 3
24	COWMAN, WILLIAM HARRIS	Flight Sergeant (W/Op/ Air Gnr)	549530	Royal Air Force – 408 (RCAF) Sqn	07/02/1943	22	Row 4 Grave 10
25	COWPER, EDWIN FRANCIS	Sergeant (Air Gnr)	1271839	Royal Air Force Volunteer Reserve – 158 Sqn	07/02/1943	22	Row 4 Grave 1

No.	Surname and Christian name(s)	Rank	Service Number	Air Force and Regiment	Date of Death	Age	Headstone Marker
26	CURRIE, WILLIAM MATTHEW	Flying Officer (Air Bomber)	J/22532	Royal Canadian Air Force – 115 (RAF) Sqn	13/02/1943	24	Row 5 Grave 8
27	DAVIES, HUGHIE FRANCIS	Sergeant (Air Gnr)	1078918	Royal Air Force Volunteer Reserve – 427 (RCAF) Sqn	04/02/1943	19	Row 3 Grave 15
28	DRUMMOND, DOUGAL	Flight Sergeant (Pilot)	778921	Royal Air Force Volunteer Reserve – 266 Sqn	15/02/1944	20	Row 6 Grave 17
29	EASEY, GEORGE	Sergeant (Air Gnr)	1331999	Royal Air Force Volunteer Reserve – 199 Sqn	13/02/1943	20	Row 5 Grave 1
30	ECKTON, ALFRED RAYMOND	Pilot Officer (Bomb Aimer)	127283	Royal Air Force Volunteer Reserve – 427 (RCAF) Sqn	15/01/1943	21	Row 2 Graves 15–18 (6)
31	EDWARD, KENNETH WILLIAMS	Sergeant (Nav/Bomber)	1118711	Royal Air Force Volunteer Reserve – 166 Sqn	07/02/1943	28	Row 4 Graves 16–18 (18)
32	FOGDEN, EDMUND DANIEL	Warrant Officer	403045	Royal Australian Air Force	12/08/1943	24	Row 6 Grave 3
33	FORD, HERBERT CHARLES	Sergeant (Air Gnr)	1206989	Royal Air Force Volunteer Reserve – 103 Sqn	16/02/1943	27	Row 5 Grave 13
34	FOSTER, RICHARD NORMAN	Flying Officer (Pilot)	149358	Royal Air Force Volunteer Reserve – 183 Sqn	31/01/1944	21	Row 6 Grave 12

No.	Surname and Christian name(s)	Rank	Service Number	Air Force and Regiment	Date of Death	Age	Headstone Marker
35	GEORGESON, LOUIS ROCKFORD	Flying Officer (W/Op/ Air Gnr)	J/27881	Royal Canadian Air Force – 424 Sqn	11/05/1944	26	Row 6 Grave 14
36	GETHING, JAMES STEELE	Sergeant (Obs)	999003	Royal Air Force Volunteer Reserve – (RCAF) Sqn	03/06/1942	Not known	Row 2 Grave 1
37	GIBSON, LEO GARTH	Flying Officer (Pilot)	J/20374	Royal Canadian Air Force – 420 Sqn	13/02/1943	23	Row 6 Grave 22
38	GIGUERE, JOSEPH EMERY ROMEO	Flight Sergeant (Air Gnr)	R/117691	Royal Canadian Air Force – 408 Sqn	07/02/1943	25	Row 4 Grave 11
39	GOAD, CYRIL ARTHUR CAREW	Sergeant (Obs)	745898	Royal Air Force Volunteer Reserve – 53 Sqn	27/03/1941	23	Row 6 Grave 30
40	GRAY, ROBERT MALCOLM	Pilot Officer (Pilot)	142040	Royal Air Force Volunteer Reserve – 166 Sqn	29/01/1943	Not Known	Row 3 Grave 4
42	GRAY, SYDNEY JOHN	Sergeant (Air Gnr)	1263851	Royal Air Force Volunteer Reserve – 115 Sqn	13/02/1943	32	Row 5 Grave 7
42	GREEN, JAMES WILLIAM	Sergeant (Air Gnr)	1310815	Royal Air Force Volunteer Reserve – 199 Sqn	09/04/1943	22	Row 5 Grave 30 (23)
43	HAMOOD, FRANK NORMAN	Flight Sergeant	409046	Royal Australian Air Force	12/08/1943	23	Row 6 Grave 7
44	HARDING-SMITH, DUDLEY	Pilot Officer (Air Gnr)	405265	Royal New Zealand Air Force – 75 (RAF) Sqn	13/02/1943	24	Row 5 Grave 20

No.	Surname and Christian name(s)	Rank	Service Number	Air Force and Regiment	Date of Death	Age	Headstone Marker
45	HARDY, DOUGLAS ERNEST JAMES	Sergeant (Air Gnr)	1212995	Royal Air Force Volunteer Reserve – 166 Sqn	29/01/1943	21	Row 3 Grave 8
46	HARRISON, ERNEST	Sergeant (Pilot)	1090941	Royal Air Force Volunteer Reserve – 420 (RCAF) Sqn	03/06/1942	21	Row 2 Grave 3
47	HILLHOUSE, JOHN BROWN	Sergeant (Air Gnr)	976567	Royal Air Force Volunteer Reserve – 61 Sqn	07/02/1943	27	Row 4 Grave 28
48	HUGHES, THOMAS VESTEINN	Sergeant (W/Op/ Air Gnr)	1215478	Royal Air Force Volunteer Reserve – 420 (RCAF) Sqn	13/02/1943	20	Row 6 Grave 20
49	JACKSON, GEORGE WILLIAM	Sergeant (W/Op/ Air Gnr)	1263933	Royal Air Force – 166 Sqn	29/01/1943	Not known	Row 3 Grave 12
50	JONES, ELWYN KNOWLES	Flight Sergeant (Obs)	1062590	Royal Air Force Volunteer Reserve – 199 Sqn	13/02/1943	29	Row 5 Grave 2
51	KEETON, ANTHONY EDWARD	Sergeant (Pilot)	1239640	Royal Air Force Volunteer Reserve – 199 Sqn	07/02/1943	20	Row 3 Grave 17
52	KEYES, ROBERT	Flying Officer (W/Op/ Air Gnr)	J/9738	Royal Canadian Air Force – 199 (RAF) Sqn	13/02/1943	24	Row 5 Grave 6
53	LAING, GERARD JOSEPH	Sergeant (W/Op/ Air Gnr)	981143	Royal Air Force Volunteer Reserve – 420 (RCAF) Sqn	03/06/1942	21	Row 2 Grave 2

No.	Surname and Christian name(s)	Rank	Service Number	Air Force and Regiment	Date of Death	Age	Headstone Marker
54	LEWIS, HERBERT DALTON	Flight Sergeant (Pilot)	R/102653	Royal Canadian Air Force – 61 (RAF) Sqn	07/02/1943	27	Row 4 Grave 24
55	LEWIS, RALPH	Sergeant (Flt Engr)	540757	Royal Air Force – 158 Sqn	07/02/1943	23	Row 4 Grave 7
56	LOUGH, WILLIAM HERBERT	Warrant Officer Class II (Obs)	R/82621	Royal Canadian Air Force – 408 Sqn	07/02/1943	20	Row 4 Grave 12
57	MACDONALD, DONALD ANDREW	Flight Sergeant (Air Gnr)	R/110187	Royal Canadian Air Force – 420 Sqn	13/02/1943	22	Row 6 Grave 23
58	MACKAY, HUGH MUNRO	Flying Officer (Obs)	415345	Royal New Zealand Air Force – 487 Sqn	01/12/1943	22	Row 6 Grave 8
59	MARTIN, BERNARD	Sergeant (Nav)	656129	Royal Air Force – 166 Sqn	29/01/1943	24	Row 3 Grave 2
60	MASON, ARTHUR JAMES CEDRIC	Flight Sergeant (Air Gnr)	1376810	Royal Air Force Volunteer Reserve – 103 Sqn	16/02/1943	30	Row 5 Grave 11
61	MILLER, JOHN DENNIS	Flying Officer (Pilot)	80363	Royal Air Force Volunteer Reserve – 266 Sqn	15/02/1944	23	Row 6 Grave 18
62	MILLMAN, THOMAS RALPH BERNARD	Flying Officer (Pilot)	J/26745	Royal Canadian Air Force – 424 Sqn	11/05/1944	Not known	Row 6 Grave 31
63	MORGAN, KENNETH LLEWELLYN	Flying Officer (Nav)	126512	Royal Air Force Volunteer Reserve – 61 Sqn	07/02/1943	21	Row 4 Grave 20
64	MUNRO, HENRY DUNCAN	Sergeant (W/Op/ Air Gnr)	1381934	Royal Air Force Volunteer Reserve – (RCAF) Sqn	15/01/1943	22	Row 2 Graves 15–18 (7)

No.	Surname and Christian name(s)	Rank	Service Number	Air Force and Regiment	Date of Death	Age	Headstone Marker
65	NEVILLE, WILFRED RONALD	Pilot Officer (Nav)	142564	Royal Air Force Volunteer Reserve – 103 Sqn	16/02/1943	21	Row 5 Grave 14
66	NORGATE, MORRIS JOHN	Sergeant (Nav)	1380915	Royal Air Force Volunteer Reserve – 199 Sqn	07/02/1943	22	Row 3 Grave 22
67	PARKER, ALFRED RAYMOND	Sergeant (Air Gnr)	908599	Royal Air Force Volunteer Reserve – 61 Sqn	07/02/1943	21	Row 4 Grave 23
68	PARSEY, ERNEST HENRY	Flight Sergeant (Pilot)	1389683	Royal Air Force Volunteer Reserve – 612 Sqn	12/03/1944	18	Row 6 Grave 11
69	PARSONS, CUTHBERT MICHAEL	Flying Officer (Pilot)	124214	Royal Air Force Volunteer Reserve – 427 (RCAF) Sqn	04/02/1943	22	Row 3 Grave 13
70	PATES, WALTER HENRY	Sergeant (Air Gnr)	1152080	Royal Air Force Volunteer Reserve – 427 (RCAF) Sqn	15/01/1943	20	Row 2 Grave 14 (4)
71	PAYLING, EDWIN	Flying Officer (Nav)	126015	Royal Air Force Volunteer Reserve – 408 (RCAF) Sqn	29/01/1943	33	Row 3 Grave 6
72	PENNYCOOK, DAVID COVENTRY	Sergeant (Air Bomber)	1552510	Royal Air Force Volunteer Reserve – 199 Sqn	07/02/1943	21	Row 3 Grave 20
73	PITT, CHARLES ARTHUR	Sergeant (W/Op/ Air Gnr)	1176419	Royal Air Force Volunteer Reserve – 166 Sqn	07/02/1943	30	Row 4 Graves 16–18 (17)

No.	Surname and Christian name(s)	Rank	Service Number	Air Force and Regiment	Date of Death	Age	Headstone Marker
74	POWELL, CHARLES	Flight Lieutenant (Pilot)	123965	Royal Air Force Volunteer Reserve – 199 Sqn	07/02/1943	24	Row 3 Grave 21
75	RAIT, THOMAS GILMOUR	Sergeant (Pilot)	1341342	Royal Air Force Volunteer Reserve – 115 Sqn	13/02/1943	Not known	Row 5 Grave 10
76	RICHARDSON, RONALD WILLIAM	Sergeant (Air Gnr)	2207432	Royal Air Force Volunteer Reserve – 466 (R.A.A.F.) Sqn	12/08/1943	Not known	Row 6 Grave 4
77	ROBINSON, STUART QUENTIN	Flying Officer (Air Bomber)	124758	Royal Air Force Volunteer Reserve – 199 Sqn	14/06/1943	22	Row 6 Grave 1
78	ROSE, DESMOND JAMES	Flying Oficer (Nav)	124400	Royal Air Force Volunteer Reserve – 115 Sqn	13/02/1943	21	Row 5 Grave 9
79	ROSTRON, JOSEPH	Sergeant (Nav/ Bomber)	1029458	Royal Air Force Volunteer Reserve – 408 (RCAF) Sqn	29/01/1943	30	Row 3 Grave 11
80	ROUX, THEUNIS CHRISTOFFE	Pilot Officer (Pilot)	80412	Royal Air Force Volunteer Reserve – 408 (RCAF) Sqn	29/01/1943	29	Row 3 Grave 1
81	SALT, REGINALD JAMES PETER	Sergeant (Obs)	657679	Royal Air Force Volunteer Reserve – 408 (RCAF) Sqn	07/02/1943	32	Row 4 Grave 13

No.	Surname and Christian name(s)	Rank	Service Number	Air Force and Regiment	Date of Death	Age	Headstone Marker
82	SANDOVER, PETER	Sergeant (Obs)	1315036	Royal Air Force Volunteer Reserve – 427 (RCAF) Sqn	04/02/1943	20	Row 3 Grave 16
83	SAWDY,] WILLIAM ERNEST	Flying Officer (Pilot)	123355	Royal Air Force Volunteer Reserve – 199 Sqn	14/06/1943	Not known	Row 6 Grave 2
84	SAYERS, JOSEPH FISHER	Flight Sergeant (Air Obs)	R/53361	Royal Canadian Air Force – 408 Sqn	07/02/1943	27	Row 4 Grave 15
85	SHARP, ROBERT THOMAS CARTMEL	Sergeant (Nav)	1530450	Royal Air Force Volunteer Reserve – 166 Sqn	29/01/1943	19	Row 3 Grave 3
86	SKINNER, DESMOND	Flight Sergeant (Pilot)	1269101	Royal Air Force Volunteer Reserve – 44 Sqn	07/02/1943	Not known	Row 4 Grave 22
87	SMITH, DEAN WILLIAM	Warrant Officer Class II (Pilot)	R/94982	Royal Canadian Air Force – 408 Sqn	07/02/1943	23	Row 4 Grave 14
88	SMITH, DONALD JACK	Sergeant (Air Gnr)	1235248	Royal Air Force Volunteer Reserve – 166 Sqn	07/02/1943	22	Row 4 Graves 16–18 (16)
89	SOMERFIELD, BERNARD WELBY	Sergeant (Nav Bomber)	658354	Royal Air Force – (RCAF) Sqn	13/02/1943	22	Row 6 Grave 21
90	STARRUP, BENJAMIN VICTOR	Pilot Oficer (Air Bomber)	J/89254	Royal Canadian Air Force – 424 Sqn	11/05/1944	Not known	Row 6 Grave 15
91	STEVENS, JOHN CHARLES WILLIAM	Sergeant (Air Gnr)	1397811	Royal Air Force Volunteer Reserve – 199 Sqn	14/06/1943	22	Row 5 Grave 44 (24)

No.	Surname and Christian name(s)	Rank	Service Number	Air Force and Regiment	Date of Death	Age	Headstone Marker
92	STUBBS, ALEXANDER WILLIAM	Pilot Officer	401568	Royal Australian Air Force – 158 Sqn	16/02/1943	28	Row 5 Grave 18
93	SULLIVAN, CHARLES BARRY	Flight Sergeant	408713	Royal Australian Air Force	07/02/1943	21	ROW 3 Grave 19
94	SWARBRICK, JOSEPH	Pilot Officer (Flt Engr)	187233	Royal Air Force Volunteer Reserve – 424 (RCAF) Sqn	11/05/1944	30	Row 6 Grave 13
95	TEMPLETON, ARTHUR MOORE	Sergeant (W/Op/ Air Gnr)	1071533	Royal Air Force Volunteer Reserve – 427 (RCAF) Sqn	04/02/1943	Not known	Row 3 Grave 14
96	WHILES, GEORGE WILLIAM	Sergeant (Pilot)	1249500	Royal Air Force Volunteer Reserve – 158 Sqn	07/02/1943	22	Row 4 Grave 27
97	WILLCOCK, ANTHONY JOHN	Flying Officer (Pilot)	122427	Royal Air Force – 169 Sqn	06/08.1943	25	Row 6 Grave 24
98	WILLIAMS, HOWARD LLEWELLYN	Sergeant (Nav/ Bomber)	1499052	Royal Air Force Volunteer Reserve – 61 Sqn	07/02/1943	21	Row 4 Graves 25–26 (26)
99	WILLIAMS, MARK ARTHUR LOTHERINGTON	Squadron Leader (Pilot)	40584	Royal Air Force – 427 (RCAF) Sqn	15/01/1943	Not known	Row 2 Graves 15–18 (18)
100	WILLIAMS, ROY ARTHUR	Pilot Officer (Pilot)	140912	Royal Air Force Volunteer Reserve – 75 Sqn	13/02/1943	21	Row 5 Grave 19
101	WINCHESTER, WILLIAM VICTOR BRYAN	Flight Sergeant	409265	Royal Australian Air Force	12/08/1943	25	Row 6 Grave 6

No.	Surname and Christian name(s)	Rank	Service Number	Air Force and Regiment	Date of Death	Age	Headstone Marker
102	WOODRUFF, HAROLD EUNSON	Flight Sergeant (Air Bomber)	1190385	Royal Air Force Volunteer Reserve – 199 Sqn	13/02/1943	26	Row 5 Grave 5
103	WOODWARD, JOHN CHARLES	Sergeant (Air Bomber)	1316223	Royal Air Force Volunteer Reserve – 103 Sqn	16/02/1943	28	Row 5 Grave 12
104	WOOSNAM, RICHARD GORDON	Sergeant (W/Op/Air Gnr)	1316368	Royal Air Force Volunteer Reserve – (R.A.A.F.) Sqn	12/08/1943	22	Row 6 Grave 5
105	WRIGHT, BRYAN HENRY	Able Seaman	P/J 40530	Royal Navy – H.M.S. Javelin	29/11/1940	42	Row 6 Grave 29
106	YOUNG, GEORGE	Sergeant (W/Op/ Air Gnr)	1380959	Royal Air Force Volunteer Reserve – 61 Sqn	07/02/1943	Not known	Row 4 Graves 25–26 (26)
107	YOUNG, CHARLES HARLEY	Pilot Officer	403065	Royal Australian Air Force	16/02/1943	28	Row 5 Grave 15
108	WINIARCZYK, HENRYCK	PLT	/	Polish Forces – 300 Sqn	11/11/1943	25	Row 6 Grave 9
109	UNKNOWN	An Airman	/	Royal Air Force	29/07/1944	Not known	Row 6 Grave 33
110	UNKNOWN	A Sailor	/	Royal Navy	01/09/1944	Not known	Row 6 Grave 28
111	UNKNOWN	An Airman – A Sergeant	/	Royal Air Force	27/06/1944	Not known	Row 6 Grave 27
112	UNKNOWN	An Airman – A Sergeant	/	Royal Air Force	18/01/1942	Not known	Row 6 Grave 26
113	UNKNOWN	An Airman – A Sergeant	/	Royal Air Force	04/09/1941	Not known	Row 6 Grave 25
114	UNKNOWN	An Airman	/	Royal Air Force	18/05/1942	Not known	Row 6 Grave 10

No.	Surname and Christian name(s)	Rank	Service Number	Air Force and Regiment	Date of Death	Age	Headstone Marker
115	UNKNOWN	An Airman	/	Royal Air Force	25/02/1943	Not known	Row 5 Grave 17
116	UNKNOWN	An Airman	/	Royal Air Force	17/04/1943	Not known	Row 5 Grave 21
117	UNKNOWN	An Airman	/	Royal Air Force	03/05/1943	Not known	Row 5 Grave 22

Notes: For the tracking of the headstones, we kept the numbering of the Rows 2 to 6 (5 rows only currently, there being no numbered Row 1) and the grave number specified on the CWGC website (in parenthesis, we noted the current situation in the row number when the information from the CWGC was unclear). Row 6 is located to the north and the numbering of the rows begins to the west.

For some graves of the Commonwealth War Graves Commission there is a collective burial (Collective Grave) or attached (Joint Grave) numbering when the burial of the remains of the crews could not be identified separately. However, a headstone for each casualty is shown.

Annexe II

List of Servicemen Temporarily Buried in Another Cemetery Whose Bodies Were Later Transferred to Guidel

Cléder Cemetery (Finistère)

- Able Seaman Wright
- Sgt Goad

Garlan Church Cemetery (Finistère)

- Fl/Sgt Drummond
- F/O Miller
- F/O Chapman
- Sgt Hughes
- Sgt Someford
- F/O Gibson
- Sgt MacDonald
- F/O Willcock

Plogoff Communal Cemetery (Finistère)

- Unknown RN (Sailor)

Lampaul-Plouarzel Church Cemetery (Saint-Egarec) (Finistère)

- Fl/Sgt Parsey
- Unknown RAF (Airman)

Étel Communal Cemetery (Morbihan)

- Unknown RAF (Sgt)

Plouhinec Communal Cemetery (Morbihan)

- Unknown RAF (Sgt)

Saint-Philibert Communal Cemetery (Morbihan)

- Unknown RAF (Sgt)

Annex III

List of Military Burials at Lorient/Kerentrech

No.	Surname and Christian name(s)	Rank	Service Number	Air Force and Regiment	Date of Death	Age	Headstone Marker
1	ALEXANDER, KENNETH JOSEPH	Sergeant (Obs)	1382705	Royal Air Force Volunteer Reserve – 156 Sqn	07/07/1942	23	Area 62 Row C Grave 4
2	ATTWATER, ROBIN AELRED	Sergeant (Pilot)	1264198	Royal Air Force Volunteer Reserve – 156 Sqn	07/07/1942	20	Area 62 Row D Grave 3
3	BARRIE, GRAHAME COWAN	Flight Sergeant (Air Gnr)	524581	Royal Air Force – 156 Sqn	07/07/1942	25	Area 62 Row C Grave 2
4	BUCKINGHAM, ROBERT JOHN	Flight Sergeant	400578	Royal Australian Air Force	22/06/1942	24	Area 62 Row C Graves 5–6 (6)
5	CHAPMAN, WILLIAM JOHN	Sergeant (Obs)	934647	Royal Air Force Volunteer Reserve – 420 (RCAF) Sqn	13/07/1942	Not known	Area 62 Row D Grave 1
6	COOPER, HECTOR THOMAS MOORE	Flight Sergeant (Pilot)	R/80234	Royal Canadian Air Force – 101 (RAF) Sqn	03/04/1942	20	Area 62 Row A Grave 2
7	CROMBIE, JAMES DUNCAN	Pilot Officer (Pilot)	68793	Royal Air Force Volunteer Reserve – 50 Sqn	25/03/1942	21	Area 62 Row A Graves 4–5 (5)

No.	Surname and Christian name(s)	Rank	Service Number	Air Force and Regiment	Date of Death	Age	Headstone Marker
8	DECKMAN, HARRY NAUGHTON	Sergeant (Obs)	924734	Royal Air Force Volunteer Reserve – 50 Sqn	25/03/1942	21	Area 62 Row A Grave 3
9	FOUNTAIN, NORMAN	Sergeant (W/Op)	1062388	Royal Air Force Volunteer Reserve – 156 Sqn	07/07/1942	Not known	Area 62 Row D Grave 4
10	GALLEY, ARTHUR FREDERICK	Sergeant (Pilot)	1288181	Royal Air Force Volunteer Reserve – 156 Sqn	07/07/1942	32	Area 62 Row C Grave 1
11	HEDDLE, JOHN DAVID ROBERT	Sergeant (W/Op/ Air Gnr)	1117365	Royal Air Force Volunteer Reserve – 156 Sqn	07/07/1942	18	Area 62 Row C Grave 3
12	HERRICK, DENNIS TREVELYAN	Pilot Officer (Pilot)	40974	Royal New Zealand Air Force – 53 (RAF) Sqn	30/06/1941	29	Area 62 Row A Grave 7 (8)
13	LEEDHAM, WILLIAM HENRY	Sergeant (Obs)	1263488	Royal Air Force Volunteer Reserve – 156 Sqn	07/07/1942	29	Area 62 Row D Grave 5
14	MANLEY, FRANK	Sergeant (W/Op/ Air Gnr)	1208601	Royal Air Force Volunteer Reserve – 50 Sqn	25/03/1942	30	Area 62 Row A Grave 1
15	MARTIN, FREDERICK ROY	Sergeant	403479	Royal Australian Air Force	22/06/1942	24	Area 62 Row C Grave 7
16	McQUEEN, WILLIAM STALKER	Sergeant	403277	Royal Australian Air Force	22/06/1942	22	Area 62 Row B Grave 1
17	MOORES, JAMES	Sergeant (W/Op/ Air Gnr)	798533	Royal Air Force Volunteer Reserve – 460 (R.A.A.F.) Sqn	22/06/1942	27	Area 62 Row B Grave 2

No.	Surname and Christian name(s)	Rank	Service Number	Air Force and Regiment	Date of Death	Age	Headstone Marker
18	MYRING, NORMAN ERNEST	Pilot Officer (Obs)	107995	Royal Air Force Volunteer Reserve – 101 Sqn	03/04/1942	21	Area 62 Row B Grave 6
19	PARKER, ROBERT	Sergeant (Air Gnr)	953678	Royal Air Force Volunteer Reserve – 156 Sqn	07/07/1942	Not known	Area 62 Row D Grave 6
20	PERRY, CHARLES RONALD CLIVE	Sergeant (W/Op/ Air Gnr)	1165304	Royal Air Force Volunteer Reserve – 50 Sqn	25/03/1942	32	Area 62 Row A Joint Grave 4–5 (4)
21	RODDY, WILLIAM GEORGE	Flight Sergeant (Obs)	R/95149	Royal Canadian Air Force – 156 (RAF) Sqn	07/07/1942	22	Area 62 Row D Grave 7
22	ROBERT, RAMOND GEORGE MARAFU	Sergeant	400333	Royal Australian Air Force	22/06/1942	23	Area 62 Row C Joint Grave 5–6 (5)
23	THOMSON, JAMES ANDERSON	Flight Sergeant (W/Op/ Air Gnr)	R/71841	Royal Canadian Air Force – 420 Sqn	13/07/1942	Not known	Area 62 Row E Grave 2 (1)
24	VALDER, CLAUDE WILLIAM	Sergeant (Air Gnr)	621311	Royal Air Force – 101 Sqn	03/04/1942	21	Area 62 Row B Grave 7
25	WILTCHER, NORMAN RIGBY	Sergeant (W/Op/ Air Gnr)	1311452	Royal Air Force Volunteer Reserve – 101 Sqn	07/07/1942	21	Area 62 Row D Grave 2
26	CIOLEK, J.	POR	/	Polish Forces – 301 Sqn	06/08/1942	25	Area 62 Row E Grave 4
27	DOMANSKI, L	PPOR	/	Polish Forces – 301 Sqn	06/08/1942	28	Area 62 Row E Grave 3
28	FRANKOWSKI, A.J.	KAL	/	Polish Forces – 301 Sqn	06/08/1942	24	Area 62 Row E Grave 5

No.	Surname and Christian name(s)	Rank	Service Number	Air Force and Regiment	Date of Death	Age	Headstone Marker
29	GOHRES, W.	ST - SZER	/	Polish Forces – 301 Sqn	06/08/1942	21	Area 62 Row E Grave 2
30	JOSZT, K	KPT	/	Polish Forces – 301 Sqn	31/10/1942	31	Area 62 Row F Grave 1
31	KUROWSKI, LTJ	ST - SZER	/	Polish Forces – 301 Sqn	06/08/1942	20	Area 62 Row E Grave 6
32	OSSOWSKI, B.	KPL	/	Polish Forces – 3015	31/10/1942	21	Area 62 Row F Grave 2
33	PILARSKI	KPL	/	Polish Forces – 305 Sqn	31/10/1942	27	Area 62 Row F Grave 3
34	ROGOWSKI, A	POR	/	Polish Forces – 305 Sqn	31/10/1042	25	Area 62 Row F Grave 4
35	UNKNOWN	An Airman	/	Royal Air Force	/	/	Area 62 Row A Grave 6
36	UNKNOWN	An Airman	/	Royal Air Force	/	/	Area 62 Row A Grave 7
37	UNKNOWN	An Airman	/	Royal Air Force	/	/	Area 62 Row B Grave 4
38	UNKNOWN	An Airman	/	Royal Air Force	/	/	Area 62 Row B Grave 5
39	UNKNOWN	A Soldier – Captain	/	/	/	/	Area 62 Row B Grave 3

Notes: For the recording of the headstones, we kept numbering of the rows to A to E (with an extra row marked F for the Polish military) and the grave number specified on the website of the CWGC (in parenthesis, we noted the current situation for the row number where the information from the CWGC was unclear). Row A is located to the north and the numbering of the rows begins to the east. As at Guidel, for some Commonwealth war graves the table shows an attached numbering (Joint Grave) when human remains of buried crew members could not be identified separately. However, a headstone for each casualty is listed.

Annexe IV

List of Military Burials at Lanester Corpont Cemetery

No.	Surname and Christian name(s)	Rank	Service Number	Air Force and Regiment	Date of Death	Age	Headstone Marker
1	BATTLE, EDWARD HULME	Sergeant (Obs)	523469	Royal Air Force – 50 Sqn	28/12/1940	23	Row 1 Grave 1
2	HEMINGWAY, MARCHANT	Sergeant (W/Op/ Air Gnr)	649426	Royal Air Force – 50 Sqn	28/12/1940	19	Row 1 Grave 2
3	MILLIGAN, PETER	Sergeant (Air Gnr)	629402	Royal Air Force – 217 Sqn	20/12/1940	23	Row 2 Grave 1
4	PLANT, WILLIAM SIDNEY	Sergeant (W/Op/ Air Gnr)	620004	Royal Air Force – 217 Sqn	20/12/1940	25	Row 2 Grave 2
5	SMITH, GEORGE GRAY	Sergeant (Air Gnr)	615035	Royal Air Force – 50 Sqn	28/12/1940	19	Row 1 Grave 3
6	TIPLADY, CHARLES MAURICE	Sergeant (Pilot)	745261	Royal Air Force Volunteer Reserve – 217 Sqn	20/12/1940	Not known	Row 2 Grave 3
7	WEB, NELSON HENRY	Pilot Officer (Pilot)	44594	Royal Air Force Volunteer Reserve – 217 Sqn	20/12/1940	23	Row 2 Grave 4

Notes: We record the numbering of the headstones as the numbering of the CWGC except for mass graves (Collective Grave 1–2 and Collective Grave 3–5), where human remains could not be separately identified.

Annexe V

List of Military Burials at Gâvres Cemetery

No.	Surname and Christian name(s)	Rank	Service Number	Air Force and Regiment	Date of Death	Age	Headstone Marker
1	DAVIES, EVAN ARTHUR	Flight Lieutenant (Pilot)	101537	Royal Air Force Volunteer Reserve – 50 Sqn	13/02/1943	32	Area S.W. Row 3 Grave 4
2	HOGG, WILLIAM JAMES	Flight Sergeant (Nav/Bomber)	R/97033	Royal Canadian Air Force – 50 Sqn	13/02/1943	Not known	Area S.W. Row 3 Grave 5
3	SMITH, HERBERT	Sergeant (Obs)	1061130	Royal Air Force Volunteer Reserve – 22 Sqn	26/11/1041	26	Area S.W. Row 4 Grave 6
4	WHITTAKER, NORMAN HORACE	Sergeant (W/Op/Air Gnr)	949600	Royal Air Force – 44 Sqn	27/07/1941	20	Area S.W. Row 5 Grave 6
5	KORECKI, EDWARD ROMAN	Lieutenant navigator	P-02216	Polish Forces – 300 Sqn	11/11/1943	35	Area S.W. Row 3 Grave 7

Annexe VI

Date, Cemetery and the Number of Men Buried in the Cemeteries of the Lorient region

Date	Guidel	Lorient	Lanester	Gâvres	Total
Not known		5			5
29/11/1940	1				1
20/12/1940			4		4
28/12/1940			3		3
27/03/1941	1				1
30/06/1941		1			1
27/07/1941				1	1
04/09/1941	1				1
26/11/1941				1	1
18/01/1942	1				1
25/03/1942		4			4
03/04/1942		3			3
18/05/1942	1				1
03/06/1942	3				3
22/06//1942		5			5
07/07/1942		10			10
13/07/1942		2			2
06/08/1942		5			5
31/10/1942		4			4
15/01/1943	5				5
29/01/1943	12				12
04/02/1943	4				4
07/02/1943	34				34
13/02/1943	11			2	13
13/02/1943	6				6
16/02/1943	7				7

Annexe VI

Date	Guidel	Lorient	Lanester	Gâvres	Total
25/02/1943	1				1
09/04/1943	1				1
01/05/1943	1				1
03/05/1943	1				1
14/06/1943	5				5
06/08/1943	1				1
12/08/1943	5				5
11/11/1943	1			1	2
01/12/1943	1				1
31/01/1944	1				1
15/02/1944	2				2
12/03/1944	1				1
11/05/1944	5				5
27/06/1944	1				1
22/07/1944	1				1
29/07/1944	1				1
01/09/1944	1				1
Total	117	39	7	5	168

Annexe VII

Table 1

Date, Cemetery and the Number of Men Buried in the Cemeteries of the Morbihan Region Other Than Those of the Lorient Region

Aircraft Type	Guidel Cemetery	Lorient Cemetery	Lanester Cemetery	Gâvres Cemetery	Total
Beaufort	0	0	1	1	2
Blenheim	1	1	0	0	2
Halifax	4	0	0	0	4
Hampden	1	2	1	1	5
Lancaster	3	0	0	1	4
Mosquito	1	0	0	0	1
Mustang	1	0	0	0	1
Spitfire	1	0	0	0	1
Stirling	1	0	0	0	1
Typhoon	3	0	0	0	3
Wellington	13	6	0	1	20
Aircraft type not known	4	0	0	0	4

Table 2

The Number of Dead Buried in Each Cemetery by Aircraft Type

	Guidel Cemetery	Lorient Cemetery	Lanester Cemetery	Gâvres Cemetery	Total
Beaufort	0	0	4	1	5
Blenheim	1	1	0	0	2
Halifax	24	0	0	0	24
Hampden	3	6	3	1	13
Lancaster	15	0	0	2	17
Mosquito	1	0	0	0	1
Mustang	1	0	0	0	1
Spitfire	1	0	0	0	1
Stirling	2	0	0	0	2
Typhoon	3	0	0	0	3
Wellington	53	27	0	1	81
Aircraft type not known	4	0	0	0	4
Unidentified casualties	9	5	0	0	14
Total	117	39	7	5	168

Annexe VIII

List of the Military in other Cemeteries of the *Département*

Vannes-Boismoreau

No.	Surname and Christian name(s)	Rank	Service Number	Air Force and Regiment	Date of Death	Age	Headstone Marker
1	BRADSHAW, DOUGLAS JAMES	Pilot Officer (Obs)	119905	Royal Air Force Volunteer Reserve	08/11/1942	31	Div.B Row 1 Grave 14
2	EVISON, RONALD GRANVILLE	Sergeant (Pilot)	1214198	Royal Air Force Volunteer Reserve	08/11/1942	21	Div.B Row 1 Graves 12–13
3	GLENN, THOMAS WILLIAM	Sergeant (Pilot)	742263	Royal Air Force Volunteer Reserve	22/11/1940	Not known	Div.B Row 1 Grave 15
4	HILL, CYRIL SYDNEY HERBERT	Sergeant (Bomb Aimer)	1319144	Royal Air Force Volunteer Reserve	08/11/1942	20	Div B Row 1 Graves 12–13
5	HULL, NORMAN WILLIAM	Sergeant (W/Op/ Air Gnr)	638879	Royal Air Force	22/11/1940	19	Div.B Row 1 Grave 15
6	NEWTON, ALEC WILLIAM	Sergeant (W/Op/ Air Gnr)	536600	Royal Air Force	22/11/1940	Not known	Div.B Row 1 Grave 15
7	PEARCE, KENNETH GARD	Flight Sergeant	416228	Royal Australian Air Force	08/11/1942	25	Div.B Row 1 Grave 10
8	SAUTELLE, CLAUDE BESNARD	Flight Sergeant	411390	Royal Australian Air Force	08/11/1942	28	Div.B Row 1 Grave 1

9	WARD, JOHN MONTAGUE	Sergeant (Pilot)	742466	Royal Air Force Volunteer Reserve	22/11/1940	20	Div.B Row 1 Grave 15

Plougoumelen

No.	Surname and Christian name(s)	Rank	Service Number	Air Force and Regiment	Date of Death	Age	Headstone Marker
1	BRADDOCK, ROBERT JACK	Warrant Officer (Nav/ Bomber)	416081	Royal New Zealand Air Force	06/08/1944	26	Grave col.
2	EUNSON, LEONARD ALLAN	Flight Sergeant	410536	Royal New Zealand Air Force	06/08/1944	24	Grave col.
3	HARRISON, GORDON FLETCHER	Warrant Officer Class 1 (Air Gnr)	R/112 810	Royal Canadian Air Force	06/08/1944	Not known	Grave col.
4	HULL, ALFRED ANTHONY	Sergeant (Flt Engr)	1588979	Royal Air Force Volunteer Reserve	06/08/1944	Not known	Grave col.
5	IRVING, WALTER NELSON	Pilot Officer (W/Op/ Air Gnr)	J/87928	Royal Canadian Air Force	06/08/1944	Not known	Grave col.
6	URU, HENARE WHAKATAU	Pilot Officer (Pilot)	39589	Royal New Zealand Air Force	06/08/1944	23	Grave col.

Quiberon

No.	Surname and Christian name(s)	Rank	Service Number	Air Force and Regiment	Date of Death	Age	Headstone Marker
1	DEARDEN, ARTHUR JOHN	Pilot Officer (Obs)	63433	Royal Air Force Volunteer Reserve – 271 Sqn	02/12/1941	24	1
2	HOBGEN, THOMAS CUNNAH	Sergeant	404313	Royal Australian Air Force	04/08/1942	21	2

3	FURZEY, WILLIAM ROBERT	Sergeant (W/Op/ Air Gnr)	993605	Royal Air Force Volunteer Reserve – 22 Sqn	02/12/1941	21	3
4	NOBLE, JOHN REGINALD	Flight Lieutenant (Pilot)	40843	Royal Air Force Volunteer Reserve – 22 Sqn	02/12/1941	23	4
5	OSTROWSKI, ANTONI	ST-SZER	/	Polish Forces – 305 Sqn	23/09/1942	32	5
6	UNKNOWN	An Aiman	/	Royal Australian Air Force	17/08/1942	/	6

Sarzeau

No.	Surname and Christian name(s)	Rank	Service Number	Air Force and Regiment	Date of Death	Age	Headstone Marker
1	DIAMOND, THOMAS	Private	3779240	The King's Regiment (Liverpool)	28/03/1942	Not known	/
2	WATKINSON, JAMES LESTER	Flight Sergeant	R/69360	Royal Canadian Air Force	16/11/1942	24	/

La Trinité-sur-Mer

No.	Surname and Christian name(s)	Rank	Service Number	Air Force and Regiment	Date of Death	Age	Headstone Marker
1	MATTHEWS, DOUGLAS ARCHIBALD GEORGE	Sergeant (Pilot)	566240	Royal Air Force	17/12/1940	24	/

L'Île aux Moines

No.	Surname and Christian name(s)	Rank	Service Number	Air Force and Regiment	Date of Death	Age	Headstone Marker
1	COOK, ALEC ERNEST	Squadron Leader (Pilot)	74329	Royal Air Force Volunteer Reserve	14/08/1944	25	/

| 2 | PYRAH, STANLEY HARRISON | Flight Lieutenant (Nav/ Bomber) | 122971 | Royal Air Force | 14/08/1944 | 31 | / |

Pénestin

No.	Surname and Christian name(s)	Rank	Service Number	Air Force and Regiment	Date of Death	Age	Headstone Marker
1	TAIT, JAMES	Sergeant (Obs)	1365802	Royal Air Force Volunteer Reserve	29/06/1942	Not known	/

Le Palais

No.	Surname and Christian name(s)	Rank	Service Number	Air Force and Regiment	Date of Death	Age	Headstone Marker
1	CHADWICK, W B	First Officer	109921	Mercantile Marine	27/03/1917	Not known	Near the southern boundary

Réguiny

No.	Surname and Christian name(s)	Rank	Service Number	Air Force and Regiment	Date of Death	Age	Headstone Marker
1	CLIFFORD, JOHN THOMAS	Flight Officer (Pilot)	52615	Royal Air Force	28/07/1944	28	Area 2 Row 3 Grave 6

Guiscriff

No.	Surname and Christian name(s)	Rank	Service Number	Air Force and Regiment	Date of Death	Age	Headstone Marker
1	OGDEN-SMITH, COLIN	Major	91977	Royal Artillery	29/07/1944	33	/

Annexe IX

Table 1 Census Date, Cemetery and the Number of Men Buried in the Cemeteries of the Morbihan Region Other Than Those of the Lorient Region

Date	Vannes	Plougoumelen	Quiberon	Sarzeau	Île aux Moines	Trinité sur Mer	Pénestin	Le Palais	Réguiny	Guiscriff	Total
23/03/1917								1			1
22/11/1940	4										4
17/12/1940					1						1
02/12/1941			3								3
28/03/1942				1							1
29/06/1942							1				1
04/08/1942			1								1
23/09/1942			1								1
08/11/1942	5										5
16/11/1942				1							1
28/07/1944									1		1
29/07/1944										1	1
06/08/1944		6									6
14/08/1944					2						2
Not known			1								1
Total	9	6	6	2	2	1	1	1	1	1	30

Annexe IX

Table 2 Census by Cemetery of the Number of Aircraft Affected by Type

Type d'avion	Vannes	Plougoumelen	Quiberon	Sarzeau	Île aux Moines	Trinité sur Mer	Pénestin	Le Palais	Réguiny	Guiscriff	Total
Beaufort			1			1					2
Hampden	1										1
Mosquito					1						1
Spitfire									1		1
Stirling		1									1
Wellington	1		2	1							4
Total	2	1	3	1	1	1	?	0	1	0	10

Table 3 The Number of Dead Buried in Each Cemetery by Aircraft Type

Type d'avion	Vannes	Plougoumelen	Quiberon	Sarzeau	Île aux Moines	Trinité sur Mer	Pénestin	Le Palais	Réguiny	Guiscriff	Total
Beaufort			3			1					4
Hampden	4										4
Mosquito					2						2
Spitfire									1		1
Stirling		6									6
Wellington	5		2	1							8
Total	9	6	5	1	2	1	?	0	1	0	25

Appendix 4
Media

Newspaper and Magazine Articles and Broadcasts

During 1944/5 and after the development of the story from 2006 onwards there was media interest which included (the first four being in the classified announcements columns of the newspapers):

'Missing on Active Service F/O E.R. Lyon', *The Scotsman*, 25 November 1944.

'On Service Colinton Flying Officer missing', *Edinburgh Evening News*, 25 November 1944.

'War Casualties', *The Scotsman*, 25 November 1944.

'Deaths on Active Service, Lyon, previously reported as missing', *The Scotsman*, 30 June 1945.

BBC Radio Scotland – Live Interview with Richard Lyon, 19 October 2007.

'Grave hopes for pilot's family', BBC Newsonline, 16 November 2007.

'Spitfire pilot may have been found', *Cambridge News*, 16 November 2007.

'Hope for end to riddle of pilot killed in war', *The Scotsman*, 17 November 2007.

'Spitfire hero found', *The Times*, 17 November 2007.

'Our uncle was just a snap in a frame', *Edinburgh Evening News*, 22 November 2007.

Colinton News, the Newsletter of Colinton Parish Church, Edinburgh, November 2007.

'Le crash d'un Spitfire à Kercavès le 27 juillet 1944', *Les Cahiers du Pays de Plœmeur*, No. 17, December 2007.

'Spitfire hero Russell found after 63 years', *Daily Record*, 28 December 2007.

'A la recherche de témoignages sur un pilote', *Ouest-France*, 24 January 2008.

'Le Comité d'Histoire à la recherche de témoignages', *Le Télégramme*, 27 January 2008.

'Quest for war grave', *Cambridge News*, 1 April 2008.

Talk by the Author given to the Cambridge Friends of the National Trust for Scotland, 8 April 2008.

'French town honours city Spitfire hero', *Edinburgh News*, 11 April 2008.

'Tribute to hero Spitfire pilot 60 years later', *Daily Record*, 11 April 2008.

'Les écoliers captivés par l'histoire d'Ernest Russell Lyon', *Ouest-France*, 18 June 2008. The story is shared with Schoolchildren in Larmor-Plage.

Conférence, Larmor-Plage, Le Comité d'Histoire du pays de Plœmeur, 25 June 2008.

'A la mémoire du pilote E.R. Lyon', *Bulletin municipal de Larmor-Plage*, No. 2, Septembre–Décembre 2008.

'Nouveau giratoire – Dédié à Ernest Russell Lyon', *Le Télégramme*, 30 October 2008.

'French honour for Spitfire hero Russell', *Daily Record*, 8 November 2008.

'Hommage – La ville se souvient d'Ernest Russell Lyon', *Le Télégramme*, 9 November 2008.

'L'hommage au pilote écossais', *Ouest-France*, 9 November 2008.

'Spitfire pilot honoured – 60 years on', *Cambridge News*, 10 November 2008.

'Family unveil roundabout tribute to city Spitfire hero', *Edinburgh News,* 11 November 2008.

Anglia TV, News Report, 11 November 2008.

'Inauguration du rond-point "Ernest Russell Lyon"', *Larmor-Plage Actualité*, November 2008.

'Flying Officer Ernest Russell Lyon (1922–1944)', *The Newsletter of Colinton Parish Church*, 2008.

'Flying Officer Ernest Russell Lyon (1922–44)', *Colinton News*, December 2008/January 2009.

Article, *The Parish Voice*, St. Johns, Hills Road, Cambridge, December 2008/January 2009

'Le pilote Ernest Russell Lyon grade son mystère', *Ouest-France*, 20 April 2009.

Conférence 'L'histoire du pilote Ernest Russell Lyon' devant des écoliers à Plœmeur, April 2009.

'Ernest Russell Lyon 1922–44 Spitfire Pilot', *Spitfire* – Journal of the Spitfire Society, Spring 2009.

'Rond-point et stèle en mémoire d'Ernest Russell Lyon', *Les Cahiers du Pays de Plœmeur*, No. 19, December 2009.

Talk by the Author to Cambridge Round Table, December 2010.

Conférence de Jean-Yves Le Lan devant les membres de la Société polymathique à Vannes, January 2014.

'Il y a 70 ans, un spitfire se crashait à Kercavès', *Ouest-France*, 26–27 July 2014.

'Campaign success for "unknown airman"', *Royal Air Force News*, 10 October 2014.

'The World War II Spitfire hero finally remembered', *The Daily Telegraph*, 23 November 2014.

'Grave of wartime pilot to be named after 10-year fight', *The Times*, 26 November 2014.

'War hero grave named at last', *The Edinburgh Evening News*, 26 November 2014.

'70 ans après, le pilote écossais sera honoré', *Ouest-France*, 27 November 2014.

'Richard wins grave battle', *Cambridge News*, 13 December 2014.

'Clear and Convincing Evidence', *Britain at War* magazine, December 2014.

'Histoire – Ernest Russell Lyon honoré', *Le Télégramme*, 8 October 2015.

'Un vibrant hommage à Ernest Russell Lyon, pilote écossais', *Ouest-France*, 8 October 2015.

Gonville and Caius College, Cambridge University, Partners Group, Talk by the Author, 27 November 2015.

'Ernest Russell Lyon, pilote de Spitfire', *Bulletin et mémoires de la Société polymathique du Morbihan*, Tome CXLI 2015.

'*Ex Corde Caritas*, Not Forgotten', *The Watsonian*, 2015/16.

'Cérémonie pour la reconnaissance du lieu de sépulture du pilote de Spitfire Ernest Russell Lyon le 5 octobre 2015 au cimetière de Guidel', *Les Cahiers du Pays de Plœmeur*, No. 26, December 2016.

Fleury, Jean, 'Les Bretons et les Écossais sont tenaces', *Le Piège: Revue des anciens élèves de l' École de l'air*, No. 227, 1st Trimestre, 2017.

'La vie et la mort de l'aviateur écossais E. Russell Lyon', *Les Nouvelles* – Le magazine de Lorient Agglomération, No. 37, November/December 2017.

Books

The following books have references to F/O. E.R. Lyon:

Caygill, Peter, *Spitfire MkV in Action: RAF Operations in Northern Europe*. Airlife, 2001, p. 212.

Walpole, Nigel, *Dragon Rampant: the Story of No. 234 Fighter Squadron.* Merlin Massara, 2007, pp. 79, 89, 96, 106, 107.

Saunders, Andy, *Finding the Fallen: Outstanding Aircrew Mysteries from the First World War to Desert Storm Investigated and Solved.* London: Grub Street, 2011, pp. 124–128.

Plœmeur et la Seconde Guerre mondiale. Comité d'histoire du Pays de Plœmeur, Sous la direction de Jean-Yves Le Lan et Emmanuelle Yhuel-Bertin, Liv'Editions, November 2017.

Internet Sites

- 'Ernest Russell Lyon' Wikipedia. https://en.wikipedia.org/wiki/Ernest_Russell_Lyon.

- Aérostèle. http://www.aerosteles.net/stelefr-larmorplage-lyon.

- ABSA. https://www.absa3945.com/Pertes%20Bretagne/Morbihan/27%20juillet%2044/ernest_russell_lyon.html.

- Les amis de la Resistance du Morbihan. http://www.lesamisdelaresistance56.com/index.php/articles-de-presse1/ernest-russell-lyon.

- Comité d'histoire du Pays de Plœmeur. http://www.histoiredePlœmeur.fr/page39.html.

- The *Telegraph.* http://www.telegraph.co.uk/history/world-war-two/11245926/The-World-War-Two-Spitfire-hero-finally-remembered.html.

- TalkingScot.com. http://www.talkingscot.com/forum/viewtopic.php?t=8676.

- *Edinburgh News.* https://www.edinburghnews.scotsman.com/news/raf-pilot-to-be-remembered-after-ten-year-campaign-1-3615187.

- Alchetron. https://alchetron.com/Ernest-Russell-Lyon.

- The Spitfire site. http://spitfiresite.com/2010/04/spitfire-pilot-life-prematurely-ended.html.

Appendix 5
Biographies

Richard Stanley Lyon MA Dip Arch RIBA

Richard with Anne, leaving an event held at No. 10 Downing Street, London, SW1A 2AA in 2014.

Born 27 September 1948 in Norton on Tees, County Durham, to Stanley and May Lyon (née Jack), with two brothers: Alastair b. 1946 and Bob b. 1950, Richard Lyon is a retired architect who ran his own private practice in Cambridge for thirty years until his retirement in 2008. Growing up on Teesside and in North Yorkshire, he was educated at Pocklington School, East Yorkshire, and Fitzwilliam College, Cambridge, where he studied Architecture and Fine Art under Sir Leslie Martin at the Cambridge University School of Architecture. During his career he worked on many residential, healthcare, commercial and Church projects in and around Cambridge, East Anglia and beyond. He has an interest in family history that led, amongst other research lines, to the story of his uncle, Russell Lyon, occupying much of his time in retirement. Married to Anne in 1972 and living in Cambridge, he has two sons and two daughters: Alexander, Amelia, Victoria and Charles; and eight grandchildren: Jack, Archie and Monty; Henry and Willow; and Freddie, Zac and Billy.

More used to the creation of three-dimensional products, this is the author Richard Lyon's first attempt at the creation of a two dimensional product of this scale.

Jean-Yves Le Lan

Né le 28 novembre 1949 à Lorient en France, Jean-Yves Le Lan est un ancien ingénieur en chef des études et techniques d'armement (ICETA). Il a travaillé à la conception des bâtiments militaires pour la Marine nationale française (batiments de surface et sous-marins). Il a été en activité à Paris et à Lorient. Après son départ en retraite, en 2002, il a poursuivi une activé d'enseignant à l'Université de Lorient tout en s'intéressant à l'histoire locale de la région et à celle de la Compagnie des Indes. Il est le président du Comité d'Histoire du Pays de Plœmeur et c'est dans ce cadre qu'il s'est intéressé à l'histoire d'Ernest Russell Lyon. Il habite Plœmeur, est marié avec Catherine et a 2 enfants: Émilie et Élodie.

Born on 28 November 1949 in Lorient, France, Jean-Yves Le Lan, is a retired chief engineer of studies and technique of weaponry (ICETA). He worked on the design of military vessels for the French national navy (surface vessels and submarines). He was active in Paris and in Lorient. He pursued a teaching career at the University of Lorient while focusing on the local history of the region and that of the East India Company. He is the president of the Comité d'Histoire of the Town of Plœmeur and it is in this context that he was interested in the history of Ernest Russell Lyon. He lives in Plœmeur, is married to Catherine and has two children: Émilie and Élodie.

Jean Robic

Jean Robic est né le 23 août 1950 et s'est marié en 1973 avec Myriam, une enseignante. Le couple a eu 3 enfants: Anne-Solène, Guillaume et Marie-Morgane. Jean Robic a vécu dans la ferme de ses parents à Plœmeur dans le Morbihan en France et a continué leur métier de paysan. Dès son enfance, il est attiré par l'aviation et tout particulièrement par les souvenirs de guerre de ses parents. Ceci l'a conduit à entreprendre des recherches sur les sites de crashs d'avion dans le secteur de Lorient, dont celui d'Ernest Russell Lyon en 2003. Cet intérêt pour l'histoire de la Seconde Guerre mondiale l'a amené à créer un « musée » sur cette période et un mémorial pour Ernest Russell Lyon.

Jean Robic was born on 23 August 1950 and in 1973 married Myriam, a teacher. They have three children: Anne-Solène, Guillaume and Marie-Morgane. Jean Robic grew up on his parents' farm in Plœmeur in Morbihan, France, and now runs that farm. From childhood, he was attracted by aviation and particularly by the war memories of his parents. This led him to undertake research on the sites of plane crashes in the area of Lorient, where that of Ernest Russell Lyon was found in 2003. This interest in the history of the Second World War led him to create a 'museum' over this period, and a memorial for Ernest Russell Lyon.

Appendix 6

RAF 234 Squadron Association

RAF 234 Squadron was formed in 1917 as part of the Royal Naval Air Service and was first based in Tresco, on the Scilly Isles, where it was equipped with early flying boats. The Royal Air Force – motto: '*Per Ardua ad Astra*' 'Through Adversity to the Stars' – was founded on 1 April 1918, and is the oldest air force in the world. The motto of 234 Squadron is: *Ignem Mortemque Despuismus*, 'We Spit Fire and Death. The formation of 234 Squadron thus precedes by just over a year the formation of the RAF, a rare accolade.

There have been two histories written on No. 234 Squadron. The first, entitled *A Short History of No. 234 Squadron Royal Air Force 1917–1955*, was written by Flight Lieutenant Robin A. Brown, and the second, the more recent book, entitled *Dragon Rampant: the Story of No. 234 Fighter Squadron*, was written by Group Captain Nigel Walpole OBE BA RAF and published in 2007.

The latter book includes references to the findings in southern Brittany of the crash site of Spitfire MkVb AR343 piloted by F/O E.R. Lyon, but printing occurred just before the Lyon family and the French researchers made contact with each other, following which Richard Lyon made contact with the Squadron Association Secretary, Derek Colborne. The author, Nigel Walpole, who commanded the Squadron in the 1960s, was the first 234 Squadron member to visit the crash site at Kercavès.

The former history by Robin Brown is a brief twenty-three-page illustrated history with selected extracts from the squadron's Operations Record Books, together with a few simple aircraft illustrations. It is barely a book, being a number of imperial-size foolscap folio pages stapled together.

Dragon Rampant is a much more comprehensive history comprising over 278 pages with illustrations.

Amongst planes flown in the squadron are the Curtis H.12 'Large American', Felixtowe F-2A and F-3 flying boats, and the Short 225 seaplane. These were followed in 1939 by three Magisters, a Fairy Battle and three biplane Gauntlets, soon to be followed by some Bristol Blenheim 1Fs. Then came the Vickers Supermarine Spitfire, and then later in the War the North American Mustang II. These were followed by the first jet aircraft including the North American Sabre 4, the Gloster Meteor, the de Havilland Vampire, the North American F6 Sabre, the Hawker Hunter and finally the BAe Systems Hawk.

During WWII the squadron included ace pilots Bob Doe and Pat Hughes. In the Battle of Britain the squadron is believed to hold the record for shooting down more enemy aircraft in one day than any other squadron.

RAF 234 Squadron suffered a number of pauses in its life, the first starting in 1919 at the end of WWI. Then it was re-formed at the beginning of WWII in 1939 and deactivated again in 1946. Starting again in 1956, it was wound down on 28 June 1957, becoming an operational training squadron until it was finally disbanded in 1994.

The squadron has flown from bases the length and breadth of the UK, from the Scilly Isles and RAF Predannack on the Lizard peninsula in the South-West, to RAF Peterhead and both the Orkney and Shetland Islands in northern Scotland. Other UK stations include RAF Middle Wallop, RAF St. Eval, RAF Warmwell, RAF Ibsley, RAF Charing Down, RAF Grimsetters, RAF Hornchurch, RAF West Malling, RAF Southend, RAF North Weald, RAF Bolt Head, RAF Hutton Cranswick, RAF Leconfield, RAF Church Fenton, RAF Portreath, RAF Skeabrae, RAF Deanland (a temporary grass airfield for D-Day), RAF Boxted, RAF Molesworth, RAF Dyce, RAF Bentwaters, RAF Coltishall, RAF Brawdy, RAF Chivenor and RAF Valley. The squadron has also flown from European Cold War bases including RAF Gütersloh, RAF Oldenburg, RAF Geilenkirken and RAF Gibraltar.

No. 234 Squadron Association Reunions gather annually over a weekend at various bases around the UK, usually but not always one where the squadron had been based. For instance RAF Marham,

RAF Valley, RAF Linton-on-Ouse, RAF College Cranwell, RAF Coningsby, RAF Bentley Priory, RAF Halton and AAC Middle Wallop.

Since its formation, the 234 Squadron Association has been carefully nurtured by the Association Secretary, firstly Ray Stebbings, followed by Derek Colborne (the Honorary Lifetime Secretary), and currently by Rob Sargent. This is no mean task, organising members and partners, now with super-numerary family guest members, and keeping everyone interested for forty hours or so during the reunion weekend. Exceptionally competent model propellor and jet aircraft flying is usual; social interaction over mealtimes revive old and new memories; and a black tie evening dinner with speeches, often preceded by a Spitfire flypast, keeps all awake before a lazy departure for home on the Sunday morning.

Appendix 7

History of the Exchanges between Jean-Yves Le Lan and Richard Lyon 2007–2018

Following the posting in November 2006 by Richard Lyon on the Scottish family history website http://www.talkingscot.com/, a few months elapsed before Jean-Yves was able to find the author of the posting, who was using an anonymous username, and his contact email address. After explanation by Jean-Yves to one of the administrators of the website the email address was provided and on 1 April 2007 the first contact was made with Richard.

This was the first of perhaps some 1,500–1,800 emails that have subsequently flowed between Richard and Jean-Yves as the story developed, and as the event of the naming of the roundabout took place in November 2008, and plans were made for the ceremony to re-dedicate the grave in Guidel Cemetery in October 2015.

Without the Internet the achievement narrated in this book would, firstly, possibly just not have started at all, and secondly, it could not have been brought to anywhere near the conclusion that has occurred.

The Internet has also been a very useful resource for information to supplement the exploration into the wider history surrounding the events of 1944 to enable the wider context to appear.

Via the Internet new friendships have been created between those closely involved with the story in Brittany and in the UK. Visits to Plœmeur in southern Brittany have happened with accommodation generously provided, and a reciprocal visit by Jean-Yves and Catherine Le Lan and Jean and Myriam Robic has been made to Cambridge.

Without the Internet F/O Russell Lyon's memory would still be just a photo in a frame in the family photo collection and in the carved name in the silent cold stones of his mother and father's family grave in Colinton, Edinburgh or on the RAF Runnymede Memorial high over the River Thames in Surrey.

His name is now generously remembered on the new roundabout and Stele at Kercavès, near the crash site where his life was extinguished. His name is now also rightly on the gravestone in Guidel Cemetery.

Several websites include aspects of the story for the wider global audience.

The story often captures the imagination of those who have heard it and it is hoped that this book will provide a fitting record of how the near impossible was achieved.

This narrative tries to pull together and present the events of nearly fifteen years of work in the UK and in France. It has not been an easy task with so many changing strands of the story. Following a strict time line has been one objective but this has not always been achieved. The authors seek their readers' patience if the story appears to swing around from subject to subject.

The authors hope also that the story may encourage others to pursue their researches without being blown away by the bureaucratic hurdles that are put in their way.

Richard Lyon and Jean-Yves Le Lan

February 2018

Appendix 8

The Little Prince, by Antoine de Saint-Exupéry

During the early contacts made with the French researchers and during the visits made to southern Brittany another person, not previously mentioned in the story, came forward. This was a retired French Mirage jet pilot, Gérard Pénobert, who lived locally to Plœmeur. He is a member of a group of Air Force veterans working voluntarily in the Salles des Traditions at Lann-Bihoué. One of the projects that have been undertaken by this group has been the cleaning, mounting and display of the parts of Spitfire BM 200, piloted by Fl/Lt Walton, shot down on 27 July 1944 and recovered from Rédené in 2005.

Another string to the bow of this retired pilot was an interest in *Le Petit Prince*, the famous and best-selling book by Antoine de Saint-Exupéry, aviator and poet, first published in 1943.

This poetic and beautifully illustrated tale appears at first sight to be a gentle children's story. Deeper analysis reveals the perplexities of life and human nature, with allegorical references that can be connected to Antoine's own life experiences. Written during the early days of WWII after the Fall of France, the book has inner moral messages about human life and relationships.

The pilot narrator of the story crashes in a remote spot in the Sahara Desert where he meets a young boy whom he refers to as 'The Little Prince'. For the eight days lost in the desert before rescue appears, the narrator and the young boy's discussions form the basis of the story. The young boy, whose home is on Asteroid B-612, has already visited six other planets and is well versed in debating deep issues with sceptical adults. At the end of the tale the young boy lets himself be bitten by a snake, which ends his life on earth, but only for his life to continue in space amongst the planets.

Antoine de Saint-Exupéry disappeared on 31 July 1944 while piloting an unarmed Lockheed P-38 Lightning on a reconnaissance mission from a base in Corsica. Gérard has been intrigued enough to draw the comparison between Russell, the subject of this story who is reported missing in action after 27 July 1944, and Antoine de Saint-Exupéry, author of *Le Petit Prince*, who just four days later became another pilot reported as missing in action.

Later, from 1998 onwards, researchers believe they found underwater artefacts and aircraft wreckage near Marseilles and an unidentified casualty grave at Carqueiranne, on the Mediterranean coast near Hyères, that are thought to be linked to Antoine de Saint-Exupéry.

A8.1 *The Little Prince* welcomes Russell to his home on Asteroid B-612. Created by Gérard Pénobert. Richard Lyon Collection.

One of Gérard's graphics linking *The Little Prince* to Russell is shown above with the prince saying: 'I am proud to make your acquaintance on my planet. The Knights of the sky are my friends.'

This is one of several similar pieces of correspondence received from Gérard linking F/O Russell Lyon to *The Little Prince*.

Reference

Saint-Exupéry, Antoine de, *The Little Prince*, translated from the French language by Katherine Woods, third printing. New York: Reynal and Hitchcock, 1943. https://en.wikipedia.org/wiki/Antoine_de_Saint-Exupéry; https://en.wikipedia.org/wiki/The_Little_Prince.

Appendix 9
Spitfire AR343 – Recovered Parts

From the time that the crash site was found in 2003 the parts recovered by Jean Robic were taken to his farm at Cosquéric. Most of these parts remain there today in his private museum of WWII artefacts. This museum is housed in the underground concrete bunkers that were built there in WWII by the Germans as part of their perimeter defences around the Kerlin-Bastard Luftwaffe airfield.

A9.1, A9.2
Jean Robic with parts recovered,
and Jean Robic, centre, with
Nigel Walpole, right, and
Jean-Michael Lepretre, left.
Photos N. Walpole.

One of the recovered parts, a metal gearing, has been donated by Jean Robic to 234 Squadron, and was received by Nigel Walpole on his visit to southern Brittany soon after the crash site was found.

This part (below) was placed in the main entrance of the RAF College at Cranwell on the occasion of the 234 Squadron reunion held there in 2007.

A9.3
The gearing part of the Merlin
engine on display over the 234 Squadron colours.

A9.4 The view in the main entrance of the RAF College at Cranwell, between the portraits of HM Queen Elizabeth II and HRH The Duke of Edinburgh. Derek Colborne, Secretary of the 234 Squadron Association with back to the camera, Alan Frost extreme right.
Photos Lyon family collection.

When Alastair Lyon, the first member of the Lyon family to visit the Plœmeur area, met with Jean Robic, he was presented with a mounted display of another part of AR343. This is one of the Merlin engine exhausts.

A9.5 An exhaust from the Merlin engine mounted for display by Jean Robic. Photo Richard Lyon.

A9.6, A9.7
The 2008 Stele at the new roundabout at Kercavès, mounted on a
piece of granite taken from the roof of the U-boat pens at Keroman.
Photos J.-Y. Le Lan.

The large and heavy cast iron propeller hub, seen on the previous page, found its way into being the centrepiece of the Stele standing beside the new roundabout at Kercavès, on the Plœmeur to Larmor-Plage road.

Other parts, including part of a burnt wooden propeller blade, a firing button AM Ref. No.5D/534 and metal brackets, were also donated by Jean Robic to Richard Lyon.

The other parts recovered are on display at the Ferme du Cosquéric.

Soon after the crash of 27 July 1944, the Germans cleared most wreckage from the site, including the Merlin engine, fuselage, wings and tailplane. If the Germans had been more efficient and had totally cleared all metal from the crash site then perhaps this story would never have been told.

Bibliography

Books and Publications (see also Appendix 4)

Aubertin, Jean, 'La Poche de Lorient', in Fahrmbacher, Willhelm and Matthiae, Walter, *Lorient: Entstehung und Verteidigung des Marine-Stützpunktes 1940/1945*. Weissenburg: Prinz-Eugen-Verlag, 1956, pp. 29–40.

Brown, Fl/Lt Robin A, *A Short History of No. 234 Squadron, Royal Air Force, 1917–1955* (Pamphlet).

Caygill, Peter, *Spitfire MkV in Action: RAF Operations in Northern Europe*. Airlife, 2001, pp 206–213.

Clamp, Arthur L. *The Hope Cove Area during the Second World War 1939–45*. April 1992.

Commonwealth War Graves Commission, Information Sheets and Pamphlets.

Fahrmbacker, Wilhelm, *Souvenirs of the Base: Keroman, 1940–45*, translation by Jean Aubertin, Liv'Editions, 2012.

Hadaway, Stuart, *Missing Believed Killed: the RAF and the Search for Missing Aircrew 1939–1952*. Pen and Sword Books Ltd. 2008.

Kipling, Rudyard, poem, 'My Boy Jack', 1916.

Le Lan, Jean-Yves, 'Cimetières militaires du Commonwealth du Morbihan', 2011.

Le Lan, Jean-Yves, *Le pays de la Ria d'Étel, entre terre et eau*. Saint-Avertin: Editions Sutton, 2014.

Magee, John Gillespie, poem, 'High Flight', 1941.

McNicol, Pam, '*The Story of a Devon Parish*', Hope Archive Group, pp. 112–113.

Porter, Richard O., *The Story of an Electrical & Mechanical Company Royal Engineers* (Territorial). Printed by Barnard and Westwood Ltd. 1946.

Saint-Exupéry, Antoine de, *The Little Prince*, translated from the French by Katherine Woods, third printing. New York: Reynal and Hitchcock, 1943.

Saunders, Andy, *Finding the Few*, London: Grub Street, 2009.

Saunders, Andy, *Finding the Fallen: Outstanding Aircrew Mysteries from the First World War to Desert Storm Investigated and Solved,* London: Grub Street, 2011, pp. 124–128.

Scarr, R.J., poem 'When Freedom Bled'.

Scutts, Joanna, 2009, 'Battlefield Cemeteries, Pilgrimage, and Literature after the First World War: the Burial of the Dead'. *English Literature in Transition*, 52 (4): 387–416.

Short, Major O.M., *History of the Tyne Electrical Engineers: from the Formation of the Submarine Mining Company of the 1st Newcastle-upon-Tyne and Durham (Volunteers) Royal Engineers in 1884 to 1933*. United Kingdom: Naval Military Press Ltd, 2009.

Sweetman, Bill and Watanabe, Rikyu, *Spitfire*. Paris: Editions Atlas, 1981.

Walpole, Nigel, *Dragon Rampant: the Story of No. 234 Fighter Squadron*. Merlin Massara, 2007, pp. 89–108.

Official Records

The National Archives, Kew, Surrey, TW9 4DU, United Kingdom.

AIR 2/6964 List of Investigations of Crashed Aircraft.

AIR 20/9305 Report on the RAF and Dominions Air Forces Missing Research and Enquiry Service.

AIR 29/1598 Operations Record Book.

AIR 27/1440 No. 34 Squadron, Operations Record Book.

AIR 27/1441 No. 234 Squadron, Operations Record Book.

AIR 55/53 to AIR 55/58 no.1 MREU Reports and Policies.

AIR 55/65 Report on the RAF and Dominions Air Forces MRES 1944–49.

AIR 55/78 Locations, postal and telegraph addresses of MREUS.

AIR 55/79 HQ MRES MED/ME Search Party Instructions.

AIR 55/80 HQ MRES (Missing Research and Enquiry Service), MED/ME: centralisation of investigation into fate of missing casualties: reports and memoranda 1945 Dec–1946 May.

Air Ministry, Air Publications 1565E and 2280A B and C: Pilot's notes, Spitfire VA VB and VC and Seafire IB IIC and III Aircraft.

Commune de Guidel, Morbihan, Brittany, Cemetery Burial Record, WWII Casualties.

Commune de Guidel, Morbihan, Brittany, Death Register.

Report on the RAF and Dominions Air Forces Missing Research and Enquiry Service AIR 27/1439. No. 234 Squadron, Operations Record Book.

The National Collection of Aerial Photography 16 Bernard Terrace, Edinburgh, EH8 9NX.

The Red Cross, Bern, Switzerland.

Press

American Press Cuttings.

Scottish Press Cuttings: *The Scotsman* and *Edinburgh Evening News* 25 November 1944, *The Scotsman* 30 June 1945.

The Times, Obituary, 27 December 1991.

Internet Sites

'George Heriot's School', https://en.wikipedia.org/wiki/George_Heriot%27s_School, consulted 28 November 2017.

'George Watson's College', https://en.wikipedia.org/wiki/George_Watson%27s_College, consulted 28 November 2017.

'Watsonians Online', https://www.watsonians.org/page.aspx?pid=329, consulted 28 November 2017.

'Royal Air Force', https://www.raf.mod.uk/history/234squadron.cfm, consulted 28 November 2017.

'RAF Bolt Head', https://en.wikipedia.org/wiki/RAF_Bolt_Head, consulted 28 November 2017.

'Supermarine Spitfire', https://en.wikipedia.org/wiki/Supermarine_Spitfire, consulted 28 November 2017.

'Predannack Airfield', https://en.wikipedia.org/wiki/Predannack_Airfield, consulted 28 November 2017.

http://spitfiresite.com/2010/04/spitfire-pilot-life-prematurely-ended.html/3

http://www.alamy.com/stock-photo/germans-surrender.html.

'High Flight', https://en.wikipedia.org/wiki/John_Gillespie_Magee Jr.

Scarr, R.J. 'When Freedom Bled', https://www.creative-funeral-ideas.com/funeral-poems-for-military-and-heros.html.

https://en.wikipedia.org/wiki/*Antoine_de_Saint-Exupéry*.

https://en.wikipedia.org/wiki/The_Little_Prince.

Other

Claude Hélias, Spitfire Losses over Brittany 1941–1944, private research.

Claude Hélias, American Advance into Brittany Aug–Sep. 1944, private research.

RAF Air Historical Branch, RAF Northolt, West End Road, Ruislip, Middlesex, HA4 6NG.

Twenty-five letters exchanged between the Air Ministry and E.H. Lyon from September 1944 to November 1949; source RAF AHB Files and Lyon family collection.

Index

Questions for Couples

Amazing Questions to Build Emotional Intimacy in Your Relationship

Sabrina Schuman

Table of Contents

Introduction

C ouples seek advice from other couples. And while there are plenty of books out there that provide you with useful insight on how to answer this or that issue, how does one go about finding the right questions to ask?

By "right questions to ask" I am not referring to questions that will get you deep into the mind of your partner, although such questions are useful. Rather, I am referring to questions that help you get a clear sense of how your partner thinks about important things in life and what their attitudes are. In other words, questions that can help you better understand your partner's views during the early stages of relationship formation.

You see, though couples often come together initially due to some physical or emotional attraction they feel with each other (perhaps because they share similar backgrounds or because one or both of possesses social prowess), it is not only these qualities that make or break a relationship in the long run. Rather, it is how well the partners understand and deal with each other's attitudes and beliefs that determines the fate of the relationship.

In fact, one of the most important aspects of successful relationships is the ability to connect over topics considered important by each partner. Couples who share similar views about these "core" topics are more likely to stay together over time, whereas couples whose views are incompatible tend to live unhappy lives and eventually break up.

The purpose of this book, therefore, is to help you better identify your partner's "core" topics by focusing on questions that will get you thinking about these very issues. Of course, the specific questions you ask will depend upon your partner and what your relationship is like at the present moment. So in addition to suggestions for general conversation topics, you will also find specific questions for use when discussing each one.

Finally, you will find some recommendations on how to identify a topic as core by paying attention to how your partner reacts when certain topics are discussed around them.

For example, if your partner shows an intense interest in a particular issue that tends to upset them (such as if they cry during an argument over said issue), chances are that this issue is core to their life and that of their immediate family.

These discussions can be quite difficult and may leave you or your partner feeling a bit uneasy. Don't worry. It's worth it! In fact, this process is essential if you ever want to have a healthy relationship.

Couples who have a hard time talking to each other without getting upset, or those who have trouble communicating in general (often in stressful situations) may find some of the issues discussed below helpful. They can be considered core to the lives of most people, and therefore they will have an important impact on your relationships with loved ones. This does not mean that just because you think one or more of these questions are relevant you should ignore any other areas that trouble you and your partner – it is still important to find out where your spouse is coming from on all matters. But it does mean that if you're having trouble communicating with your partner, then these questions can be a good starting point for useful discussion.

This book is a compilation of questions on many topics related to how couples live their lives. Some are broader and some are more specific, but most will help you to talk with your partner about how you feel and think. Some of these questions have been around for years, while others were inspired by recent events in modern psychology research and literature. The point is that all of them have been selected because they make people think, and that's the key to a good conversation.

This book can provide useful insights in various situations: when you're picking up your partner at the airport, when you're shopping with your wife or husband, or even while sitting down with your kids at dinner. You could even use these questions for talking with friends, family members or other loved ones.

Most of these questions will help you to talk about the things that are important in your life. So keep them in mind next time you and your spouse want to have a meaningful conversation. It doesn't matter if one of you wants to talk about work and the kids while the other wants to talk about politics, religion, or philosophy — just start asking questions!

NOTES

Chapter 1:
Questions on Trust

T rust is a vitally important element in any healthy, loving relationship. Being able to trust your partner is the bedrock of the love you share. Without it, it's impossible for either of you to feel secure in your relationship.

But what does it mean to trust someone? To most people, trusting means believing that the other is being truthful and genuine in their actions, thoughts, and feelings - that they have your best interests at heart without an ulterior motive. But, in practice, this can be difficult to assess, especially in the early days of a relationship. And if you're wrong in your assessment and you trust someone who turns out to be untrustworthy, it can be devastating.

If you have difficulties with trust in your relationship and would like to build a greater sense of security and stability between you and your partner, try asking these questions for couples. They are likely to help you explore what it means to trust as well as define what makes you both feel comfortable with each other.

1. Have you ever felt like you shouldn't trust me?

Couples who trust each other have better, more stable relationships. When you trust your partner, you feel secure in the knowledge that they won't hurt you or let you down. And when they know that they're trusted, they feel better about themselves and their relationship with you. So, if you don't trust your partner, it's normal to feel nervous about what they're doing when they're away from you and whether they are faithful.

If that's the case for you, try to work out why – have there been times when your partner has behaved in a way that made you distrust them, or do you just get the feeling that they aren't as committed as you are? Be sure to talk to each other about how much trust matters to both of you and how important it is in a successful relationship.

2. What if my spouse was unfaithful?

This isn't a question about infidelity itself; rather, it's a question about one possible outcome if your partner were to cheat on you. Like many of the questions in this book (and in life), this one comes from "The Five Love Languages" by Dr. Gary Chapman. His theory is that there are five major ways to "speak" and show love to your partner – through words (quality time), acts of service (physical touch), receiving gifts (words of affirmation), quality time, or through physical touch or acts of service. Some people speak in all five languages; others speak only in one, two, three, while some speak only in the one language in which they're fluent.

3. What are the most important things I have to do to build your trust?

This and the following question (what are the most important things you have to do?) come from "For Better or For Worse: the Science of a Good Marriage" by Tara Parker-Pope.

The opposite of trust isn't expectation — it's betrayal. If you can't trust your partner, then all of the expectations in the world won't make a difference. What we want is for couples to have both trust and expectations; this allows them to work together toward common goals, both at home and in their relationship generally. If you want to build trust in your relationship, you need to find out what your partner needs. When it comes to building specific expectations, each of you has different expectations of the other, which can lead to disagreements (or worse) if you don't make a point of discussing them.

What are the most important things I have to do? What are the most important things I have to be? The answers will help you and your partner focus on your highest priorities for improving your relationship and keeping it strong.

Various therapists who work with couples often ask these questions of partners during an initial session.

4. Do you want to know more about my past relationships?

Couples don't have to share their entire past or even their present with each other. If you do feel like being open about things, then this question is a way to ask it gently and indirectly.

You should never force your partner to share things, but if you're talking about it and they seem hesitant, this question and the next provide ways to encourage your partner without being pushy.

5. What are the most important things I have to do to build your trust?

If you really want to build trust, you have to know what your partner needs. If your partner can't tell you what those things are, you need a more direct question like: what happens when my partner doesn't trust me? Those with a history of betrayal will struggle the most with this question because they may need to think about it carefully before they answer. So be patient while they work through their answer – if it's important enough for them to tell you, then it's important enough for you to wait for them.

5. What would help you feel more comfortable when talking about things in our past together?

This is the mirror of the previous question and one way of asking gently that might cause your partner less anxiety when you do choose to talk about past relationships.

If you do talk about your past relationships, and you and your partner are both willing, it's a good idea to keep a positive frame of mind. That means avoiding the past tense as much as possible when talking about interactions with exes. So say, "I love how so-and-so did this during our last encounter," not "I loved how so-and-so did this...(sniff)...last encounter."

7. How can I build my trust in you?

This question comes from "For Better or For Worse: The Science of a Good Marriage" by Tara Parker-Pope.

The opposite of trust isn't expectation — it's betrayal. If you can't trust your partner, then all of the expectations in the world won't make a difference. What we want is for couples to have both trust and expectations; this allows them to work together towards goals, both at home and in their relationship more generally. If you want to build trust in your relationship, you need to find out what your partner needs. When it comes to building specific expectations, each of you has different expectations for the other, which can lead to disagreements (or worse) if you don't make a point of discussing them.

If your partner has trouble trusting because of past relationships, then this question will help them start working through that issue with you and finding a way they can be more at ease taking new risks together.

8. What do you think we should do if we find out that someone is lying?

This question comes from research I conducted at the University of Toronto's Rotman School of Management and Baruch College in New York City. We found that couples with clear rules for what to do if one or both partners lie were more confident in their relationship and felt less distressed.

In fact, these clear rules for handling relationship problems were more important than both how many problems the couples reported and how satisfied they were in their relationships.

This question is a great way to add a little structure to your relationship and get your partner in the habit of working with you to figure out ways you can handle problems and work through conflicts more effectively.

The technique is based on research by Dr. John Gottman, considered the top relationship researcher in the world

9. Would you trust me if I asked a friend or relative to spy on you?

Asking someone to do this would be an act of distrust, so if your partner said yes, that would be a sign of trouble.

When you ask this question, you are thinking about what to do if your partner lies, so the answer is particularly important. Another reason for asking it is that if your partner says "yes" that would be an alarming indication that they do not respect your boundaries and privacy. Even if they say no, it still may mean they lie too much or feel comfortable doing things behind your back without telling you about them. Secrets breed lies and lying breeds secrets. It's a vicious cycle in relationships.

10. How would you feel about me having a close relationship with someone I work with?

Women tend to be more jealous when it comes to their partner having strong relationships with co-workers of the opposite sex, but men are nearly as bothered by opposite-sex friendships as they are by same-sex friendships — either way, they're concerned about losing their partner through a relationship with someone else. If the work environment is a source of stress in the relationship, then this question can help you or your partner work through the issue.

It's important to understand that no one person is the source of all of your happiness. It's okay to have outside friendships – it just needs to be without secrets. If you think about what makes close friends special, it's probably because they listen to you, tell you the truth about yourself and others. They help and support you, and they're always there for you. You want a relationship with someone at work with those same qualities.

These questions will help you and your partner work on trust issues together. This chapter is designed to help you understand what trust means, how to go about building it in your relationship, and how to deal with problems that arise due to or because of a lack of trust.

I've found that these questions work well during couples counseling sessions. I suggest that all of the couples I work with print out this list and discuss the questions together. It's also a good idea to keep answering them and discussing your answers with your partner even after you complete the exercise in counseling.

If you are having trust problems or have been hurt or betrayed by your partner, it's important to understand that trust issues often take time to heal. It's impossible to get over a past betrayal in one conversation. You and your partner need time and space for healing – plus, of course, good communication skills – so you can work through any problems together and come out stronger in the end.

NOTES

Chapter 2:
Questions on Communication

C ommunication is one of the most important aspects of a healthy friend or family relationship as well as significant other relationships because it fosters understanding between two people who are sharing their lives. But the importance of effective communication in a relationship is often overlooked, especially in the early days when you are caught up in the excitement of being with someone new who seems to understand you like no one ever has.

If you want to enhance your communication with each other and build a stronger sense of emotional intimacy, try asking these questions for couples. These questions are likely to help you explore your feelings about each other as well as enhance your ability to talk honestly and openly about any issues that might be holding you back.

Vital Questions for Couples to Discuss Together

1. What am I going to do about certain areas in our relationship? What are we going to do about them?

2. How should we communicate with each other?

3. What is one thing I need from you but we haven't done yet? That you feel we can't do yet? How can we work on these things together?

4. What is one thing that you as my partner needs from me but I haven't done yet? That you feel I can't do yet? How can we work on those things together?

5. How are you feeling about our relationship right now, right here?

6. What are the most important things you have to do to build trust in our relationship? What happens when we can't trust each other? What happens when trust is broken between us?

7. How is it different when we communicate about positive things versus when we talk about negative things in our relationship? In our lives in general?

8. What is one thing I do to make you feel less comfortable communicating with me and makes you feel less in control of the way we communicate?

9. How are you feeling about our communication right now, right here?

You and your partner need to create a plan for how you'll deal with areas of disagreement or problem behavior. You should agree to decrease your anxiety.

When there is a problem or an issue you see with your partner, have a plan in mind to address it with them. Plan on doing the following:

• Ask yourself if you are really upset. If so, ask yourself why this is upsetting you and what exactly about the situation might be causing it.

• Let yourself feel what comes up for you emotionally at the moment. Let yourself feel your feelings.

• Think about what you are going to do, say, or change in the situation or the way you react to it.

• Take a deep breath and step back from the situation. Rather than being sucked into reacting immediately, take a moment and consider how you might want to respond or act differently.

• Communicate with your partner (without nagging or yelling) in a calm manner about your feelings about the situation or behavior upsetting you. If possible, try to state your feelings in terms of feeling needs: "I felt disappointed when..." vs "You did such-and-such..."

• Communicate with your partner about what you are going to do differently.

• Agree on what you'll both need to do to make things different.

2. Ask how should we communicate with each other?

You and your partner should agree on how you can best communicate with each other, especially when an issue or problem needs addressing. You want communication with your partner to be as effective as possible so it can help you create a good relationship. You don't want communication to cause more trouble or conflict.

You want to the communication to be:

• Respectful

• Honest

• Focused on shared positive goals

• Based on the idea that both of you have good qualities and are trying to be a good people...not just that you have shortcomings.

• Based on the fact that your relationship is not about idealism but grounded in reality. This means it is based on shared interests, shared values, and what makes sense for the relationship. It's okay to have different opinions about some things as long as those differences don't threaten the core values or interests of the relationship: "We may differ about politics, but we can agree to disagree about that one topic without threatening our relationship."

• Based on the importance of the relationship to you and your partner individually. You care about each other and want to do what is best for yourselves and for the relationship. It's easier to focus on positive goals rather than negative ones.

3. What is the one thing that I need from my partner, but they haven't done yet? That they feel they can't do yet? How can we work on this thing together?

You should discuss what it will take for them to be able to create a sense of trust in the areas where you are struggling with trust. This may be about sharing personal information, behaving in certain ways, or in any other area you feel they need to build trust.

What can you do together to help the other person feel comfortable with issues that concern trust? What can you both do together as a couple that will help your partner trust you more? What is one thing that you want so badly that it creates doubt for them about your ability to handle whatever the issue is? (Maybe they don't want to see pictures of your ex, for example, but you don't understand why they would have a problem with it when it's just pictures?)

4. How is it different when we communicate about positive things versus how it is when we talk about negative things in our relationship? In our lives in general?

Again, this is a good question to ask if you are having problems in your relationship. If there are persistent issues that need to be addressed, pay close attention to how you and your partner communicate when talking about them. If you find yourself being harsh or using a lot of judgment, you might be dealing with some anger or resentment. If you find yourself coming across as overly accommodating, you may be suffering from fear and anxiety. If you find yourself avoiding the whole subject, there's a good chance that some anxiety is creeping into the relationship and causing stress.

Now how are you feeling about the relationship right now, right here? This is a more general question that might be helpful for you and your partner to keep returning to in the future. If you're worried about how your partner feels, ask about it! It might seem obvious from their actions (or lack of action), but sometimes we have a hard time articulating how we really feel about something in words.

What else could you bring up if it seems like they aren't doing a good job at communicating? What can you do together to improve this aspect of the relationship?

What are the most important things you have to do to build trust in the relationship? What happens when we can't trust each other? What happens when trust is broken? These questions will help you both understand the core issues of trust for your relationship. They can also give you an idea about what to do together if trust is an issue.

If your relationship seems relatively healthy, but there are still issues of trust here and there, it might be helpful for you and your partner to work on building trust in other aspects of your relationship. Perhaps you need better communication about how you're feeling or perhaps there's something they need to share more often.

This can be a long list, but it will help you both develop a better understanding of the issues that relate to trust. Use this list along with your own ideas about what is most important for you and your partner in order to improve this aspect of your relationship.

If something is an issue, but you don't see it here, feel free to add it. These things aren't to be taken too seriously. This is just meant to be a resource for you and your partner. However, I have seen these issues cause major problems in relationships. If any of these items are a more serious issue, consider working to solve them together.

You'll also want to pay close attention to the terms used to describe everything and everyone in your life. With constant negativity, the words used to label everything can be more black-and-white than need be. There's a good chance that such a relationship will fall prey to a particular kind of cognitive distortion, called, "all-or-nothing thinking."

When it comes to communicating about positive things and your relationship, keep an eye out for biased language. In other words, when you communicate with your partner about positive things, where are you coming from? Are your judgments and evaluations equally as harsh as they would be for negative things?

Looking into your mode of communication can help you spot issues that they may be having with their own communication. Try to inspect what you do and look for ways that your behavior could be affecting your partner's ability to communicate effectively with you. Are there times when you interrupt them? Do they ever feel like they can't express how they're feeling? Are there ways in which your attitude could be interpreted as controlling?

Asking yourself these questions can help you develop a better understanding of some of the factors that might be involved in your partner's inability to communicate freely and openly with you.

Other relevant questions: what is one thing that my partner does to make me feel less comfortable communicating with them? To make me feel less in control of the way we communicate with each other?

There are two sides to every communication, and even the most respectful, open communicators will have their fair share of issues with how they communicate.

Inspect what your partner does and look for ways that their behavior could be affecting your ability to communicate effectively with them. How are you feeling about our communication right now, right here?

In this chapter, we've covered a lot of areas where trust can be built, and issues of trust can occur. You want to consider how your relationship is coming along in terms of the way that you communicate with each other on a daily basis. This is the basis for all of your relationship.

Your answer depends on where you are right now, and it's important to acknowledge that you will have good days and bad days. That's not a problem – all relationships go through ups and downs. Just try to answer these questions as honestly as you can, even if it takes more than one try. You may want to discuss your answers with your partner to extend the conversation.

When thinking about communication in your relationship, pay attention to how you both feel about the way that you communicate with each other on a day-to-day basis. Is there a difference between how you feel about communicating in general and how you feel when you two communicate specifically?

These questions are designed to help you and your partner communicate in an effective way that will build the trust in the relationship. They are also designed to help you both build a better understanding of how each of you impact the other's ability to communicate effectively with each another.

That said, there is a wide variety of communication styles out there, so don't feel boxed into these questions if they don't work for you and your partner.

NOTES

Chapter 3:
Questions on Fun

F un and playfulness are often overlooked in relationships, especially in the beginning when you're more focused on falling in love and discovering who you are. But it's important to remember that all relationships need to have moments of fun and playfulness to make them strong and healthy, because the love you share is enriched by the joy you have just being together.

If you want to bring more fun into your relationship, try using these questions for couples. They are likely to help you explore what it means for you both to have fun together as well as what makes each of you feel playful around each other.

Use these questions at any point during your relationship they're especially helpful when getting to know each other better. It's important to have fun with each other, so have fun answering these questions!

1) What do you like most about being with me?

This question is a great way to get things started. It helps you focus on the good, which will naturally lead into deeper conversation. The key to having good playfulness in your relationship is having a sense of humor about yourself and each other.

2) What does it feel like when we are enjoying being together?

What actions do you take? What do you say? How do your bodies move? This question will help you focus on physical playfulness in particular, which can be important if you want to have more physicality in the relationship.

3) How do you like to spend time by yourself?

How do you like to spend time with me? It's important to know that the playfulness and fun in your relationship isn't just about making sure each person is happy all the time. It's about acknowledging each person's separate interests, activities, and joys, as well as bringing these things together.

This question helps you understand what brings joy into your own life and makes it a question of sharing that joy with each other. When that happens, it allows you both to be more playful with each other while still maintaining your own individual characteristics. Which leads us nicely to the next question.

4) What do you like best about me?

This question can be a bit more difficult, because you might not always know how to answer it. You might feel like there isn't much to say or that your love for each other is already apparent. But trust me, this question is a great way to bring deeper conversation and fun. Try answering from different perspectives, such as, "What do you appreciate about me?", "What do you find attractive about me?", or "How have I grown as a person?" You may also want to ask each other questions that allow you both to put yourselves in the other's position for a change.

5) When do you feel most playful with me?

This question is a great follow-up to the previous question. It requires that you think about what it feels like when the two of you are being playful together. A lot of people find this question hard, because they don't believe they have been as playful as they could or that their partner doesn't have the same ideas about playfulness as they do. But focus on what does feel fun to you, and try to understand why some it makes you want to be more playful with each other. Then, think about answering this next question...

6) What do you think I might appreciate about being with you?

If you want to see more fun in your relationship, this is an important question to ask. It requires that each person focus on the other person's perspective, allowing for a deeper understanding. If you don't feel like you know how to answer the question, ask your partner what it might feel like being with them. This will give each of you some insight into how the other person feels.

7) What physical activities do we enjoy together? This is a great question if you're trying to bring more physicality into the relationship. Especially if you aren't used to being physical or don't have a lot of shared interests, this question can be a good way to come up with new ideas of things you can do together. Even if you already know what kinds of physical activities the two of you like, answer the question again. This time, think about it from another person's perspective. What would they find fun and exciting about the two of you being physical together?

Now we move on to some questions more focused on the relationship as a whole...

8) How do you feel when we're having fun?

This is an important question because it's important to remember that each relationship is different. Some people don't feel much of anything when they are enjoying them-selves, while others feel a lot of emotions. Some people really notice a change in their body, while others don't. Or maybe you really get into the fun and are more playful than normal. This question will help you understand your partners feel-ings about being happy and having fun together.

Because each relationship is different, each relationship needs to find its own balance of fun and serious talk. If you don't have time for deep discussions every day, that's okay! For some relationships, it might be more important to set aside some time on the weekend for getting to know each other better, while other relationships thrive on constant communication.

Whatever you need to make your relationship work, you can find ways to add playfulness throughout the week. Maybe try to ask a question during a fun moment together!

For some questions, you may need to think about your an-swers for a while and spend some time together reflecting. If this is the case, feel free to write down your answers and share them with each other later!

It can be hard for us to remember why we fell in love with each other in the first place. And sometimes we get so caught up in day-to-day life that we don't remember to appreciate what makes our relationship special. That's why it's important to take some time to think about these questions and what they mean for you and your partner. If you're constantly communicating with each other, you'll stay connected during the fun and the hard times. And even if things change, it can help to remember why you fell in love in the first place!

After answering these questions about fun and playfulness with each other, take some time to discuss what it was like to answer them. What did you learn about each other? Did one of your answers surprise the other? Did anything you said make you feel differently about each other, or about your relationship?

Now it's time to get playful!

NOTES

Chapter 4:
Questions on Respect

W hen a man is motivated by a desire for respect, he will often give you everything you ask, no matter how unreasonable it is, and no matter whether you deserve it or not.

Respect is the outward expression of approval; it can be given only by those who have control of some kind over the person who receives it. "Give me respect" means "Make me feel important." To inspire respect in others we must convince them that we are superior to them in some way. But their position in relation to us is not important; what matters is the way they feel about themselves compared with how they think we feel about ourselves.

This is why we respect those who are self-assured and we usually feel contempt for those who have no doubts. In other words, it is not so much their positive qualities that inspire us to give them respect as the absence of negative characteristics.

When people are aware of their weaknesses, they automatically become unsure of themselves. They want to cover up their inadequacies but do not know how to do so. Though they fear the judgment of others, they can never be quite sure what other people really think of them. In this situation there is only one way for them to be accepted, and that is by constantly trying harder than everyone else. There are only 10 questions important for you and your partner to answer regarding respect:

1. What do you think makes you a better person than me?

To answer this question, you must first ask yourself the following what good qualities do I have that my partner does not? What are the things that I would like to change in my partner—the things that prevent him from being as good a person as I would like him to be?

When a person realizes that his partner is more talented or better at something, he feels inadequate and inferior. And when a person feels inferior toward someone else, he will try to develop feelings of jealousy or hostility so strong that they overpower his feeling of inadequacy. But if your partner has something you want and you don't think you can get it by competing, you will feel tremendous resentment rather than jealousy. Resentment is a powerful emotion that can be used to control and dominate others, and it is one of the most dangerous feelings that can develop in a relationship.

Those who ask this question are often not really interested in the good qualities or abilities their partners possess, but instead they are looking for a feeling of security in relation to something they consider a weakness. For example, if your partner is very generous with her time and energy and knows quite a few people, you might worry that she will find someone else who will take up more of her time than you do.

2. If I tried to behave the way you want, what would stop me?

When a person feels guilty, inadequate, or inferior, he usually has a kind of inner barrier that prevents him from acting the way he wants to. This barrier is like a series of self-imposed negative attitudes that give him something to feel guilty about even before he does anything wrong.

For example, an individual who feels guilty when he shows anger will make sure that his partner is never angry at anybody else; but whenever she gets angry with him, she will be expressing mistrust or resentment because he had thought of doing something she would not have wanted him to do.

People use their personal feelings as an excuse for not taking responsibility for themselves and their relationships. They feel that it is not their fault if their partners don't behave the way they want them because they are naturally good people and would never hurt anyone. But in relationships, they allow themselves to get upset even though they know that at any moment they can change their feelings. The idea that they have done something wrong becomes an excuse for getting upset and blaming others for their negative feelings.

3. What makes a man friendlier and more responsible than he actually is?

When people feel guilty or resentful toward someone for some reason, they act friendlier toward him than he deserves. This is called "being nice." While this may seem like it is being friendly to the other person, it is actually something very different. When a person sees someone of the opposite sex who attracts him, he will usually act in a way that indicates attraction. If he is friendly or nice to her, then he will assume that she will feel good about herself and want to be closer to him because she will think she is so desirable. In fact, if a woman feels attracted to a man and wants to be close to him, she will act more attractive toward him as soon as possible.

Women are usually more direct and open about their feelings than men; they don't have as much trouble being open and honest with their partners. This is why men, when they are un-confident and insecure about their attractiveness, will often try to act friendlier or nicer to the women they would like to be close to than is necessary or justified. Men will show off their ability to be friendly and supportive by offering favors that are not really needed, since they don't feel secure that the woman in question would want them for herself.

4. What can I do that will make you feel that my presence raises your status?

People are so used to acting in a certain way around others that they don't realize how others feel about them. Even though your partner might be loyal and loving, she will still see that something is missing in you, such as more money or better looks. If you can think of a way to act that will make her feel that your presence is not only comfortable but actually elevating her own status, then she will be more attracted to you.

5. How does a person who is incompetent and irresponsible act when he wants to make others feel good about themselves?

Even though many people are not in touch with their own feelings, they usually know if their actions make them feel good or bad about themselves. This is why incompetent people often act in ways that make others feel guilty or ashamed.

They do things that cause them to feel good about themselves by making others feel bad. If a man does something wrong, he will try to make others feel responsible. For example, if a man is poor and can't take his wife out on weekends, he may try to convince her that it's unfair for him to have all the responsibility for supporting the family while she doesn't have any at all. He makes himself seem like the victim, and she feels guilty for not being more supportive.

6. How can I improve my relationships with those people who are already friendly toward me?

If you want to improve your relationships with people who are already friendly toward you, then make an effort to be with them more often. People who are already friendly toward you may feel honored if they can be around you, and this would improve the relationship. If you have people in your life that like being around you, see if there is some way that the two of you could become closer.

7. What emotions do I feel towards the persons who are already friendly toward me?

If you have people in your life who are already friendly toward you, look at what emotions you feel toward them. Are you happy they think so highly of you, or do you feel some jealousy that they have a better relationship another person than you do? If you can be honest with yourself about your own feelings, then it will be easier to find ways to fix these relationships by addressing such issues. If you are close to becoming friends with someone and still harbor jealousy or envy toward them, it will be hard to make your relationship solid because you will always feel like they have something you don't. This isn't the way a good friendship should be, and it's better to address your feelings head on.

If there are people who dislike you, do not immediately assume that they have valid reasons. Someone who dislikes you might simply resent something about your personality. Sometimes people try to improve themselves by learning about how other people behave.

7. How can I be a better person if my friends try to make me feel that I can improve my status?

If your friends were to try to make you feel that you have improved your status by making a lot of money, getting published, or achieving something important, then it is possible that you will change in the way they want. But if your friends are honest and accept you as you are, there is no way that they will try to make you feel like this. So this question re-quires some serious concern on our part.

If your partner has asked any of these questions about her-self—questions about her good qualities and desirable char-acteristics—we can assume that she is aware of something good about herself and probably has a few qualities that at-tract people to her.

8. How would you like me to act for the two of us to get along better?

If your partner has asked you this question, she probably feels that you are not as close to her as she would like you to be. She will feel very frustrated if she feels that you are not close enough because she has the deep feeling inside that there could be something great between the two of you. The chances are good that there is something negative between the two of you, but it is better to look at what's positive as well.

9. If people were constantly trying to put me down, what can I do about it?

Many people have the idea that if someone were to try to hurt them or make them feel bad about themselves, they would act right away to defend themselves. But in reality, if someone always makes you feel bad, you will probably just keep trying to avoid that person. For example, if your partner doesn't want you in his life because he doesn't like himself and can't accept his own mistakes, then he will try to get back at you by making you feel guilty for something. Then when you are feeling guilty and insecure about yourself, he will start telling you that it is your fault for not being supportive enough because he needs your understanding.

10. How can I give people more respect than they give themselves?

If you can figure out how to do this, you and your partner will be able to make the most of the relationship. If your partner feels that you respect him more than he respects himself, he will probably feel much better about himself.

These questions are designed to help you respect each other as couples. If you believe that your partner has good qualities, you will want to be close to him. If you are interested in improving your relationship, you can begin by finding out what is holding you back from getting closer to each other.

NOTES

Chapter 5:
Questions on Quality time

Quality time is one of the most important aspects of a relationship. It doesn't have to be fancy or expensive. All you need is each other; and sometimes that's all you need to make things seem right in the world again.

Grab some popcorn, settle down for a cozy night in, and ask each other these questions to get things going! You'll be surprised at what you learn.

1. What do you enjoy doing together?

This question is extremely open-ended, and it will allow both parties to talk about their favorite things to do as a couple. It can be as simple as walking around the block or going out for a milkshake, but it's rare that couples get the chance to discuss little joys like this!

2. Where would you like to go someday?

This question is a good one for those who are married and have already been on various vacations. It's also perfect for those who simply want to travel and need some inspiration! Asking each other where you've always wanted to go is a great way to have fun dreaming and planning your future adventures together.

3. What is your favorite memory of us together?

This question is all about reminiscing. It will allow both partners to share the funniest or most touching moments of your time together. Even if you've heard these moments a million times before, asking this question again is a great way to spark renewed joy and laughter in your relationship!

4. How would most people describe the two of us as a couple?

Couples rarely take the time to stop and think about what others think of them as a unit. This is an opportunity for you both to step back and see how others see you, which can provide insights into the type of people that the two of you are as a couple!

5. Who is the most important person in your life, besides me?

This question is all about getting better acquainted with each other. It will allow you to see how important your partner is to you outside of the relationship. Often, it can spark conflicts because one partner may not appreciate the amount of time the other spends with family or friends. When dealing with this issue in a relationship, it's important for both partners to be open and honest so that these types of conflicts can be addressed early on before they get blown out of proportion.

6. What do you like most about being married?

This question is a fun one that will allow each person to reminisce about the reasons why you got married in the first place. It will provide renewed joy and reason to be grateful that you're together. It's also a good tool for those who may have been together for so long that you've forgotten what you saw in each other in the first place.

7. If I could change one thing about myself, what would it be and why?

This question can ignite a firestorm of honesty which is always needed between partners. If your partner says that he wishes he were taller or she wishes she had bigger boobs, it will make you think about your own self-image and how those things impact the relationship as a whole.

8. Why did we decide to get married in the first place, and how is it working out so far?

This question can be extremely important because it will allow you to see what the big picture in your relationship when you got married. It may reveal that you both expected very different things from marriage, which may lead to an unexpected conflict. It can also provide a good way for both of you to reflect on your individual expectations of marriage before it became a reality.

9. What is the best thing about having kids?

If you have any little ones running around, this question will generate some serious laughs (and probably a few tears). Not only is it a great way to enjoy a night in as parents if you have the kids at home, but it can also be a good way to see just how much the two of you have in common. If your opinions are polar opposites on this topic, some tension needs to be addressed!

10. Where do you see us in five years?

This is another question that allows both partners to step back and look at the big picture. It will allow both parties to reflect on where they see themselves and their relationship going forward. It's also a great tool to provide perspective on how you've both grown in your relationship and whether or not it's heading in a positive direction.

These questions are all great tools to help you get to know each other on an intimate level. They'll spark discussions and allow the two of you to look at your relationship from a different perspective. If you and your partner can answer them together, it will provide a safe place for both of you to share some vulnerability that will strengthen your bond as a couple.

NOTES

Chapter 6:
Questions on How to fight fair

I n order to fight fair, you need to have a clear understanding of what is it you are fighting for and why. What is it about the situation that upsets you? Is this an issue that can be resolved through constructive discussion? Do you want to make your partner aware of something they do not realize? Are you trying to change a current behavior pattern by putting pressure on the other person?

Don't focus solely on what's wrong in your relationship. Focus also on the positive aspects and possible solutions; there might just be ways in which both parties could compromise and work together. Whatever your goal is when fighting, be fair and try not to put blame or throw judgmental criticism at each other. This will only cause the other person to react defensively. If your partner is capable of accepting responsibility for his or her actions, you can actually make them feel more secure. If your partner is defensive, try not to take it personally. This is a sign that you have done something wrong and need to correct it.

When fighting fair, remember to listen and understand what the other person has to say before you continue with what you were saying. You may be surprised to find that the root of the argument was not even related to what you originally thought. We often enter into arguments thinking we know exactly why because we tend to focus on ourselves—our own feelings, beliefs and wants—rather than our partner's thoughts and feelings.

Here are questions for couples to ask each other. Use these questions to guide your discussions and try not to get into the same arguments using the same words, each time.

1. What do you consider to be a healthy relationship?

A healthy relationship is one in which the couple has empathy towards each other. They listen to each other and appreciate what they do for each other. They have a sense of mutual trust.

2. What is love? How do you show your partner that you love them? Love is an action, not a feeling. Showing your partner that you love them means taking the time to do little things for them. It could be as simple as doing their laundry or giving them a foot massage.

3. What does intimacy mean to you in a partnership/marriage/relationship and how can we create more intimacy in ours?

4. What is a healthy balance of individuality and together-ness?

5. What would it take for us to move forward and make the changes we want to make in our relationship?

6. Do you think we can make these changes or is it time to move on? (If one or both don't want to work on things, then it's time.)

7. What is respect and how can we show respect in a healthy relationship?

Respect is treating each other with dignity and kindness, no matter what the situation - right or wrong. This includes having patience with one another, listening to each other and considering what the other partner has to say before responding instead of reacting defensively.

8. Why do we have conflict in our relationships?

Conflict occurs whenever there is a difference of opinion or point of view. The main source of conflict is when there is disrespect, or one partner feels as though the other does not appreciate him/her or care about his/her feelings. This can happen when we are under stress, tired or frustrated. One way to prevent this from happening is by being genuine with your words and actions; in other words, mean what you say and do what you say you are going to do!

9. How did our family influence how we handle conflict and deal with each other as adults?

Our families, whether they be immediate or extended, have an immense impact on who we are as individuals. Perhaps one or both of you had a parent who was overly strict and demanding, or perhaps one of your parents was always yelling at you to do well in school (or did not encourage you enough). You felt as though you could never get enough praise. Your family taught you how to deal with conflict in an unhealthy manner; the sooner we learn to deal with conflict positively, the better off we will be in our relationships.

10. How did growing up together or apart affect how we relate to each other as adults? (separated couples only)

It is important to remember that your past does not have to determine your future. When people who are abused and/or neglected come together in a new relationship, they often find themselves repeating the same unhealthy patterns of communication and behavior that they experienced in their families. This is because they had no one in their lives telling them at an early age that what was happening was wrong, and no one teaching them how to deal with conflict in a healthy way.

This is a big reason why people leave their partners; most of the time, it is not because they don't love them or want to be with them but because they can't get out of those unhealthy patterns of behavior and/or they can't stand to see the pain in their partner's eyes.

11. What does intimacy mean to you in a partnership/marriage/relationship and how can we create more intimacy in the relationship?

Intimacy means closeness and connectedness. It is not, as many people think, sexual activity. Too often, couples wait to discuss important issues until after they have had sex. This only allows the issue to fester and grow into something bigger than it was when it started. If you really want a healthy relationship, you have to make time for intimacy.

12. How do we go about setting up boundaries and rules to promote a healthy relationship?

It is important that each person be clear with their partner what their boundaries are and that they respect one another's boundaries as well as those of their extended family and friends! Role-playing is a great tool for helping couples set up boundaries in an easy way that does not hurt anyone's feelings!

13. How do you feel about money? Do you think that it is important to share financial responsibilities?

Money can be an issue in any relationship. Many people never get over their resentment and anger toward their parents for the way they handled money when they were growing up. Some people use money to keep score, while others are afraid that if they have too much, their partner will leave them or take it away, etc. If money is a problem for your partner, then you must deal with it and find a way to make the other person comfortable with the situation!

10. What are your life goals for the next 20 years?

Knowing where you want to be in 5, 10 or 20 years is an important part of any relationship. If both partners share the same goals, then it can help build a rewarding and loving relationship. If one person has no interest in reaching their dreams, then they may resent their partner for holding them back.

You might want to take turns answering the questions. As you talk, listen for underlying feelings and unspoken expectations that need to be understood and resolved. Remember to focus on feelings and not on right/wrong, good/bad or whose fault it is. Keep the discussion focused on issues and not your partner or yourself.

Also note that some of the questions above will be more relevant for couples who have been together for a longer time than those who have been together for just a few months. After all, there is a lot to learn about each other during courtship, but there is even more to learn about each other after many years of marriage. You will want to add more questions based on your situation and experience as well as any concerns you might need to discuss with each other.

It is important that the questions not offend, upset or otherwise trigger your partner in an unhealthy way. If you notice that a question upsets your partner, it is best to replace it with another question.

If you use any these questions in a discussion, record the responses recorded for future reference. It will take time and requires patience but it is possible for both of you to learn and grow from the process of fighting fair. Once fighting fair is understood by both parties, it will only become a matter of time before you realize how much progress you have made together as a couple.

NOTES

Chapter 7:
Questions That Make you Think

S ometimes, our days are so busy that we barely have time to think. And when you're in a relationship, it can be hard to find moments where you can see the big picture and make decisions together. But it's important to set aside some time for this because it will have a huge impact on your relationship. Start by thinking about how you and your partner feel about each other right now in general and then narrow it down to how you feel about specific things like communication, sexuality or relationships with parents and friends. The more you know about each other, the easier it will be to discuss the issues that come up along the way.

When answering these questions about how you feel in general, think about everything, including the little things. Rate your feelings on a scale from 1 to 10. And if you need help deciding how to rank each item, ask yourself these questions: is this feeling something I am totally comfortable with? How much do I support it? Does this feeling make me want to change anything in my life?

To get started with these questions, ask yourself:

1. Am I making a decision about my health because I understand my options?

This question will help you focus on whether or not you really understand the options that have been presented to you. If your decision isn't based on understanding and knowledge, it will be hard for your partner to trust that you're making the right decision for yourself and the relationship.

If you need more information, ask your doctor or a trusted family member or friend to help explain things in a way that makes sense to you.

2. Am I making the decision that is best for me?

This question will help you focus on what's most important. It will help you think about your wants and needs, and the wants and needs of your partner. It will also make sure you're not being influenced by things that have nothing to do with your health or treatment plan.

If your decision isn't what's best for both of you, talk with your doctor or a trusted friend so they can help to make sure it fits with all the other parts of your life.

3. Have I thought about how my decision will affect my partner?

You may feel that you're making a decision for yourself and not your partner, but your partner's opinion matters. They have the right to decide how they feel about your decisions and whether or not they are okay with it. If you aren't thinking about how your decision will affect them, it might not be the best decision for either of you.

If you don't know how your partner feels about what you're doing or would like to include them more in this process, talk with them.

4. Have I explained the treatment decision to my partner?

You may not want to tell your partner every detail about the problem, but it is important to talk it over with them. Your partner may be able to help you understand things like cost, the process of treatment, and the potential side effects. Plus, you might find out that your partner is uncomfortable with a certain choice or may have questions of their own.

If they don't understand what you're doing or don't approve, don't be afraid to talk about their feelings and try to come up with something that works for both of you.

5. Will my decision be good for me in the long term?

This question will help you focus on what will happen after your treatment. It will make sure that you're not just thinking about what happens immediately, but also down the road.

Keep in mind that health problems change over time, so you may need to get more treatment or have a different option later on.

If you feel like your choice doesn't address future issues, talk with your doctor, a friend or partner about it.

6. Have I thought about how this decision fits into my life as a whole?

Think about things like school, work plans and social activities that are important to you. Are there other things in your life that may make this decision harder to accomplish?

For example, some of the decisions you might need to make are hard if you have a job, kids, or a family. But if your decision fits into all the parts of your life, it will be easier to follow through.

If this decision doesn't fit in with the rest of what's going on in your life, however, talk with your doctor or trusted friend about it so they can help you find a different option.

7. Do I understand how to take care of myself if I decide to have treatment?

Some treatments can be hard and may need special follow-up care. It's important that you know what your treatment will be like, who will help you with it, and what kind of follow-up care you'll need.

Sometimes this information is hard to find, so talk about what kinds of things you'll need to do after the treatment is over.

8. Am I sure about my choice?

Ask yourself if there are any doubts in your mind about making a decision now. If you're not sure whether to have treatment or not, you should talk with your doctor or someone you trust. After a while, decide if you'll have treatment or not. If you decide to wait for now, add the following question to your list:

9. Have I talked about my decision with family and friends?

If there are things in your life that are important to other people (like your friends, family, and religion), involving them can make things easier. It can also help with making big decisions (like whether to have treatment or not).

How do you get started? You may feel a lot of pressure to "just get started." But take it easy because you're the one who is going to be doing all the work, and none of it has to be done all at once.

Next, follow these seven steps:

1. Make a list. Write down the things that are important or interesting for you at this point. Your list could include things like your disease and its symptoms, treatment decisions, or important life questions (like what kind of work you want to do or where in the world you want to live).

2. Make a timeline. When are you going to think about your choices? Maybe you want to make a list of questions at the beginning of each week, or maybe you want to talk things over with your partner once a month. Then decide when you're going to review and update your list so that it's always ready when you need it.

3. Pick up the pace. As time passes, some of these questions may feel less important or urgent, so don't stress if it takes longer than expected to finish your whole list; just do what works best for now and adjust as needed later on.

4. Keep it all in one place. If you're going to have more than one list, keep them together so all your questions are easy to find. Maybe you want to keep a notebook with your list of questions or put your questions on sticky notes that are easy to move around.

5. Share the load. It can be good to talk about big issues with friends and family who care about what happens next or who can offer a different perspective on your future plans. But remember that it's your decision so don't let anyone else make it for you, especially if they don't know what's best for you or your relationship.

6. Give yourself some space. It can be hard to think about a lot of things all at once, and you might find it easier to think about some parts of your list one at a time. If that works for you, schedule time: I'll work on my list on Mondays and Wednesdays from 12:00-1:00 (or whatever works best for you).

7. Take charge of your own health care by getting the information you need and make sure that all your questions are answered before making a decision.

After answering these questions about your health, feelings and views about relationships and life in general, take some time to discuss what it was like to answer them. Get an idea of your partner's responses and how those views are different or similar to yours. Then put these questions away for a little while and work on other exercises.

While you're both working on other exercises, stop thinking about the list of questions and try to let go of whatever feelings or thoughts they brought up. When you're ready to move back to this list, go through them one at a time so that your partner has a chance to answer them too.

If you find yourself getting upset as you think about answering these questions, try breathing slowly (inhaling and exhaling for five counts each) until you feel more relaxed. If that doesn't help, try to distract yourself by thinking pleasant thoughts or do something that takes your mind off the stressful situation. For example, you might try talking to a trusted friend or doing things you enjoy that don't involve thinking about your health.

Making the decision: finally, when you reach the point where you feel ready to make a decision (and have made sure that all your questions have been answered), consult with someone who has gone through this process and whose opinion you value. Choose someone unbiased and supportive of your decision, if possible. This person can be your counselor, doctor, a friend or family member. They will help you think about your situation and get a fresh perspective on the issue.

When you're ready to make a decision about your health, it's important to make it on the basis of good information and not just strong feelings. Use the following questions to guide you through the decision-making process. These questions are designed for after you have made some choices about treatment options and want to make sure your decisions are based on solid information and good thinking.

When dealing with important issues like these, it may be hard for you to keep your focus on the right things. If that's the case, take a break and come back to the questions when you feel ready. Or talk with someone you trust who can help to keep your thoughts grounded or find another way to get through it.

NOTES

Chapter 8:
Questions on Conflicts with In-laws and Extended Family Members

R elationships with in-laws and extended family members can be a source of stress and frustration for everyone involved. In this chapter, we'll look at the root causes of these conflicts, potential solutions to reduce future conflict, and learn how to have better communication with each other.

Are you interested in knowing how to deal with your spouse's in-laws or extended family members? Take a look at our list of 10 questions for couples!

1. Does you feel as strongly about the issue as I do?

This question could be the most important one on the list. It is vital to figure out if your partner is as invested in solving the issue as you are. Perhaps you have differing opinions on dealing with certain conflicts. Discuss these differences and how you can come to a solution that works for both of you instead of going your separate ways.

2. How would you describe your relationship with my family members?

Sometimes your partner may be unwilling to open up about his or her family relationships due to various reasons, including fear of creating conflict or embarrassment, or anything else that may cause distress. Be patient and find a quiet time to have a non-confrontational conversation with your partner where you can discuss your concerns.

3. How does you feel when around my family members?

Sometimes conflicts between family members may be related to differences in cultural upbringing or opinions. For example, one spouse may have limited contact with his or her parents due to differences in religion or lifestyle, while the other one maintains frequent contact and visits often. If you ask this question and find that your partner is uncomfortable when you are around their extended family, it could be because he or she feels embarrassed about the differences in opinion, lifestyle or culture between the two families.

3. What would you like to see happen in our relationship with family members?

The answer will let you know what your partner thinks about the current state of his or her relationship with his or her relatives. You can then work together to find a solution that is mutually beneficial for everyone involved.

4. What have you done so far about this issue?

If your partner feels as strongly about the issue as you do, it may be because he or she has already brought it up in conversation with family members before and even come up with a solution to fix it. If this has happened before, make sure to understand what steps have been taken so far and if they were successful.

5. What will you do if I don't want to deal with the issue anymore?

It is important to know what both of you will do if one of you is unwilling to continue dealing with this issue. If multiple attempts have been made at solving the problem and it still exists, this may be a good time to re-evaluate your relationship.

6. What else would you like to share on this topic?

This question is useful for couples seriously considering taking action in resolving a family conflict or who are already taking action. You can discuss your plans and make sure that both parties are on board before making any decisions.

7. Are there any ways you would like to improve our communication?

There are times when conflict arises due to poor communication between the couple, and extended family members become collateral damage. Sometimes, the best way to avoid getting into conflicts with family members is to talk about it with your partner first. If talking about family conflict does not work out, you may need professional help. Seeking a couple's counselor could be a good step forward in resolving disputes with your partner's relatives. The counselor can help you identify potential causes of conflict and how to deal with them once they arise.

8. How do you feel when we spend time together without your family members?

Some conflicts between families may be due to one partner feeling neglected by the other, or vice versa. Try doing fun activities with each other — without the interference of family — and see if your relationship improves. This will let you know if your partner is comfortable enough to spend quality time with just you. If the answer is no, perhaps you should try spending less time with his or her family and more time with each other.

9. What do you want to be said about our relationship with your family members?

Everyone wants to feel validated. Once you know that the topic of conversation is not going to end in an argument, it will be easier for both of you to talk and come up with a solution that will improve your relationship with extended family members.

10. What is the most important thing for both of us to remember when dealing with this issue?

This question is helpful if the conflict seems overwhelming and you both need something to take away from it. This way, if one or both of you forget about what was discussed after a while, talking about it again will be easier. After this conversation, hopefully you will have a better idea of how to mend your relationship with your partner's family members. If talking about it doesn't work out, you can see a couple's counselor to help improve communication and avoid future conflicts.

NOTES

Chapter 9:
Questions on Money Matters

G etting along with someone's financial habits can be just as important as getting along with them. Just like a couple has different tastes in food and music, they also might have different ideas about how they spend their money. Even in a relationship where both people earn an income, there is always the possibility that one person spends more than the other. This can be a sensitive area for some couples, and it can also cause resentment – and possibly even arguments! That's why it's important to talk about money issues together.

The next time you're together, find a place where you can have a conversation in private. Make sure that you have enough privacy to talk comfortably. If your partner is not very open about money issues, you might want to start off the conversation by asking what he or she thinks about money matters. Even if your partner is more open about their feelings on the subject, it can feel more natural if one person asks questions first.

If you want to have a friendly conversation about money, it can be helpful to have a few discussion points lined up. Here are some of the most important money topics that people might like to discuss:

1. What are your priorities when it comes to money?

This question will help you to understand what is important to your partner when it comes to spending and saving. A person's first answer might not be their final answer, so it is important to follow up with the following question:

2. How do you want to handle money as a couple?

If there are current habits you don't agree with, then it will be helpful to talk about how you can handle these differences moving forward. If the person you are dating has different spending habits than you, it is also helpful to talk about how much of an influence these differences might have on the future of the relationship.

3. Does my spending bother you?

This is a good question to ask if one of you is more frugal or spendthrift than the other. This could cause problems in the future, especially if one person likes to splurge and the other likes to save.

4. How can we work together on our money issues?

This helps both people understand how they can compromise moving forward. It also helps couple focus on only their money issues and not on other important relationship issues as well.

5. What are your financial goals?

It is a good idea for both partners in a relationship to have an understanding of each other's' financial goals, even if they are very different. If a couple has different goals, they should figure out how these goals will affect the relationship moving forward.

If you are dating someone you know casually, there are even more important issues to talk about. These include where each person sees their financial future in a year or two, and how much responsibility they want in the relationship. If both people earn money, it is also helpful to talk about who will be responsible for the household expenses.

These points might help your conversation along, or you can come up with other conversation points that are more relevant. The important thing is to have an open conversation and be honest with each other about your feelings on money matters.

The financial health of a household can be tied to the overall health of the relationship. Couples have a higher risk of divorce if they are neither financially satisfied nor financially compatible. One way to assess the health of a relationship is by looking at your credit reports, which provide a wealth of information about your relationship status and spending habits.

The lesson here: don't give yourself more credit than you deserve, and don't blow up your past or present successes out of proportion. Remember that you are just as fallible as your cohorts and future endeavors are no guarantee of success. Be patient with yourself and your money; try to be realistic in your expectations. It's easy to let the past determine the present and future.

That's why it's important not to compare yourself with others, especially when it comes to finances. The truth is that there really is no right or wrong way to handle money, and it's all about what works best for you. While there are always new methods of saving money coming out, the most important thing is to find what works best for you and your family. Here are more questions.

1. How would you describe our money situation? How do you feel about it?

2. Have there been any major changes in our finances recently? What caused them? Where do you hope they'll lead?

3. Are there things in your relationship that cause disagreements about money or make it difficult to talk about it?

4. What kind of help or advice do you want from regarding our money situation?

5. How can I support you financially?

6. Is there anything else we should discuss about our money situation?

If you have trouble talking to your partner about money, now is the time for a discussion! You might not always see eye-to-eye with your partner when it comes to financial decisions, but that doesn't mean that you shouldn't talk about the subject. After all, it is a very important thing in a relationship and needs to stay healthy for the relationship to stay healthy. If you're afraid to start a discussion about money because you don't know how to talk about it, try doing it in a fun way!

NOTES

Chapter 10:
Questions on Intimacy

Yes, intimacy is important! It's the foundation of our relationships and allows us to experience satisfying connections with the people we love. Intimacy is also a dynamic process that involves all of our senses: physical, emotional, intellectual, and spiritual. It means paying attention to what someone is saying while they are speaking, but also noticing their tone of voice, body language, and facial expressions.

Intimate communication goes beyond talking; in fact, it often happens through touch (like a hug or a kiss) or when we connect with someone "viscerally" by listening closely to their words and letting ourselves feel their emotions.

Intimacy isn't easy especially in the early stages of relationships. You may be wondering if you can really trust this person who seems so different from you. You'll need to be patient and open and take the time to get to know each other. If your partner wants the same thing, then intimacy can grow in the relationship, and may even get better over time.

If you want more intimacy in your relationship, you both need to be willing to share what turns you on as well as what turns you off; that is the only way you can truly find out what feels good for each partner. For instance, if he tells you that he enjoys watching pornography, or she reveals she has a foot fetish, those things may turn off or weird out a lot of people.

If you want to become more intimate, you need to be willing to reveal things you have a hard time talking about with just anyone (or maybe even at all). The more open and honest communication you can share, the closer you will feel.

However, giving and receiving intimacy is often a two-way street. If you want your partner to give of him or herself sexually, then in turn you need to be willing to open yourself up sexually as well. If your partner has sexual fantasies they would like fulfilled but won't ask for them, you need to be willing to fulfill their needs. It's important to have fun with each other, so have fun answering these questions! Ask them of each other.

1. When you think of me as your partner, what are the first things that come to mind? What associations do you have with me? What do I represent in your life? What do I mean to you and how so?

2. Were there moments when we were close to each other that you recall as being particularly special, romantic or intimate? Can you share those moments with me now? How did they make you feel?

3. In what ways have you been intimate that are important to you? Have there been times when you felt especially close to me?

4. What do you feel is the most important element of an intimate relationship? Is it sexual, emotional closeness, or something else? Why do you feel that way?

5. What are the differences in being intimate with a partner compared to a regular friendship? Are there differences in being intimate in a long-term relationship versus a new relationship or hooking up with someone for one night?

6. How often do you find yourselves not sharing enough "inner" things about yourself? What keeps you from being more open and vulnerable with me? At what points during our relationship have you felt especially open and intimate?

7. How much of your self-worth and sense of being has the relationship with me come to represent? What have been the most intense moments in our relationship?

8. What is it like for you to share something with me that you haven't told another person before? Be concrete. How does it feel? Are there things that you have tried not telling me, but I make you feel comfortable talking about?

9. How do different types of communication relate to intimacy: physical touch, sexual activities, intellectual connection, emotional sharing, spiritual connection?

10. What are the things that you do that allow for a deepening of intimacy? What do you need to do differently in order for the level of intimacy to grow for us?

11. How does the degree of intimacy in our relationship differ as a man and a woman? When does it work better? When is it worse?

12. What are good ways to introduce more emotional and physical closeness in our relationship? Be specific.

13. What are some of the challenges you have faced when trying to be more intimate in our interactions, in general and sexually?

14. How do you express your feelings about the closeness that we share?

15. What are some of the most intense moments in our relationship? Be concrete. How does it feel?

16. What has been most challenging about sharing sexual intimacy together? How can you overcome it?

17. Is there anything I have asked that made you feel nervous, uncomfortable, or a little self-conscious? Would you like to share with me what it was and why it made you feel that way?

18. Is there anything I have asked that you really liked talking about or being intimate with me? Would you like to share what that was and why it made you feel good?

19. Do you genuinely enjoy spending time together? What are some of your favorite activities together? What do you feel is important about doing these activities regularly with each another?

20. When you recall your best experiences in a relationship, what comes to mind? What are some of the most intense moments when you thinking back over the years at the beginning, middle and end of the relationship or a particular phase in it?

NOTES

Chapter 11:
Questions on Reconnecting with Your Spouse

T his chapter includes questions to get to know your partner better. They are designed to be used during personal time together. If you choose to answer them all, consider spending 30 minutes talking about the questions one night a week for 6 weeks. Or if you choose to only answer a few, consider picking questions you would like to work on for the coming week and talking about them at a time that works best for both. Make sure you are in a quiet place where the two of you can sit comfortably. Read the questions (there is one for each of you) and ask each other the questions in order. Discuss what was said and how you feel about it. You don't have to answer all the questions at once. You can pick the ones you want to work on together.

Here we go!

In your relationship, it's important to be open with each other and share things about yourself that you wouldn't share with others. Take turns answering and try not to hold back! If it makes you uncomfortable, that's a good thing because sharing feelings may help you both better understand each other.

1. What is one physical thing that you love about yourself?

This question is designed to help you understand what your partner likes about his/her body. Some of you are probably thinking, "I'm happy with my body," or something similar. If so, ask the follow-up question: what one physical thing would you like to change about yourself? (You could say, "What's one thing you'd like to change about your appearance?") This will get both of you thinking and talking about physical attributes.

2. How is our sex life?

This question is designed to further tap into feelings that may be difficult for both of you to talk about. Try to relax and share what you feel. If you are uncomfortable with the question, think about what things in the bedroom could be improved. If you choose to answer this question together, it may be helpful to answer what do we do that you like but I don't? Could we try that?

3. What do I do that frustrates / annoys / bothers you?

The purpose of this question is to identify frustrations in the relationship so they can be addressed and worked on. This will also give you insight into your spouse's personality and help the two of you become closer by becoming more understanding of each other. For example, if you find out that being late frustrates your spouse, arrange to leave early or have more communication about the plan ahead of time.

4. Do I do things that have made you proud?

Many of you are probably thinking, "Yes! Of course!" But there's a great truth in this question: if your spouse made you proud for doing something in the past, then he/she will continue to do so in the future! It is important to understand what your spouse thinks is a win-win situation and what makes him/her feel good about himself/herself as well as the relationship.

5. What do I need to be more comfortable around you?

This question is designed to get you talking about things that might be uncomfortable. For many of you, it will touch on sexual feelings. Don't be afraid to share "intimate" feelings with each other. Remember that the point of this book is to have a loving and intimate relationship in which you are comfortable sharing your inner thoughts and desires.

6. What are some things I can do for you that will have an impact on your life?

This question is designed to help us all think about how we can make a positive difference. We want our spouses to feel like they can count on us and that we truly care about them. It is important we do things to show our support. What are some things that your spouse does that have made a positive impact on your life? What would you like them to do in the future?

7. What would you never want me to do?

This question is designed to help you think about boundaries in the relationship and respecting those boundaries. There may be something you want to do, but because of your spouse's personality or past experiences, it might not be something he/she feels good about. This is an important area for discussion. It's better that those feelings come up now than later when both of you have invested more in the relationship.

8. What would you do if I got fired from my job?

This question is designed to provoke feelings and thoughts about what life would be like if one of you were not in the same place. This can be a difficult question for some because it deals with an unpleasant subject that might cause feelings of sadness, fear, or guilt. It is good to talk about these things now so that you understand each other's reactions and plans ahead of time.

9. What's your happiest memory with me?

This question is designed to help you focus on positive memories from the past, present, and future. It is important to identify the things that made your relationship stronger in the past, as well as the things that will make your relationship stronger in the future. Even though this is a tough question, try not to be negative when talking about the memories you have. It is important to remember that even though people change over time, your love for each other should not change.

This brings us back to the importance of communicating in a positive way and remembering our love for one another.

10. How did I make you feel during _____ (a past experience)?

This question is designed to get you thinking about how you can communicate with each other better in the future by learning from past experiences. It is important to remember that you have different communication styles. It may be that in the past, your spouse reacted in a negative way to something you did because his/her communication style was different than yours. You want to learn about each other's communication styles so you can talk about things in an effective manner going forward.

After going through these 10 questions, it is good to go back and focus on the first one. You should be able to remember what your spouse said to you in response to each of the 10 questions. This will make it easier for you both to communicate with each other going forward. It is important for you to remember that by doing this exercise, there was a deeper level of communication and understanding between you. You were able to talk about things that can be uncomfortable for some couples and were still able to have a good, positive conversation about them. This kind of communication will help your relationship grow stronger from this point forward.

NOTES

Chapter 12:
Day-to-day Conflict Resolution

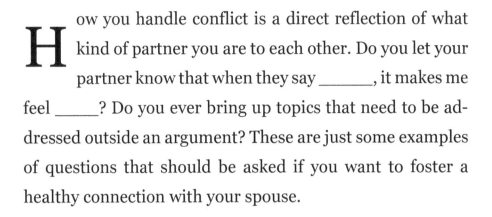

How you handle conflict is a direct reflection of what kind of partner you are to each other. Do you let your partner know that when they say _____, it makes me feel _____? Do you ever bring up topics that need to be addressed outside an argument? These are just some examples of questions that should be asked if you want to foster a healthy connection with your spouse.

This book explores 10 important questions for couples and offers insights on how to answer them. Trust is the foundation of a healthy relationship. Do you know if your partner has an online presence? Is he or she active on social media? As with everything, check the comments for any signs of negativity.

When couples have the same vision of what they want to achieve together, their dreams are more likely to be realized. For example, if one partner wants to start a business or buys a house and the other is unwilling (or has different plans), then that partnership may dissolve. Firmly aligning your goals in life will help you make decisions together as a couple.

These are just some examples of the questions that should be asked if you want to foster a healthy connection with your spouse. You already know how important communication is in any relationship. It is the foundations of all good relationships, and it applies whether you're married or not.

Remember that when answering these questions, honesty is always the best policy, and when in doubt, err on the side of carefully considering your words.

It's normal for partners to disagree sometimes (even married couples). With this question, ask yourself whether you find yourself falling into that trap often. If so, it may be valuable to have a conversation about how to approach conflict more effectively in the future.

If your partner constantly brings up past mistakes (or yours), it may be time to talk about how to approach the subject differently. A relationship is a living thing, and it's important to nurture it properly.

How do you feel when you get in fights? Are they draining? Does it seem like you're repeating yourself? Do you have confidence that your partner is listening to what you say (even if he or she doesn't agree)? These questions should be discussed. Ask yourself if your goals in life are compatible with your partner's.

This applies to both short-term and long-term goals. For example, if one partner decides to take a year off from school, the other might not be on board with that decision. As a result, problems arise when one is trying to move forward and the other is trying to hold him or her back.

If you have different visions of what you want in 10 years, then talk it out. Maybe your partner wants children, and you want a career. Maybe your partner wants to live on the beach, and you want to live in the mountains. As long as both partners understand each other's life dreams, then they're more likely to come together and decide on a compromise that works for both of them.

NOTES

Conclusion

T here are many ways to communicate in a loving relationship. As an example, consider the "no contact" rule. It basically dictates that partners must separate themselves from each other during arguments or other intense discussions and not initiate or accept contact until they have cooled off. If this rule is not followed, much harm can be caused to the relationship, especially if the argument escalates to physical violence.

It is also important that people understand why they argue with their partners in the first place. It helps them realize what could be causing conflict within their relationship and what they can do to work together to fix it before it gets worse. There is a vast array of methods to resolve conflicts, from mediation to couples counseling. Whatever route people decide to take, it is extremely important that they are aware of the potential consequences. If not, a small disagreement could escalate into something more serious.

It is also important for partners to remember that there are some things that can never be solved. If this happens, it is best to learn how to carry on with life without dwelling on the argument as if there is no hope of a resolution. This will allow them to avoid getting caught up in the conflict and possibly causing further harm to the relationship as a result of their refusal to compromise.

The whole point of communication is for couples to understand each other and work out differences together rather than losing patience or taking sides against one another.

The list of 20 questions provided aims to help couples understand and appreciate each other, talk about their feelings, listen to each other more and share their thoughts.

These questions are for all types of relationships - same gender or others, married or not married. We also encourage you to use the answers as a starting point for discussions about things not included in this list.

Thank you.

CPSIA information can be obtained
at www.ICGtesting.com
Printed in the USA
BVHW062006260221
601199BV00004B/256